Students and F~

The Exploding Cities

The Exploding Cities

Peter Wilsher
and Rosemary Righter

With an Epilogue by Barbara Ward

ANDRE DEUTSCH

First published 1975 by
André Deutsch Limited
105 Great Russell Street London WC1

Copyright © 1975 by Times Newspapers Limited
All rights reserved
Second Impression January 1977

Printed in Great Britain
by Ebenezer Baylis and Son Limited
The Trinity Press, Worcester, and London

ISBN 0 233 96665 X

Contents

List of Illustrations

1*

Preface

Nineteen seventy-four was designated by the United Nations as World Population Year. As a practical contribution Harold Evans, Editor of The *Sunday Times*, organised, in co-operation with the United Nations Fund for Population Activities, a major international conference at Worcester College, Oxford, under the title of "The Exploding Cities". This brought together a globe-spanning group of political leaders, planners, administrators, consultants, journalists and radical critics to discuss the many-layered problems which have arisen from the recent hectic and unprecedented growth of the world's great urban agglomerations. This book is a distillation and an elaboration of that week's debate – between practitioner and theorist, between police chief and pollution protester, and between the eminent architect, who jets easily from one city's spatial inadequacies to another half a world away, and the social researcher who sees those inadequacies from the festering, unrelieved underside.

The central topic was most succinctly set out by one of the UN's senior officials, Rafael Salas, the Executive Director of the United Nations Fund for Population Activities, in his opening address. "Before the end of the century," he said, "the size of city populations will be radically altered. By the year 2001, perhaps as many as half the world's population will be city-dwellers; and this in a world which will be supporting twice the number of people that it did in 1970. Our world now is having great and apparently increasing difficulty in feeding, clothing and housing itself. How shall we accommodate another world on top of this one?"

The debate around this question took many forms, from formal presentation to late-night argument and the showing of hand-held, bullet-disrupted cine-film of a Colombian squatter invasion. It also, because so many participants were already expert in the subjects concerned, took a great deal of basic information for granted. For ease and coherence, therefore, the authors of this volume have added much additional material which did not

directly form part of the conference. We have also made no
attempt to follow the precise chronological order of the Oxford
proceedings. Instead, with the kind permission of all the contributors, we have divided the book into four main sections, and
drawn on the various speeches, papers and discussions where
these appeared most telling and appropriate.

The first section sketches the global background, assembling
the raw demographic and statistical material on urban growth,
disentangling the contributions of natural increase and migration
from the countryside, and setting out the main economic and
social theories of city development.

Section II looks at the cities of the already-developed world –
the nineteenth- and twentieth-century cities which embodied the
achievements and the aspirations of the Industrial Revolution.
With all their manifold failings, they have firmly set the pattern
for what a city should look like, contain and be, and that pattern,
rightly or wrongly, is still being followed throughout the Third
World. But where are the New Yorks, Parises, Tokyos and
Londons of the West actually proceeding as we approach the
twenty-first century? Can they handle their own proliferating
tensions and financial difficulties, let alone offer useful guidance
to the people desperately trying to tackle the problems of Saigon,
Ankara or Bogotà?

The third section looks in detail at the vast, shapeless, barely
controlled, brutally poor, but often hugely lively "super-
conurbations" of the developing continents. Hope and despair,
Malthus and Pangloss, run a close race, and temperament, rather
than scientific impartiality, probably decides finally between the
optimistic and the apocalyptic view. But there is, at any rate,
general agreement that, either way, the swarming cities of Asia,
Africa and South America represent a major new political factor
in our time, and that any serious solution to their problems must
imply a large measure of political change – peaceful or otherwise.

The fourth section, therefore, considers civic policy as applied
in the main alternative societies – the Chinese People's Republic
and the USSR. Both enjoy, or suffer, the existence of vast cities:
deliberately developed in Russia, inherited, with some considerable reservation, by the peasant-backed revolutionaries who took
power in Peking. Both are now trying, by an assortment of fiscal,
physical and ideological methods, to control, curtail and re-

direct unwanted urban growth. Some, at least, of their ideas might be worth consideration by the West and the non-aligned world, though none has yet so clearly succeeded as to sweep the board.

The bulk of this book, although based on the important and authoritative exchanges at Oxford, and owing a great deal to the help and stimulating advice of various contributors, is, in its final version, the work of the authors, who must take the responsibility for the facts, judgments and opinions which it contains. There are, however, two exceptions. The chapter, "The Self-help Society", in Section III, has been specially written by the architect, John F. C. Turner, and the sociologist, Dr Bryan Roberts, who have spent many years studying the achievements of self-help builders in the cities of the Third World, and speak with unique knowledge and sympathy in this controversial area. And the final, summing-up chapter, by Dr Barbara Ward, is virtually the full text of the keynote speech with which she opened the conference. It seemed to us to express precisely the right mixture of urgent concern and bracing responsibility that the middle 1970s require. But as this whole book shows, the megalopolitan time bomb is ticking uncomfortably fast. There is little margin for anyone to take a leisurely defusion course.

London, 1974

SECTION I

The Explosive Ingredients

Should the population continue to expand at the current rate, it will be only 3,500 years before we have converted into people all the matter that can be reached during that period.

DR I. J. GOOD

CHAPTER I

The Noise and the Smell
and the People

God the first garden made,
And the first city, Cain.

ABRAHAM COWLEY,
The Garden

Aristotle, writing shortly after Plato had laid down the ideal size for a community of citizens as 5,040 – the number who could comfortably gather into the Athens market-place – said that men came to the city to live, but that they stayed to live the good life. In the last fifteen years, something like 577 million extra citizens have been born or have moved into those communal aggregations of 100,000 or more people now generally signified internationally by the word "city", and in the next twenty-five years, saving pestilence, famine or thermonuclear war, they will be joined by a further 1,467 million – more than half the world's entire population as it stood at the beginning of the 1960s. How will they live, these almost unimaginable hordes, and in what sense is it possible to hope that more than an infinitesimal, privileged fraction will succeed in living anything resembling "the good life"?

The crude figures, compounded from the still-high birth rates, the accelerating flow of peasant migration, and the rising life expectations now enjoyed by even the most primitive and backward of nations, are sufficiently disturbing as they stand. But they look far worse once you start breaking them down. The situation would be serious enough if the world's expected population increases were being spread evenly. Unfortunately this is far from the case, whether you look at the division between urban and rural populations, or between the relatively advanced, stable towns and cities of Europe, North America and Australasia, and the exploding metropolises of the Third World. In 1960, when there were some 3,000 million people in the world, two-thirds of them made their living on the land, and the rest were split more or less equally between the "developed" and the "developing". By the turn of the century, however, this balance looks like being totally overturned – with anything between 6,000 and 7,500 million to accommodate (according to your choice of demographer), the countryside's share will be down to one-third, and the new "great wens" of India, Nigeria, Brazil, Indonesia and the like will have outstripped the Parises, Londons and New Yorks by a factor of around two and a half to one.

What this means, in effect, is that three out of every five of the 2,000–3,000 million additional faces who will swell the human race during the next three decades, can be expected to join the teeming hordes of those Asian, African and Latin American cities which will have most difficulty in feeding them, housing them, transporting them and finding them jobs – and which are already, in many cases, bursting at the seams (not to mention the sewers, the water supply, the tramway system and most other aspects of civic life). In Manila, in Caracas, in Kinshasa, in Cairo, anything from a tenth to a third of the people are not accepted tax-paying "citizens" at all, but illegal squatters – families in tents or tin shacks or waterless, drainless hovels, hanging on to a precarious toe-hold in the urban jungle which is just one step better than the starving village which they left behind – and this proportion could easily rise to 50 per cent or more in the next few years, as more and more authorities abandon any systematic attempt to stem the flood.

The "urban squatter" – the man who arrives with nothing but a determination to make it in the big town, prepared to hole up in any filthy corner while he accumulates his initial stake – is a phenomenon as old as history. Excavations at Ur show that even 8,000 years ago the fringes of the city were befouled with shanties. But now, across the world, there are millions upon millions of such sub-minimal city-dwellers, with their own way of life, their own social stratifications, in many cases their own "laws" and "institutions", and to an ever-increasing extent their own potentially formidable political strength. It is here, in the purulent enclaves and festering outskirts of Istanbul, Karachi, Rangoon and Rio de Janeiro, that the true city explosion is building up.

Such "spontaneous settlements", as the more optimistic sociologists like to call them, have naturally generated, in every country, an indigenous vocabulary and nomenclature. Even a short sample list shows the ubiquity of the problem. In Brazil they are *favelas*, in Chile *callampas*, and in Argentina *villas miserias*. In Turkey, where perhaps half of Ankara's 1·5 million live this way, they are *geçekundu* – acknowledging the fact that, to avoid instant legal destruction, any temporary dwelling has to be erected in a single night between dusk and dawn. In the Soviet Union, where many of Stalin's "new cities" initially consisted of little else, they are *zemlyanki* – half tent, half hole in the ground. In Calcutta they are *bustees*; in the Philippines *barong-barongs*; in Tripoli *barracas*. In Venezuela they are *cerros*, if built on hillsides, and *quibradas* in ravines. In Zaire they are *villes outre-coutumiers*, and in Porto Alegro *vilas de malacas*, while in Mexico City, with a full third of the population on a squatting basis, there is a whole hierarchy: *tugerios*, if you have a one-room hut round a central courtyard; *jackales* if you live in a scrap-iron hut; *colonias proletarias*, or more graphically, *colonias paracaidistas*, "parachutists' neighbourhoods", a bit higher up the squatters' scale. The most recent official counts showed 1,200,000 illegal homesteaders in Seoul (one in four) and over 785,000 in Ankara (two in three), while even in Hong Kong, where the most sustained and determined efforts have been made, over the last twenty years, to grapple with the problem, there are still 275,000 people clinging illicitly and desperately to more than 100 separate sites in that tiny colony.

Calcutta is of course the awful example: the suppurating image of what all these other cities – maybe the whole world – could so easily become, under the inexorable influx of too much humankind. Kipling summed it up, nearly eighty years ago, when the population was perhaps a tenth of its present boiling 8·2 million (with the prospect of 12 million and upwards by the time the twenty-first century arrives):

> As the fungus sprouts chaotic from its bed,
> So it spread . . .
> And above the packed and pestilential town
> Death looked down.

Nothing much has changed, except for the worse, since Kipling wrote those lines. Calcutta and its attendant towns and districts now stretch like a rotting narrow ribbon for sixty miles along the foetid banks of the Hooghly River, and in every possible way that a city can go sour, this one has gone sourer.

Already, by 1921, the density of population in the central metropolitan area was higher than that of present-day Manhattan. Now, fifty years later, it has trebled – 84,896 people live in each square mile – and an estimated 600,000 all told sleep in the streets every night. Almost half of this suffocatingly populous area is totally without sewers, and even a moderate shower floods the shallow *kutcha* channels which act as drains, and sweeps the filth and effluent through thousands of *bustee* basements, and even middle-class kitchens.

Even the parts that have sewers do little better. The basic system was dug between 1896 and 1905 to serve a population of 600,000. Nothing of serious consequence has been added since, and in the meantime, thanks to sloppy maintenance and slipshod removal methods, some 7 million tons of silt have accumulated, cutting the city's totally inadequate drainage capacity in half. The twenty-two trucks, twenty-five trolleys, and occasional tractors on which the corporation relies to collect the daily accumulation of "night soil" from Calcutta's 40,000 public privies can barely cope with a third of the stuff, while the rest pollutes the air and ultimately overflows.

Garbage disposal, similarly, is 25 per cent below minimum strength, and periodically the trash mounts so high in the streets that the State government has to draft in the National Volunteer Force on an emergency basis to reduce it to tolerable levels, so that people can move around.

The Hooghly, which supplies most of the water, often gets so salty with the tide flow from the Bay of Bengal that salinity reaches twelve times the supposed limit for human consumption. Overstretched pumping machines, creaking away in the overworked and superannuated water mains, often break down completely for twenty-four or even forty-eight hours at a stretch, while sewage meanwhile seeps in through the massive cracks that are gradually developing throughout the 700-mile system. But anyone who is actually on the mains, with more or less filtered water, counts as lucky. The great mass of the squatters and the pavement dwellers have to make do with the unfiltered supplies

originally intended for street washing and fire-fighting – and that
system too is now so heavily used and silted up that the fire
brigade usually has to transport its own water in tankers or bring
it by bucket-chain from the nearest open pond.

The situation is perhaps summed up most neatly in a reported
exchange recently between the Calcutta Metropolitan Development Association, which now has overall responsibility for attack-
ing the impenetrable tangle, and the Calcutta Corporation: "We
sent a note to the Corporation," said a senior CMDA official,
"requesting them to clear the gully pits. They replied with a note
saying that the gully pits could not be cleared because the inlets
were choked, the inlets could not be cleared because the manholes were choked, the manholes could not be cleared because the
sewers were choked, and the sewers could not be cleared because
pumping stations were weak." And as one knowledgeable com-
mentator added, the chain of disaster could easily be extended
further. Even if the pumps are working, the sewage often cannot
be cleared because the outfall canals are silted up, and during the
monsoon months, the Hooghly and the Kulti rivers, which finally
receive the discharge, are often swollen to levels above the
capacity of the city's drainage system. Frequently, in any case,
the pumps are not working at all because of systematic load-
shedding by the overworked Calcutta electricity agencies. Also,
it must always be remembered that Calcutta itself is a jewel of
competence and efficiency beside its thirty-six associated muni-
cipalities – many of which, like Howrah, Barrackpore and North
Dum-Dum, are growing from anything between twice and nine
times as fast as the central zone, but have little or no water or
sanitation at all.

It is easy to write poems of despair about Calcutta; about the
agony and desperation; about the graft and corruption; about
the clapped-out city tramways which carry only three-quarters
as many people today (despite the concurrent doubling of population) as they did twenty years ago; about the pathetically
inadequate public housing programme; about the ludicrous
£500,000 finally set aside, on the very eve of the 1971 elections,
for "slum improvement"; about the fact that, thanks to modern
technology and capital intensive investment, there are fewer
factory jobs in Calcutta today than there were a decade ago.
Bengalis themselves take an almost British delight in cataloguing

the horrors, listing the political ramps and the gross income disparities of their chief city, and masochistically detailing the failings of such districts as Howrah, which with a population of 740,000 – larger than many of the world's capital cities – can only be described as a colonial monstrosity and a vast, unmitigated slum. And yet there is a fundamental ambiguity about even the worst of these flooded *bustees* and stinking shanty towns, an ambiguity which underlies any assessment of the world's erupting cities and which is perhaps most neatly summed up in the distinction made by one sociologist between "slums of hope" and "slums of despair".

To many, officials, politicians, journalists, doctors, academics, planners, who have tried and failed to wrestle with the bursting, milling, grimy, disease-ridden, illiterate, unskilled, detribalised, unurbanised hordes who arrive each year to clog up the world's housing lists, elementary schools, bus lanes and social services, the cities of the late twentieth century, especially in the Third World, can only be described as "cancers not catalysts". They tend to argue that, unlike the nineteenth-century cities of Europe and North America, which became the engines and midwives of change and prosperity, the new urban monstrosities of the developing countries can only rot and sink under the weight of their cumulative malfunctions. Indeed, in the view of the more gloomy and apocalyptic, those burgeoning slums and septic shack-villes could only too easily provide both spark and tinder for a revolution sweeping away all that has been achieved in ten thousand years of civilisation – which is, of course, the culture of cities.

Even in Calcutta, though, it is possible, through the murk and misery, to take a very different and more positive view. The pages of an International Labour Office report are not perhaps the first place one would look for an eloquent statement of hope, but here is one of their officers, Harold Lubell, discoursing in an internal memorandum on the "hallucinatory quality about Calcutta which goes with the two faces of its patron goddess, Kali as the goddess of destruction, and Durga as the goddess of fertility". The city, as he records, "is a nightmare of crowds, of poverty, of organised and unorganised violence, of maimed beggars, of pavement dwellers, or pot-holed and ill-lighted streets ... and yet its main impact is a feeling of vitality, of creativity, of irrepressible exuberance. In its heyday the city was a trading, financial, industrial, political and cultural centre for all of India. After two decades of decline it is still all of these."

Lubell, in other words, like the Filipino sociologist, Aprodicio Laquian, in his classic Manila study, *Slums are for People*, or the British architect, John F. C. Turner, who for a decade has been writing and lecturing about the immense reservoirs of talent and self-help to be found in the *barrios* and *barriados* which form a ring of apparent squalor round most South American cities, does not accept the vicious-circle theory that "the city in the Third World is doomed to being a necropolis even before it becomes a metropolis or a megalopolis".

The holders of the darker view argue a many-stranded thesis. First they say that the sheer numbers of the squatter hordes imposed on already crumbling or inadequate city administrations, must quickly lead in many cases to irreversible breakdown. Then they point to the job pattern of all but a handful of Third World cities: the proliferation of "tertiary" employments, market traders, pedlars, porters, cycle-taxi drivers, casual labourers, and low-grade bureaucrats, as against high-productivity, high-technology, high-skill posts in manufacturing industry. They adduce the grinding pressure of poverty, sickness, worry, extra-legal existence, poor schooling and dismal prospects as reasons why the slums and shanties should form ideal seed-beds for unthinking radicalism and the worst type of demagoguery – especially when, as in the extreme case of Lima, where 4·5 million of the expected 6 million population by the year 2000 are expected to be squatters, the have-nots and outcasts form a clear voting majority over the haves.

In Barbara Ward's well-known statement, first published some years ago, and widely quoted since, the argument ran as follows: "All the world over, often long in advance of effective indus-trialisation, the unskilled poor are streaming away from sub-sistence agriculture to exchange the squalor of rural poverty for the even deeper miseries of the shanty-towns, *favelas*, *bidonvilles*, that year by year grow inexorably on the fringes of the develop-ing cities. They are the core of local despair and disaffection – fuelling the *jeunesse* movements of the Congo, swelling the urban mobs of Rio, voting Communist in the ghastly alleys of Calcutta, everywhere undermining the all-too-frail structure of public order and thus retarding the economic development that can alone help their plight. Unchecked, disregarded, left to grow and fester, there is here enough explosive material to produce in the world at large the pattern of a bitter class conflict, finding to an increasing degree a racial bias, erupting in guerrilla warfare and threatening ultimately the security even of the comfortable West."

Now, obviously, it is possible to give chapter, verse and copious examples to back up every clause in that conspectus. The Shiv Sena riots in Bombay in 1966, when Marathi-speakers rose to deny jobs to non-Marathis; the massacres of the Chinese communities in Kuala Lumpur in 1968; the full-scale military eviction of the squatters from Manila's Intramuros quarter in 1963; the shooting at Peru's San Salvador in 1971, when the *barriados* pitched camp too close to the Pan-American Highway and the rich residential suburb of Monterrico; all these illustrate the electric tensions always present in the situation. And yet, may it not be even more significant how few, relatively, such incidents have been? Given the provocation, the ever-present, only too visible contrast in most Third World cities between the air-conditioned, Cadillac-driving, property-speculating, servant-pampered, lawn-sprinkling lives of the affluent few, and the sub-subsistence struggle of the huge majority, is it not the sparseness of urban guerrilla activity, the low levels of theft and violence, the absence of political mob-rule which are the really striking phenomena?

In such a massive, complex and infinitely varied development as the urbanisation of the Third World, observing the extremes is of little value – it is the averages and relativities that count. A good deal of the detailed work that has been done on the ground among the new-city communities suggests there may be rather more hope around than the doomsters give credit for.

To start with, there is the character of the squatters themselves. As they crowd into the unwanted interstices of the cities – buying their four posts and a tin roof from the *geçekundu* merchant in Istanbul, camping in the parks and on the traffic islands of Bogotà, colonising the city garbage dumps in Bombay or Caracas, erecting their hardboard "casbahs" round the outskirts of the North African capitals – they may well look, to the police, to the authorities, to upright private householders, like the worst kind of threat. Undoubtedly, some of them are. But in fact there is often as stratified and hierarchical a social order among the squatters as among the sober, established citizens whom it is their dearest wish to emulate. Frequently, it is the most intelligent, capable, and ambitious inhabitants of a country who migrate to the city – not the most feckless and irresponsible. By and large, red or any other revolution is as far from their thoughts as from those of the Lord Mayor of London.

The Australian sociologist, Maurice Juppenlatz, for instance, has reported that in Manila, squatters come in five quite distinct varieties. There are the foreshore people, who camp out on the river banks and estuaries, to fish and run their boats – they account for about 10 per cent of the city's 400,000 or so illicit occupants. Then there are the 30 per cent who are refugees from the typhoon and famine-stricken Visaya islands. With another 30 per cent of economically-depressed villagers, driven from the land by necessity (but often retaining a hankering to return) these represent the most intransigent and intractable part of the problem. Another 10 per cent were "professional squatters" – fully or semi-criminal – out to exploit the system, using blackmail and strong-arm methods to acquire and trade sides. Beyond them, however, there are a clear 20 per cent – some 80,000 people – with some education and enterprise, who are quite frankly squatting because it is cheap, and gives them the chance to save for the legal housing which is at present quite beyond their reach.

These are what Turner, in a South American context, calls "the improving squatters" – the families who, given half a chance, will upgrade mud and tarpaulin huts into brick and concrete houses, club together to run nursery schools, hire lawyers for their self-protection, and harry the authorities, by every means in their power, to legalise their tenancies, sell them their sites, however illegitimately acquired, and generally allow them to organise their lives on the approved pattern of bourgeois success. Among the 5,000 or so forcibly evicted from Manila's Intramuros fort in 1963, for instance, there were solicitors, journalists, an actress, policemen and nine professional golf caddies. And in another study, on squatters in the new Malaysian capital of Kuala Lumpur, it was notable that some of the more prominent residents in the illegal settlement just below the President's Palace were police, promoted from provincial forces, who just could not afford to live any other way.

At Davao, another fast-growing urban centre in the Philippines, it is possible to see solid squatter-built houses – and shacks as well – bristling with TV antennae, and notices saying "Master Plumber", "Dental Clinic", "Notary Public" and "Wanted: House Maid". Similar evidence of self-improvement is to be found all round North Africa, Kinshasa, Brazzaville, the eastern Mediterranean (where one of Athens's earliest squatter colonies, on the north slope of the Acropolis, is now legitimised as the artists' quarter, the nearest thing Greece has to Montmartre), and above all in South America. Not all such communities have the luck and pugnacity of Rio's Jacarezinho *favela*, who managed to tap a main running along the north slope of the site, defended it against all comers, and enjoyed free water for years. But throughout the Third World there is ample evidence of people's stubborn determination – first to get a toe-hold in the city, then to build it up, and finally to shame or pressure the authorities into recognising the situation and giving it a legal gloss.

In Peru, where between 1949 and 1956 the government built 5,476 houses while 50,000 families went ahead on any plot they could grab and built their own, it is estimated that "self-help" housing now accounts for half the dwelling space in the country. Turner, who has studied the development with enormous sympathy, finds clear patterns emerging on lines that he elaborates later in this book. First the "itinerant" arrives from the backlands, often with nothing but what he stands up in, and camps wherever he can find a corner to lay his head. Then, as a "tentative" squatter he joins up with others to invade some tip, or swamp, or railway embankment – usually within walking distance of possible work – and erects a "transient" shanty. If the group succeeds in repelling police action, as frequently happened in Chile, Columbia, Mexico and Peru in the 1960s (not to mention in Manila and Ankara) it quickly achieves an "established" status (no legal rights, but now effectively secure) with more solid "provisional" buildings. With time, it is usually possible to coax the authorities into extending some limited legal recognition – perhaps running in a stand-pipe or an electricity line to avoid the worst kind of health or security hazard – at which point the squatters start planning and building on a permanent basis. Finally, and hopefully, full title is granted, however reluctantly, and the *barriada* evolves into a fully-fledged district or suburb of the city.

Many of the signs are very encouraging, even in the earlier stages. There are plenty of examples of co-operation and fore-thought – squatter groups laying out not only houses, but schools, playgrounds, clinics and public meeting places, sharing the cost as best they can. And despite the original illegal seizure, respect for property – washing, fuel, and other people's unbuilt-on-land – is often very high.

That is one of the explodable myths about Third World city growth – that squatters necessarily lack respect for law and order, except when it is used directly against them (and not always even then – as in the Manila evictions of 1963, when it was the known criminals, of the Oxo and Sigue-Sigue gangs, who turned out to be among the most responsible parents and citizens). Another is the notion that city poverty is no improvement on the rural kind – Juppenlatz found that his Manila squatters, though only one-tenth as well off as even their poorest established neighbours, were still ten times better off than they had been in their villages. For them, the slum and the shanty town are still the first way-station on the road to a better life. And even the Third World dependence on simple, service-sector jobs which causes so much concern can turn out a blessing in disguise – it is amazing how many people can be found jobs, of a kind, round the markets, or helping with the minutiae of food preparation, where the rigid structure of a Western-style factory denies all but the lucky any place at all.

But having said all that, and giving human beings the maximum credit for toughness, tenacity, survival-power, ambition, and bootstrap-raising ability, the fundamental question still remains: can the people and institutions ostensibly in charge actually cope with the mountingly chaotic pressures which come together in these huge new urban ant-heaps? When Paris still has its *bidonvilles*, and London, Tokyo and New York their deplorable slums, what hope have Calcutta, Kinshasa, Mexico City and the rest, with maybe one-tenth or less of the developed world's *per capita* income available to finance their multifarious tasks?

More important than that, even, is whether they have actually identified the right tasks. The West, over-impressed by smells, dirt, sewage floating in the streets, and the general air of bottom-less dilapidation, tends to call for standards of housing, sanitation, and services which anyone with the back of an envelope at hand can calculate are beyond the means of Thailand or Indonesia or Ecuador. The local political élites, usually trained and frequently financed to a large extent by the West, adopt these same standards, fail to see how they can be applied on any mass scale, and tend to throw up their hands in despair, concentrating instead on personal wealth-gathering and the appurtenances of authoritarian power. But this is not the only possible approach.

The most promising alternative appears to lie in accepting the implicit message of the millions who continue to flood into the cities every year. Their tolerance of what appear appalling conditions is amazingly high, so long as they can acquire the things that only the city, for most of them, can provide – a variety of job opportunities, and the chance that their children, at any rate, can get an education and a foot on the first rung of the ladder which the Western nations have so painfully climbed.

Given this, what is needed, surely, is not a policy to knock down these laboriously constructed shanty towns and rehouse a pitiful few in the solid, ugly concrete boxes which can only become the slums of the next seventy years. It is rather a determination to improve the shanty town – to put in the water, and the power, to legitimise the land-holding so as to encourage people's self-help instincts, and at the same time to set up new, far better-chosen sites, planned for best and cheapest access to mass-transit systems, properly laid out, even with the barest minimum of those services, like main drainage, which people cannot provide for themselves, so that they can get on with building what they can.

Charles Correa, architect and planner in Bombay, must be on the right lines. He calculates that, to catch up with India's staggering housing shortage – 12 million units, without even starting on the necessary roads, sewers, shops, schools and so forth – would cost an astronomical £3,840 million, even to the barest Western standards, and demand rents more than double the capacity of the people involved. Instead, he proposes that such standards should be wholly abandoned, so that India can concentrate on those traditional mud structures, and houses of brick set in mud mortar and roofed with country-made tiles, in which large numbers of the people already quite happily live. These can be built for less than a third, and in the case of mud huts, only a thirtieth of the cost of the alternative "standard" structure. And the fact that they would only last about fifteen years he regards as a virtue, not a drawback. "After fifteen years, if our economy improves, we shall presumably have more resources to deal with this problem of housing. To build slums, permanent slums which last seventy years (as done by most housing boards throughout the country) is really the act of a pessimist. What it really does is say: our economy isn't going to get any better."

That is the line of thinking which is so conspicuously missing throughout so much of the Third World. One or two small but increasingly rich countries like Hong Kong and Singapore feel they can go the other way – Hong Kong, by a colossal effort, has evicted and resettled 1·8 million Hong Kong-born Chinese, and refugees and their children, in high tower blocks over the past twenty years. But there are still over a quarter of a million squatters, and many more live in "tolerated but illegal" structures (many of them perched on the roofs of other people's buildings), after constant efforts since 1954 – when 50,000 shacks burned down in a firework-factory fire and spurred the government to action. To house everybody adequately – the aim for the early 1980s – will entail rehousing a further 1·5 million, at a cost of over US$1,000 million at 1973 rates. It is virtually impossible that any larger, less economically ebullient country could even begin to match such a line of attack. For the rest, the only long-term policy must be to help the teeming, toiling millions of the Third World cities to do as much as they can, and want, to help themselves. Otherwise, the pessimists in the end will turn out to be right – 1,467 million desperate and dispossessed people will use their physical and political power to help themselves in other, far more cruel and dangerous ways.

CHAPTER 2

Abou Ben Adhem,
May His Tribe Increase

It is worth reminding ourselves that the end of
the century is not far away. About two-thirds
of the people now living on earth, if mortality
continues downward, will still be alive by the
year 2000. The projected urban trend, should
it come to pass, will therefore put a substantial proportion of present humanity into
cities of a size that no human being up to now
has ever come close to experiencing.

KINGSLEY DAVIS,
World Urbanisation 1950–1970, vol. II

The smallest British city is Ely, in the Fens, with just over 10,000
people, and several other proud United Kingdom upholders of
ancient civic dignity – Elgin, Truro, Bangor, Ripon – are not
much bigger. None of them would count even as urban
agglomerations (minimum 20,000) under the United Nations
demographic definitions, which set the lower limit for fully-
fledged cities at 100,000. Big-cities start at 500,000; million-cities,
as their name suggests, are in the seven-figure class; multi-
million cities weigh in at 2·5 million; and super-conurbations,
like Tokyo–Yokohama and Greater New York, range from 12·5
million upwards. New categories, however, may soon be required.
By 1985, the present trends suggest, there may be three or four
countries with metropolitan areas containing over 25 million, and
possibly one (Calcutta? São Paulo? Mexico City?) with over
50 million. And the mathematical extrapolation of current
developments suggests that there could even be one monster of
100 million or more by the end of the century.

Basically, there are two ways of predicting the future course of
world urbanisation. You can either take figures for what happened

in the recent past – say the years 1950 to 1970, as was done by Kingsley Davis in his authoritative study of the subject – and extrapolate them into the future. Or alternatively you can find a typical country where the urbanisation process has gone a great deal further than it has in the world as a whole, and use its experience as a pattern for the way things are likely to happen elsewhere. Britain's townscape probably developed too slowly, and too far in the past to provide a good contemporary guide, and Japan, at the other end of the scale, has been expanding her cities too rapidly and too recently. But the United States, which had about the same distribution of rural, urban and city population in the 1880s as the world as a whole had attained in the 1950s, might reasonably be expected to show the way, so long as you do not put too much unsupported weight on the evidence it provides.

In fact, the two methods, though widely differing in their premises, turn out to generate remarkably consistent results, given all the obvious problems about deciding just who is a town-, city- or country-dweller at any particular moment. Certainly, there is a substantial spread in the figures – but often more marked between the various ways of extrapolating the 1950–70 data than between extrapolation and the US-based forecast. This, based on Davis's calculations, is the way the world population picture is likely to unfold – barring major catastrophes and unforeseen events – over the next twenty-five years:

(*Unit: million*)

Year	Total population	Rural	Urban
1970	3,628	2,229	1,399
1975	3,925–3,981	2,300–2,352	1,625–1,660
1980	4,223–4,368	2,362–2,484	1,861–1,969
1985	4,521–4,794	2,404–2,621	1,118–2,336
1990	4,818–5,261	2,424–2,767	2,394–2,771
1995	5,112–5,773	2,432–2,921	2,680–3,287
2000	5,400–6,335	2,430–3,083	2,971–3,899

For comparison, the UN's latest global estimates for the year 2000 put total population at 6,494 million, which is slightly above Davis's high figure, with urban and rural components running almost level, at 3,234 million and 3,260 million respectively.

Whichever way you look at them, the implications of these

predictions are quite staggering. The proportions themselves are moving fast enough – the urban proportion moving from 38·6 per cent in 1970 to almost 50 per cent, even on the lowest estimate, inside three decades, and "citification" proceeding twice as rapidly – but it is the absolute numbers which really take the breath away. Within a generation, the world's urban population will double, even on the most conservative assumptions, and quite possibly treble. The higher up the scale you go, the more dramatic the acceleration becomes. City populations (over 100,000) will go up at least two and a half times; big-city populations probably three times; and million-cities between three and four times. Even that understates, if anything, the magnitude of what is happening. By the end of the century, if even the most conservative of predictions comes true, half the world's city dwellers – around 1,200 million people, or one in five of the world's entire population – will be living with more than 2·5 million neighbours. As Davis says, this is not so much "urbanisation" as "metropolitanisation", on a gigantic scale.

City Populations   (*Unit: million*)

Year	100,000+	500,000+	1 million+
1970	863	571	448
1975	1,014–1,043	683– 700	546– 562
1980	1,182–1,260	809– 856	658– 704
1985	1,371–1,522	954–1,048	789– 883
1990	1,596–1,838	1,119–1,283	939–1,106
1995	1,851–2,220	1,307–1,570	1,112–1,387
2000	2,131–2,681	1,520–1,922	1,309–1,738

The projections for individual cities – the ones that throw up the prospect of nightmare beehives, with 50 or 100 million people apiece – look a good deal less securely based. They arise from the observation that, in the past, when you arranged city sizes in logarithmically equal classes, there always turned out to be exactly twice as many cities in each class than in the one immediately above it. With a bit of statistical sleight-of-hand it is then possible to take any total population and see how many cities of each given size-range it will divide itself into. On this basis, it would appear that, if the world continues to urbanise itself at anything like its present rate, there will have to be at least one city in the world

Always room for an extra couple of hundred – commuters and "pushers" in Tokyo.

Van Dyke estate, New York (top) and Aylesford estate graffiti, London. The "city in a park" becomes the city in a parking lot and, while planners debate alternatives, the citizen scrawls his protest.

with over 100 million inhabitants – in fact, strictly following the
conditions of calculation, it will have to have over 140 million.
Even if you bend the sums quite a bit, you still come out with
three cities of over 64 million, of which at least one is likely to be
at the 100 million-end of the spectrum.

Naturally, the mind rebels at such notions. How could any
nation, or indeed any continent, feed, clean, house, transport or
in any way tolerate such unimaginable hordes? But the logic of
the figures does not thereby go away. If 140 million people are
not to be accommodated in one city, they will have to be spread
around elsewhere. Already the prospect is that there will be
somewhere between fourteen and seventeen places by the
year 2000 which are more heavily populated than New York.
Dispersing their 500 million or so inhabitants to smaller and less
congested locations will be no snap-of-the-fingers task. In fact,
it is clear that population growth and population concentration
on the scale envisaged here must tax human ingenuity, will-power
and technological skill to a degree quite unimagined by most
people quietly going about their business in the relatively well-
managed cities of 1975.

Let us turn then, to the cities as we know them today, and
particularly to those which already have over one million inhabitants, or are likely to reach that level of density and complexity
over the next ten years. These, essentially, form the location for
the ticking fuse and the incipient city explosion.

As recently as 1950, the list would have been relatively short.
Only seventy-five places would have qualified, with a total of
only 173·9 million inhabitants. But already the picture has been
transformed. In 1975, there were 191 entries, with new names
like Curtiba in Brazil and Lyallpur, West Pakistan, joining such
slower-developing, but longer-established arrivals as Vancouver,
Damascus and Odessa. The numbers involved had, at the same
time, risen to 515 million.

A decade further on, in 1985, the roll-call will have stretched
out to 273, with Siberia's Krasnoyarsk and Madagascar's Tanana-
rive coming in alongside Dublin, Aleppo and Kabul. By then
it is expected that more than 800 million people will be living in
one or another of these sprawling urban monsters – one in six of
the human race. But also by then there is every likelihood that
Mexico City, São Paulo, Los Angeles and Shanghai (despite

2

China's much-trumpeted efforts at decentralisation) will have joined New York and Tokyo in the super-conurbation class – with Peking itself, London, Bombay, Calcutta, Osaka-Kobe, Seoul, Buenos Aires, West Germany's Rhein-Ruhr complex, Paris, Rio de Janeiro and Cairo-Giza, each with well over 10 million, coming up fast behind. This group alone, aggregating some 262 million people, will easily outstrip the world's whole major-city population as it stood as recently as ten years ago.

No detailed and systematic attempt has yet been made to extend these forecasts ahead, on a city-by-city basis (and certainly no local authority, as far as is known, is consciously planning the first 100-million megalopolis). But whatever checks and balances, Malthusian or otherwise, come into effect at some stage, the immediate scenario is fairly clear. Within less than half the average lifetime, some 1,900 million people can expect to be living in places the size of present-day Newcastle-upon-Tyne or Marseilles or New Orleans. And meanwhile, if present trends continue, another ten centres, Karachi, Moscow, Teheran, Delhi, Chicago, Bangkok, Manila, Lima, Bogotà and Jakarta, will all be moving into the super-conurbation division – or worse.

It will be noticed that no fewer than eighteen out of the twenty-seven really big metropolitan complexes predicted here by the year 2000 are to be found in what are normally known as the developing countries. This is typical – on UN figures, urban population in Europe, North America and the more developed regions (including Russia, Japan and temperate South America) will merely double over the period 1960–2000, while that of the Third World will multiply five-fold. From 1950 to 1970, the poorer parts of Asia, Africa and Latin America contributed more than 50 per cent of the growth of the world's city-based population. Between 1960 and 1980, the UN expects them to account for three-fifths of all the expansion in the big- and multi-million-city categories. Yet at the same time it is these impoverished, under-capitalised, under-industrialised nations which are also carrying the brunt of the parallel population explosion which is taking place in many of the world's rural areas. While the number of people in urban areas is expected to grow from 985 million in 1960 to 3,234 million in 2000, the numbers still in the countryside will also multiply, from 1,997 million to 3,260 million. But the crude figures conceal the fact that, during the period, the rural portion of the developed world will show a net drop of 119 million. Their poverty-stricken neighbours on the other hand will have to feed, support and accommodate an extra 1,383 million mouths, on land which in many cases can barely sustain a starvation economy as it is. These are the statistical mill-stones – massive natural increase, and potentially massive migration from the hungry hinterland – between which the fate of most of the world's great cities will be ground out in the next few years.

What makes cities grow, and why do some grow so much faster, and others cope so much more successfully than others? Is it possible to explain the distribution network of large, medium and small urban settlements around the world, or do the cities, towns and extended villages in which half mankind will soon be spending its life form a completely random pattern? What constraints prevent all the people of a country – or indeed a region, or a continent – congregating into one giant conurbation? And might not the most efficient form of human organisation turn out ultimately to be one such global super-city, sustained perhaps by hydroponic food production, and stretching from Cork to Boston, Massachusetts, by way of the Aleutian Bridge?

A framework for answering such questions is required before one can even begin to assess the true seriousness of the present exploding-cities phenomenon. Trees do not grow up to the sky, for well-understood botanical reasons, so it is not necessary to worry about the consequences if they did. Similarly for cities: however dramatic and appalling the current trends, and some of their side-effects, may happen to be, there would be less reason for concern about the future if some effective self-limiting and self-balancing mechanism were quietly at work. But does it exist?

According to the vehemence of one's belief or disbelief in such a mechanism, the current state of affairs in the *favelas* and *bidonvilles* of the developing world – or, come to that, even in the bullet-swept and mugger-ridden streets of downtown Detroit – can still be interpreted neutrally, if hardly optimistically. By no means all the best-regarded experts are committed to the apocalyptic doom-view. Even the global super-sprawl idea cannot be dismissed out of hand as an unthinkable futurologist's nightmare. Scholars as reputable as Harry Richardson in Britain, N. V. Sovani in India, and Koichi Mera in Japan have all argued recently that no nation so far has come near to exhausting the various economies of scale and opportunities for human improvement that are essentially available only in the largest cities. Mera, writing from the heart of the Tokyo-Yokohama complex, which already contains almost 18 million people, states flatly that even the largest metropolitan area in the world is likely to be less than the theoretically "optimal" size.

Naturally, none of these careful analysts suggests that such "optimality" – even if the concept has any clear, universally-applicable meaning, as Richardson tends to doubt – can be achieved without a great deal of thought, planning and probably pain along the way. But to reject their generally rather hopeful point of view out of hand requires the critic to offer an alternative assessment of the forces at work. Growth in the human body can be cancerous or benign, and it often takes considerable medical skill to tell the difference. In the much more complicated and ill-understood area of urban pathology the difficulties are even greater. So how should we, in fact, set about testing the patient and trying to distinguish between imminent morbidity and excessively rude health?

Essentially, as the statistics spell out in detail, there are three separate though interrelated sets of demographic phenomena at present turning the screws on the world's major cities: the very rapid growth in population overall; the accelerating switch everywhere from rural to urban life-styles; and the apparently universal tendency for this change to concentrate itself on the largest available settlements.

For the individual city, though, the main components of population expansion boil down to two. First there is natural increase among those already established in the city – the excess of births over deaths. And second there is migration – the net balance between arrivals and departures. So far, so simple. But what the Oxford conference brought out very clearly was the immense variety of influences acting and re-acting on these factors, within the diverse and heterogeneous communities that make up the reality of any substantial metropolitan area. It is just this diversity which makes it so appallingly difficult to see what is really happening.

Take, for instance, fertility – the birth side of the natural-increase equation. One of the great hopes, underpinning the work of all the multifarious national and international groups concerned with birth control, family planning and the like, is that the process of urbanisation itself is the best guarantee that the average number of children per family will be gradually reduced towards the "replacement" levels supposed to be characteristic of the developed nations. But as Sir Maurice Kendall, the Director of the World Fertility Survey, told the conference, the point is still very much unproven.

"Historical data from most of the countries where human fertility is fairly low have established the existence of an inverse correlation between fertility and the degree of urbanisation of a community. There is also substantial evidence of urban-rural differentials in fertility having existed in many European countries for at least the last century. It appears that as natural fertility began to decline in those countries, the differentials tended to widen owing to a more pronounced fall in urban fertility; whereas after the recovery of the birth-rate following the Second World War there was a narrowing of the differentials. The reasons for this phenomenon are by no means clear. The most favoured theory is that birth control attitudes and practices conducive to the lowering of fertility were first adopted by the higher social groups in cities, and then transmitted over the course of time to the lower social groups and thence to the rural population. We know less about the developing countries."

It is to repair this gap in demographic knowledge that the Survey is currently engaged in a massive, world-wide research programme. But it would be several years, Sir Maurice thought, before there was enough reliable data to form a considered view of the effect of urbanisation on birth-rate throughout the world, and meanwhile the emerging picture was pretty mixed. In some countries of Africa, Asia and Latin America there appear to be fertility differentials "of the usual kind", but in others either the difference is insignificant at the moment, or, even worse, it actually goes the wrong way – people in cities produce even more babies than they did before they left their native village. On the latest UN figures (Demographic Survey 1972) Mexico and Panama are examples in the first category, while Guatemala, Liberia and Nicaragua stand out in the second.

Kendall spelled out some of the general reasons why this might happen. "The average couples living in some of these societies are bound by cultural and religious practices which do not work so powerfully in the developed countries, such as taboos of sex, taboos of widow remarriage, prolonged breast-feeding of infants and so forth." But more vivid and practical illustrations were provided by some of the delegates who actually work in the shanty towns and high-rise blocks where the "urbanisation" magic is actually at work.

It is, in fact, said Professor José Arthur Rios, of Rio de Janeiro's Catholic University, only when people move out of the *favelas* into the modern apartment blocks, that they become "contraceptive conscious". In the shanty towns – which for many purposes are more like country villages re-erected on a scrap of urban wasteland – children are an asset. They start work early, often at five or six years old. They help their parents and relations with the poultry-raising and the vegetable-growing that goes on amidst all the stench and chaos, on the tiny plots occupied by the cardboard and corrugated iron houses. "But in the apartments, in the narrow confines of high-rise living, parents become conscious of the need to limit families." They forfeit all the tiny jobs and chances for buying and selling which used to supplement their minute *favela* incomes – and for which any extra child came in very handy – and have to rely instead on one meagre salary. "The minimum wage now in Rio is around US$50 a month – and the minimum wage is still a privilege many people have yet to aspire to," said Rios dryly. "It is very difficult for a family who had multiple small sources of income to adjust to the new situation. To make matters worse, the apartment complexes have been built in the outskirts of the city far away from the places of work, so the single source is substantially decreased by transportation costs."

But the net effect of this on Rio's total fertility remains far from clear. Rio has built up tremendous systems of housing finance, to support one of the world's most massive city building programmes. But after ten years, and the spending of £3,000 million, the number of families actually relocated out of the *favelas* does not probably amount to more than one million. Meanwhile the shanty town population of Rio alone, according to Rios, still numbers over 500,000 (out of six million in the inner city) and is growing at 7 per cent a year – more than twice the overall average.

Out of those half-million people, he estimated, perhaps 150,000 had already achieved, or were in the process of achieving, the lower-middle-class status which goes with the sort of savings needed to buy an apartment on a twenty-year loan – and presumably also with urban attitudes to family limitation. But does this apply to the much poorer 350,000 – or to the 500,000 additional Rio citizens "who live in ghettos and other different forms of urban pauperisation"? And will it apply now that the Brazilian authorities, accepting the impossibility of rehousing the whole pauper community with public money, are increasingly switching resources and emphasis to a "self-help" programme (through CODESCO, the Community Development Corporation) which will encourage the shanty-dwellers to improve their own houses inside the *favelas* – complete with gardens and chicken houses?

Far away, in the Philippines, and in Turkey, the International Development Research Centre team, directed from Ottawa by Dr Aprodicio Laquian, have detected another trend which may have considerable bearing on the urban fertility question. Traditionally the pattern of migration from country to town, widely documented in the IDRC's work on *Town Drift*, has centred on the figure of the young, single male, seeking his fortune and sending home for a wife, often years later. Now there is an increasing likelihood that, in Manila and Istanbul, as also in Accra and in Caracas, the new city arrival will turn up complete with wife and ready-made family. Provisionally this change is being related to an increasing rate of urbanisation – and it certainly looks like creating even greater housing problems for city authorities. But is it likely to increase or decrease the average child-bearing levels among the wives involved? And how does it relate to another migration phenomenon, emphasised by Professor Buu Hoan, alternate director of the Asian Development Bank – the flight to the cities of the more educated country children? Even after as little as three or four years' schooling, the chances that a farmer's son will return to the land move towards zero in most countries of the developing world. Instead, he tries his luck in the urban environment for which he feels he has been prepared (but which is often deeply reluctant to offer him a job). Does his education and its effect on his likely choice of wife, raise or lower his desire to procreate? With primary education expanding at 6 per cent a year in South-East Asia – thus doubling every twelve years – this is not a trivial question. But so far neither the World Fertility Survey or the many independent researchers in the field appear to have produced an answer.

Fertility, in any case, is only one of the factors of natural increase. Whatever doubts there may be about the effect of urbanisation and citification on birth, there are very few about their impact on death. City air may or may not make people free, but in almost every recorded case in recent years it makes them a great deal healthier and longer-lived. The sewers may overflow, and the sky be thick with sulphur and carbon monoxide, but mortality rates come crashing down. This is due partly to the higher proportion of young, fit people in city populations, and partly to public health activities – even the most unsatisfactory drainage or clean water system tends to be better than none at all. In many cases, too, it may result from the overwhelming concentration of Third World doctors and nurses in the towns, and particularly in the capital cities. Bangkok, for instance, monopolises two-thirds of all Thailand's surgeons and physicians, although it has only 8 per cent of the country's population; and this order of distortion, according to Buu Hoan, would be quite typical of Asia as a whole.

These lower urban death rates partly, and often completely, cancel out the effects of lower fertility in the cities. On the UN's global figures for 1960, which are the most detailed available in this area, natural increase was running at 16 per thousand of the population in urban areas, and only slightly higher in the rural sector, at 21 per thousand. In many individual cases, the cities are far outstripping the countryside. In North Africa, Gerald Blake found natural increase rates of between 30 and 40 per thousand for Tunis, Algiers, Tangier and Casablanca, accounting for virtually the whole of their recent growth.

These rates would be exceptional. But Kingsley Davis, in his own wide-ranging survey, calculates that natural increase was responsible for anything between three-tenths and two-thirds of the urban and city expansion recorded in the past twenty years. He breaks the figures down like this:

Proportion of Growth Attributed to Natural Increase

% urban	Urban population		City population	
	1950–60	1960–70	1950–60	1960–70
0–15	30·5	44·7	27·8	36·5
15–40	42·9	40·8	36·7	38·5
40–65	53·8	44·3	44·3	35·3
65–80	58·5	64·9	57·5	52·1
Economic level				
Developed	45·6	48·2	42·4	41·1
Less developed	42·4	43·2	34·4	38·4

This indicates that a great deal of every city's future expansion problems is already resident within its own walls. Merely keeping out or discouraging the migrants will only moderate the pressure, and in some cases, as in the North African examples, barely affect it at all.

CHAPTER 3

Now That They've Seen Paree

It is better to be the head of a village than the
tail of a city.

Corsican Proverb

How far the migrants bring their rural fertility with them, how
long it takes them – and particularly the women – to adapt urban
ideas of family size, whether it may not be rather their reduced
death rate than their still-high birth rates which represents their
true contribution to city population, whether the situation can be
modified by specific policies, on housing, education, health care
and so forth – all such questions remain largely unresolved. So
too, unfortunately, do many of the key problems relating to
migration itself.

What makes people move? And what makes them move in
particular ways – usually those most irritating and incompre-
hensible to the responsible authorities? If the answers were
known, agreed and unambiguous, it should be possible to create
policies which would appropriately control, curb or redirect this
massive folk-wandering which is taking place across three-
quarters of the world. But as it is, the rather desperate-sounding
official metaphors are usually constructed around images of floods
and dykes and holding back the tide. To the individuals involved
the answer lies in just a simple decision to try something new and
better. To governments and international agencies, these mass
movements often look more like an inexorable and implacable
natural force. So what precisely are the dimensions of this force,
and how successful has any nation been in mitigating its impact?

Putting accurate figures on migration is in fact an extremely
difficult technical feat once you start dealing with communities of
several million people. Census takers find it hard enough in many
cases just to count heads every few years. Keeping the heads still
for detailed questions of the where-were-you-five-years-ago-and-

why-did-you-leave variety are virtually impossible, except on a small-sample basis. The key observation, though, is that, in country after country, urban population, despite the lower fertility and lower natural-increase factors, is sharply growing faster than rural. City populations (over 100,000) are growing appreciably faster still. Migration must account for a large part of the difference – as observation, deduction and a mass of varied survey material amply confirm. Greater Seoul and Greater Pusan, for instance, gained respectively by 45·6 per cent and 31·5 per cent in population between 1966 and 1970, while the nine other South Korean provinces showed either very small increases or actual loss. These enormous shifts – involving almost 1·6 million people in less than five years – can be almost wholly ascribed to people physically moving themselves and their families to the big cities (possibly not unconnected with the fact that *per capita* income in Seoul and Pusan is exactly twice that of the rest of the country).

Some idea of the overall dimensions of such movements can be obtained by looking at the seventy-five cities in the world which already counted their population above one million by 1950. Since then the fifty-one located in the developed countries have added another 72 million, and the twenty-four in the developing world almost 85 million. All told, this represents migration to the tune of 95 million people – 53 million of them pouring into an all-too-limited number of impoverished Third World metropolises like Cairo, Havana and Jakarta. And the flood is hardly moderating – the UN projections suggest that another 37 million or so will descend on the same twenty-four over-strained reception centres between now and 1985, while the old major cities of Europe and North America need plan to accommodate only 21 million newcomers between them. Even that, though, looks quite a task when you recall that, in the whole of the nineteenth century (indeed, right up to 1940) the vast migrant wave which crossed the Atlantic to people the New World amounted to rather less than 40 million.

One very important fact to bear in mind about contemporary migration is that, although it is normally at the expense of the rural and agricultural population, it is only among the rich nations that it is relatively large enough to cause an actual decline among the country-dwellers. Everywhere else, rural numbers continue to increase, despite the scale of the departures. This in itself creates a formidable engine for gearing up the pressure on the towns. In an area like South-East Asia, which is still only 15 per cent "citified", it only takes the migration of one in six of the naturally-increasing rural teenagers to double the natural growth-rate of a Manila, a Bangkok or a Jakarta. As Buu Hoan said grimly: "Precisely because urbanisation is concentrated in a few primate cities, the rural influx will continue to accelerate, thus taxing urban infrastructures to the extreme; concurrently the rural population will continue to increase unabated. This is in full contrast with the process of urbanisation in the West. The point at which the absolute number of rural workers started to decline was a key event in the economic history of the Western World. Perhaps it will never be reached in South-East Asia (with, of course, the exception of Singapore)."

Faced with this complex of problems, some countries have tried deliberately and directly to halt the flow of migrants to their cities. Probably the most comprehensive attempt was the "closing" of Jakarta in 1970 by its governor, Ali Sadikin. Under the decree limiting entry, any rural arrival must first apply for a "short visit" card and register with the city government. He deposits enough money to cover twice the cost of transporting him back to his native village or island, and six months later has to return and prove that he has acquired a job and a home. If he can he gets his deposit back, less 10 per cent for administration costs, and is allowed to buy an identification card for "Jakarta Citizenship", costing about 9 US cents or 3½p. If not, he gets a one-way ticket home. This system is claimed to have cut migration by 50 per cent, down to 1,400 people a month, but many expert visitors have doubts. The numbers involved are huge – 13,000 arrests for violation of the decree in a single night on one famous occasion – and there is a swelling market in faked cards and papers. The scared and the law-abiding stay away, but as one writer said, the Indonesian capital still "'leaks internal migrants like a sieve" – mostly the bold, the reckless and the wholly unscrupulous, who may or may not be the kind of future citizens the authorities wish to encourage.

Sometimes the discouragement of migrants can be a relatively simple affair. Benjamin Pogrund, the well-known South African journalist, told the Oxford conference about the recent case of Botswana, a tiny African country of about 500,000 people, where a year or so ago a brand new hotel with a casino was opened in the new capital of Gaborone. "Word got back hundreds of miles away that if you put 20 cents into this machine (and 20 cents would be about 12p or 13p) you could get back Rand 40 just by pulling a lever – £25. The Botswana government found, to its embarrassment, extraordinary numbers of people pouring into Gaborone and living in shacks on the edge of the town. This was basically a simple problem because the way it was met was simply to impose a levy of 50 cents (about 30p) on anyone wishing to enter the casino, and the poor people coming from vast distances away could not even afford that."

More usually, though, governments and city administrations try a varied mixture of policies in their attempts to moderate and redirect the flood. Aprodicio Laquian, describing the full-scale anthology of methods which has been attempted in the Philippines, divided the possibilities into five basic categories: keep them on the farm; throw them out of the cities; take them back to the farm; rechannel them to smaller, intermediate cities; tackle the problems where they arise, in the city itself.

To improve conditions in the rural sector – "to solve the problem of the urban areas before it even reaches the urban areas" – the Philippines are pushing hard with the new "miracle rice", with the intention of doubling yields per acre, and have also, with United States help, embarked on a major electrification programme. "Interestingly, the immediate impact has been to create a lot more leisure activity. The planners thought electricity would bring industrialisation and manufacturing. It brought juke-boxes, movies and cabarets. But again, surprisingly enough, it is keeping people on the farm: after all, bright lights mean not just neon signs, but dances, and we Filipinos like to live very well wherever we are." Also the curriculum for medical education is being revised to make doctors, nurses and social workers spend at least one year in a village before they can take their degree. "Then there are attempts at rural housing aid, undertaken in the hope that if a person has a mortgage to pay in a small town, he won't move to a large city."

Restrictions in the Philippines have not been carried as far as in Jakarta: "perhaps we do not have as good an identification system as the Indonesians, or maybe Filipinos are more inventive about getting out of the wild and into the city". The main local variant is to restrict city services to *bona fide* city residents, so that in order to get, say, free education in the public school system, it is necessary to produce an affidavit or birth certificate or some other document to prove "right of residence" in the city of Manila (which, being ten times bigger than the runner-up, Cebu, creates most of the difficulties). Such efforts are then reinforced with a vigorous (and often very funny) campaign on radio, television and in the magazines to paint the evils of city life and the beauty and ideal nature of the countryside.

This has not noticeably worked. It has been reinforced, from time to time, with a programme of "relocating squatters to suburban areas", which, as Laquian says, is too often a euphemism for dumping them out of sight. "The inner city has to keep up appearances, to remain an admirable aesthetic object; for the tourists and for the Pope's visit – you don't want him to see all those squatter and slum communities. So they are being relocated 15 or 20 kilometres out of the city, where there is no work. In one centre where I was doing research there were 5,000 families and eleven artesian wells – six of which promptly dried up because they were over-pumped. In one relocation community people were spending from 10 per cent to 15 per cent of the income they earned in the city for transportation alone. Obviously this kind of situation cannot last."

The squatters, he explained, originally agreed to be relocated because they were land-hungry. "They are speculating just like any good bourgeois or Filipino who wants to invest in land because land is the highest incremental investment obtainable. So the squatter invests, and then often puts his family in the relocation site, and rents a bed-space in the centre of the city (sometimes there are two workers renting the same bed-space and sleeping there in shifts). He works on the piers or he drives a jeepney, and he commutes. He returns to his family on Friday afternoons or Saturday mornings and goes back to the city on Mondays – and does this to save on transportation. Pretty soon, however, men being what they are, he has two families, one in the relocation centre and the other in the centre of the city – the *casa chica* is just as much an institution in the Philippines as in Latin America – so that then he has to work harder. And then what happens to UN Population Year, I don't know."

Laquian's view, as a sociologist (and also, as he proudly describes himself, as an "upwardly-mobile slum-dweller"), is that many such policies founder because the authorities concerned fail to realise that urbanisation is an irreversible process – especially when you have step-wise migration, whereby the people move from the village to a small town, then to an intermediate city, and then to the primate city. "By the time he arrives in the primate city he is a complete urbanite. So you send him back to the village and the farm – nothing doing. He will move to another rural place, maybe, if he is really down and out; but go back to his own village he will not. In the first place, he probably left the village bragging that he was going to make it in the city and come back a multi-millionaire. If he is asked to return as a failure, an insurmountable loss of face is being demanded of him. Failure to appreciate this produces ludicrous results: the government provides transportation for the person to return to his home village because it is difficult to support him in Manila. He takes the ride, spends a sabbatical there, several weeks of visiting relatives, and then he drifts back into the city."

A few more fruitful attempts have been made, Laquian admits, to decongest the cities by setting up more modern and industrialised forms of agriculture. Malaysia's Federal Land Development ment Schemes, for example, gives farm workers paid employment in a managerial system, rather than expecting them to go back to work as small farmers. But in the long term, Laquian doesn't think the policy of returning them to the rural areas has any chance of survival. There might be a better case for "re-channelling" families towards the medium-sized cities, taking some pressure off the swollen capital, but such efforts can be enormously costly and dubious in their effect. Under martial law in the Philippines it is now illegal to set up a new industry within thirty kilometres of the centre of Manila, and much existing industry is being relocated beyond this point, outside the designated "urban area", in an attempt to free the city from some of its congestion and pollution. But there are many hazards. "Conditions which will govern activities can be set, but it is very difficult really to control people and move them bodily. You can, by allocation of infrastructure priorities, by tax moratoria and by fiscal policies, influence the growth of intermediate cities, but this is a very expensive process. The Canadian case shows that to create the same type and number of jobs in Halifax, you have to invest four times as much as you would in Montreal or Toronto. In a developing country, where the infrastructural development is not quite so advanced, it may be much higher."

These, then, are the main methods adopted to alleviate the stresses and strains of Manila – a city of 3·4 million, nearly a tenth of its country's entire population, with perhaps a third of its inhabitants living in various types of slum or squatter settlement. The centre city itself is growing quite slowly – only 1·2 per cent a year – but the surrounding areas, like Quezon City, thanks to the government's "premature suburbanisation", or squatter-dumping activities, are expanding at rates of up to 12 per cent per annum. Surveys, by Laquian's teams and others, have shown that in many of the shanty areas 80 per cent to 90 per cent of the residents are migrants, many of them having arrived within the past ten years.

Why, then, do they come – these and the millions upon millions like them clinging on to marginal jobs, marginal houses, marginal lives in the swelling cities of the late twentieth century? Why do they accept, let alone seek out, the flooding, the smells, the electricity breakdowns, the police harassment, the gang wars, the juvenile delinquency, the underemployment and the squalor that make up so much of modern urban life in the Third World?

Asking them directly, as many teams of researchers have found, is not a particularly fruitful approach. Motives for a major shift in a person's life are complex and interwoven, and even if the respondent can actually remember what was in his mind when he moved, he is likely to give the interviewer only a very simplified and often distorted version. More helpful, so the International Development Research Centre groups found in their work on Bandung, Seoul, Manila, Caracas, Kuala Lumpur, Lima, Istanbul and Lagos, was to ask people first whether they were satisfied or dissatisfied with their new life. Apart from Seoul, where the authorities have been conducting a particularly brusque and effective onslaught on new squatter buildings, a predominant – and in the case of Kuala Lumpur's 95·4 per cent an overwhelming – response was in favour of living in the city against their previous life. When the question was reversed, would they be willing to return home? – the "no's" varied between 70·7 per cent and 81·9 per cent.

Economic motives are often important – better pay, better

chances of jobs, wider opportunities – but these can easily be exaggerated. Much more solidly based seems to be the migrants' feeling that the move to the city, however tough on them, must open new doors for their children. Laquian quotes an eloquent old man in a Manila slum:

> I am already old, with perhaps a few more years to live. But I decided to gamble and leave my farm, living in this stinking community. I did not do it for myself. I was happy in the village. But my children, what would they become? I was a farmer. I owned three hectares. My father was a tenant, a *kasama*, and I was lucky to have owned land, when he died without ever achieving that. But my children – I have six of them. If I die, how will they divide three hectares among them? So I decided to try out my luck in Manila. Maybe they can at least get an education, a job. Who knows?

Only in Caracas and Seoul were less than 60 per cent of parents confident that the city was better for their children than their place of origin, and in Istanbul the figure ran as high as 88·9 per cent. Parents alone, if they found the city intolerable, would always be free to move out. Very often, it seems, it is for the children that they cling on.

Where they cling appears to depend directly on the way that the migrant was introduced to the city, and this, in turn, involves all sorts of links with friends, relations, and fellow-villagers who may have led the way, sent back invitations to visit, written about the golden opportunities, and often extended a helping hand. The IDRC study emphasises the danger of treating the migrant as an individual, some sort of economic atom adrift on the metropolitan swamp. He is much more likely to arrive in the city as one of an already-established family or regional community – a sort of "urban village", where all the preliminary problems of job, accommodation, money to tide over the first days, will be taken care of by already-established acquaintances. And even after he is established in his own right, the pattern of his life and his aspirations and responsibilities will often take much more of a group than an individualistic form. His ambitions may be boundless, and ultimately he may well push off on his own, but initially it is the existence of such links, acting as a "reception area" or a "launching pad" for the new country-bred arrival which eases and facilitates what might otherwise be a forbiddingly traumatic transition.

"In general then," writes Laquian, "the findings of this study show a pattern. Migrants move to the city expecting better things. When the community they enter is somewhat like the one they left behind, the sense of satisfaction they get from the community serves to outweigh their initial individual frustrations related to jobs, separation from loved ones in the village, etc. When the community is not really a community at all, but characterised by friction, anonymity, even conflict, the migrant tends to be dissatisfied and expresses a desire to move to another community."

Considering the strong motivation of migrants to improve themselves, then, it appears that "policies that move along with the ebb and flow of migration tides will be more successful than those that try to stop them, or go against them". But to evolve and implement such policies, while still fulfilling all the other functions of good city management, requires a really top-notch city administration, backed by a national government with a coherent and detailed policy for general urban and indeed rural development. How sound and well established is the intellectual and analytical framework for such policies, even in the self-satisfied and rich cities of the West? To grapple with that question it is necessary to stand back a bit and look at the present state of city theory. You can, in principle, build and fly an aeroplane without any knowledge of aerodynamics, but your chances might be regarded as slim. How good, then, are the books that tell you how to run the city of Calcutta – or more generally, predict the likely pattern of its growth, decay, and possible death?

CHAPTER 4

Models for Megalopolis

the vast metropolis,
Fount of my country's destiny, and the world's;
That great emporium, chronicle at once
And burial-place of passions, and their home
Imperial, their chief living residence.

WILLIAM WORDSWORTH,
The Prelude, Book VIII

Cities and urban settlements are not restricted to a few favoured corners of the world – they are a universal phenomenon. Every country, every geographic region has its scatter of small villages, medium-sized towns and metropolitan agglomerations, and everywhere scientists and statisticians, looking at the size-distribution figures, have been struck by apparent regularities. Graphed, computed and analysed by various established mathematical techniques, they often appear to follow some general law. But does such a law really exist?

The question is of quite fundamental importance. As Sir Maurice Kendall said: "The various considerations which make people live in towns instead of the country, and vice versa, are numerous, complex and difficult to measure. But if they merge together . . . into a single force, we might be able to construct a fairly simple model of the growing city." It might then be possible to observe or predict the effect of changes in the relative strength of the factors entering the equation. For although many people would, quite properly, criticise such a model as over-simplified, "sometimes very simple models can represent quite complicated systems. A complex causative system can merge so as to produce a pattern which is very easily and simply expressed"; for example, Sir Maurice cited Pareto's law, which states that high incomes in all societies tend to distribute themselves along exactly similar curves.

Sir Maurice surveyed the mass of work first triggered off with the observation (by Feliz Auerbach in 1913) that in quite a few countries the size of any given city is in inverse proportion to its rank in the hierarchy of all the other cities. In other words, if the population of the capital is P, that of the second city will be $\frac{1}{2}$P, the third city $\frac{1}{3}$P and so on. Unhappily things do not always work out quite as neatly as that. But other people, most notably the American, George Zipf, have extended the idea to show that, virtually everywhere, it is possible to show an almost equally pretty (though slightly more complicated) connection between city rank and city size.

Mathematically, if the population size is P and the rank number R, then according to Zipf there exists a relationship of the type

$$RP^n = K$$

where n and K are constants. In terms of logarithms,

$$\log P = \frac{\log K}{n} - \frac{1}{n} \log R$$
$$= a - b \log R$$

If you take the sixty-three towns in Great Britain which had more than 100,000 people in 1971 – apart from London itself – and graph log P against log R, the result will be an almost straight line. Zipf himself showed that such a neat relationship applied to American cities, throughout the period of their fastest and most competitive growth, produces results much the same in the totally different conditions of India, if you try out the formula on the 1971 census.

The main interest in all of this, of course, hinges on the interpretation of the constant b, which defines the slope of the straight line, and varies quite widely from country to country and from situation to situation. Zipf himself suggested that the proper way to interpret this constant was as the ratio between two effects which operate in every society – one tending to aggregate human beings into groups, and the other tending to disperse them. In the case of Britain in 1971, b was about 0·8, implying that the forces of concentration were only 80 per cent as strong as those favouring dispersal. "The existence of patterns of this kind, which can be reasonably described as laws, arouses a good deal of emotional resistance, because some people regard them as akin to laws of Nature, and infer that it is useless to struggle against them," said Sir Maurice. "This is a mistaken attitude; I think there are lessons to be learned from such laws, if only to bring us to realise how powerful are the forces against which we have to struggle."

Unfortunately, however, not all resistance to the Zipf hypothesis can be dismissed as emotional. The whole subject is riddled with scholarly disputes, and there is no sense in which Zipf's Law can be regarded as definitively established. There is argument about the mathematics (whether the distribution is really by rank size, or whether lognormal or Pareto-type equations would give a better fit); about the lower end of the scale (why the relationship should apparently cease to work when populations drop below about 2,500); about the nature of the mechanism really at work inside constant b (economic functions, size and population of hinterland, etc.); and above all about the problem of the primate city – the Budapest or Manila or Buenos Aires which dwarfs all other urban centres within its region, and falls far outside Zipf's otherwise elegant and uncluttered straight lines.

Even the straight lines themselves sometimes tend to bend a bit, unless some pretty extreme statistical ingenuity is applied. This is always possible, of course, given the chaotic nature of urban statistics. As Sir Maurice Kendall says, "whether London contains 5,000 inhabitants, or 4 million, or 15 million, depends on where you draw the boundaries – or where someone else draws the boundaries". In the equally sceptical words of Professor Harry Richardson, "in many cases, the use of a single linear slope may require fitting the city size distribution into a Procrustean bed". Often you get a much better fit if you divide a country's cities into two separate groups – above and below 200,000 in the case of Switzerland, above and below 720,000 in the case of the USSR. Australia appears to have a clear break-point around the 65,000 mark (above which the forces of concentration appear to be a good 50 per cent stronger) and India, similarly, and even more dramatically, at 500,000. For smaller cities than that the dispersion forces predominate; for larger ones, the balance tips very significantly the other way, which could be bad news for Calcutta and Bombay.

This departure from uniformity can be fudged round by doctoring the definitions, or introducing artificial exclusions. But often it does seem to accord with reality. Australia and India, for instance, are characterised by possessing three or four cities of roughly equal size, with none of them clearly holding the first rank. Other countries, the United States, the USSR, Belgium, Holland, Switzerland, have made sustained efforts to control the growth of their largest centres, and concentrate instead on developing substantial alternatives – in the United States and the Soviet Union, around the million mark. Sometimes, too, the awkward "steps" in the otherwise smooth rank-size graph seem to be explained by the fact that two or three cities are fighting hard and consciously for second place in the hierarchy. Lyons looks as though it may be drawing away from Marseilles (after passing it in the late 1950s), but the struggle is by no means over yet. And in northern Italy the battle is three-sided, between Milan, Turin, and the Italian government, which would like to clamp down on both of them.

Even if such deviations can be explained away as "exceptional", however, the size-rank rule still breaks down very seriously when it comes to the vast, dominating primate cities – particularly those in the Third World, which has far more than its fair share. For every Paris and Copenhagen, seven to eight times the size of its nearest rival, there are three sprawling equivalents in Asia, Africa and Latin America. Montevideo, Guatemala City, Lima, Manila, Colombo, Saigon, Tunis, Beirut, Santiago, Havana, Mexico City, all run out at anything between five and thirteen times as large as the local runner-up (see table on facing page).

Some people have tried to explain this phenomenon in terms of the capital-city syndrome. As one geographer wrote grandiloquently in 1939: "All over the world it is the law of the Capitals that the largest city shall be super-eminent, and not merely in size but in national influence. Once a city is larger than any other in its country, this mere fact gives it an impetus to grow that cannot be affected by any other city, and it draws away from all of them in character as well as in size. . . ." Exceptions, like Italy, Canada, Spain and Russia, which have no "primate city" in this sense are treated as aberrations, which is not very helpful for analysis. More constructive, though, is the type of theory which tries to relate degree of primacy to the stages of national economic development. On this view, metropolitan dominance reaches its height during the early stages of economic take-off, and moderates thereafter, back to the normal size-rank pattern. But this unhappily fails to explain either the 600-year-old preponderance of

The Dominant Cities

NAME AND COUNTRY	POPULATION RATIO TO SECOND CITY	
	1950	1970
Budapest, Hungary	13·2	11·0
Manila, Philippines	9·8	8·1
Lima, Peru	7·3	7·4*
Buenos Aires, Argentina	9·1	10·6
Havana, Cuba	7·3	6·1†
Vienna, Austria	7·3	5·2
Copenhagen, Denmark	7·7	5·9
Bucharest, Rumania	8·0	5·6
Dublin, Eire	4·7	5·0
Colombo, Sri Lanka	4·6	3·5
Paris, France	7·5	7·5
Santiago, Chile	4·8	9·2
Teheran, Iran	5·1	6·7
London, United Kingdom	3·4	3·7
Seoul, South Korea	3·0	2·9

* New figure would be 14·1 now that Lima-Callao is counted as one conurbation, and Arequipa becomes the second city.

† Figures for 1966.

Paris, or the fact that, over the last century, eight of the major South American nations, which used, in colonial times, to possess a very neat rank-size structure in their cities, have now developed symptoms of almost uncontrolled – some would say malignant – primacy. In sixteen out of the twenty-two Latin American nations, more than half the total urban population is now packed into a single metropolitan area. All sorts of hypotheses have been tested – links between primacy and *per capita* exports (good for many countries, but not for Mexico), ex-colonial status (pretty strong), degree of industrialisation (negative), general population growth (mildly positive), and so forth. No really conclusive picture emerges. Nor is it clear how far the existence of primate cities is responsible for stunting the growth of other urban areas in the country: are they being positively drained by their large, vital competitor, or are they just basically unattractive? A United

Nations study in 1969 gloomily concluded: "The causal relationship, if any, between first-city dominance and regressivity in
size-distribution of the smaller cities cannot be determined at
present."

All that is clear, judging from the work of Koichi Mera, is that
growing strength in the primate city, when it exists, tends to go
together with general economic expansion. Urban São Paulo
may suffer from being five times larger than any other Brazilian
city, bar Rio de Janeiro, but its *per capita* income is six times that
of rural Piau, and even the impoverished gutters of Calcutta and
Bombay support a standard of living 40 per cent above that of the
surrounding countrysides. Mera has in fact drawn up tables
relating annual growth of average Gross Domestic Product for
various countries to the rate at which their leading city is increasing its predominance. Although no absolutely clear relationship
emerges, the nations with the most cuckoo-like capitals – South
Korea, Puerto Rico, Iran, Ivory Coast, Spain, Jordan, even Eire –
tend also to come pretty high in the growth league. Certainly,
there is no evidence, as some people suggest, that these capitals
are holding back progress and acting as parasites on the rest of the
economy. In fact, Mera calculates that economic development
must inevitably be slowed down, especially in the early stages of
industrialisation, by any attempt to "ration" the big city and
spread its resources more widely. Working on Japanese figures,
he reckoned that an equal sharing out of the "social capital"
concentrated in Tokyo and Osaka would cut national income by
30 per cent, if the population remained where it is at present, and
by 15 per cent even if they all moved in the most rational manner
to take advantage of the new opportunities. Results would be even
more discouraging to the regionalists if a similar process was
applied to less advanced countries than Japan.

What, then, is it that prevents people from crowding themselves
into one giant city, if the economic advantages are so clear? And
would it be a bad thing if they did, once the preliminary pains and
stresses had been absorbed? The quick, easy arguments – congestion, squalor, diseconomies of scale, psychological preference
for living in the country or in small towns – tend to wilt under
analysis. People adjust themselves to the congestion and the
squalor; diseconomies often turn out to be more apparent than

real when someone seriously attempts to cope with the problems; and an artificial village life for the favoured few who have made their money in the big city hardly constitutes an effective counter-thrust. To provide a complete answer requires much deeper consideration of the way a city works. As Kendall said: "From a much longer viewpoint, we have to consider whether a city has a natural period of life, in addition to its daily rhythm. Are we deceiving ourselves by supposing that we can set up our cities on a permanent basis? Or must we consider the city as an organism which grows and matures and then dies, carrying within it, like all forms of human systems, the seeds of its own decay? Has it a life cycle? Or a reproductive cycle?"

The most elaborate response to such questions has probably been made by the American scientist, Jay Forrester, who has since become famous – or notorious – for his part in the controversial world resources forecasts which make up the Club of Rome's report on *The Limits to Growth*. In his earlier book, *Urban Dynamics* (1968), he elaborated a method for constructing mathematical models of the way that a city grows, matures and, in certain circumstances, decays. He was particularly concerned with the plight of urban America, and the failure of so many expensive and apparently well-intentioned plans to cure its varied ills. But his approach – which is essentially to formulate the key factors and relationships that knit together to make a working city in such a way that a computer can be programmed to simulate the short-, medium- and long-run effects of applying suggested policies for improvement – is fully relevant to the cities of the Third World, where the real problems (and the opportunities for disastrous error) will be concentrated in the next few decades.

Forrester states his basic position as follows: "An urban area is a system of inter-acting industries, housing and people. Under favourable conditions the interplay between parts of a new area causes it to develop. But as the area develops and its land area fills, the processes of ageing cause stagnation. As the urban area moves from the growth phase to the equilibrium phase, the population mix and the economic activity change. . . . If renewal is to succeed and a healthy economic mix is to continue, the natural processes of stagnation must not run their normal course. But the interactions between economic and social activity are so complex that intuition alone cannot devise policies that prevent decay."

Obviously the situation in Caracas, Lagos or Saigon is not the same as that in New York or Chicago. Frequently the stagnation, the collapse of urban services, and the spread of the slums is taking place, on a huge scale, before their "growth phase" is even fairly begun. But the underlying analysis remains the same. People come to the city because its "attractions" outweigh those available elsewhere, and they will only move out when this situation is reversed. Once there, their prime concern is with housing and jobs. A few of them are highly paid managers and entrepreneurs, with houses to match. Many more of them are established workers, with reasonable wages and tolerable accommodation. And a further group – sometimes quite small, but often, especially in some of the teeming new cities, very large indeed – contains the un- and under-employed, existing on the margin of subsistence, both in cash and in shelter terms.

Out of these three elementary groups Forrester constructs a simulacrum of the city. New industries are started, attracting more managers, creating more jobs, causing the building of more good houses, generating more tax revenues for the development of urban services. Then, as the industries mature and decline – unless they are suitably replaced – the jobs and opportunities diminish, the houses age and slip down the scale, more under-employed need more welfare services, but there are less taxes to pay for them. The financial, social and environmental balance starts to slip, and new corrective policies are devised – subsidies for new industry, more low-cost housing, slum clearance programmes, training for lower-grade workers, and so forth. All, rightly or wrongly, are in day-to-day use in the cities of the developing world.

To discover which of them, in what combinations, are most likely to work – and why some, often after a period of initial promise, so disastrously fail – Forrester creates an intricate network of equations, setting out the way in which his basic factors interact. So much new industry creates so many jobs, requires so much new or second-hand housing; decline of a mature business generates such-and-such a degree of under-employment, income decrease and slum-spread; and so on. He is then ready to programme any proposed new policy-mixture into his computer, and show how the results interweave in a developing future – not just for tomorrow and the year after next, but fifty or a hundred years ahead (which is, after all, the expected lifetime of most of Britain's housing stock).

Forrester's results are often surprising (and depressing). He finds, for instance, that intuition and common sense are rotten guides: that slum clearance programmes on their own produce more slums, not less; that low-cost housing attracts more low-skill people, makes it harder for them to improve themselves, drives productive industry away, and does not even, overall, produce any more cheap accommodation; and so on, down a rather glum trail. What it does suggest though, which is of prime importance, is that it is far more useful to devote resources to the provision of jobs than to anything else. If the jobs are there, the incomes, the better houses, the improved services, the upward mobility and the newer industries will tend to follow. And it is often beneficent, in the longer term, to clear out the low-cost housing to make room for them.

It is not the detailed results, though, or even the precise mode of analysis, which are important. Different figures, different equations, different categories may well be more relevant to the problems of any given city. It is the approach that is important: the determination to grasp the essential complexity of a city's growth, and project into the future the effect of the decisions being made so painfully, and often so misguidedly, today. Forrester's type of model does not have to embody truth, accurate to three places of decimals. What it offers is a graspable and usable metaphor for truths which are too manifold, too fluctuating, and subject to too many random influences to be encompassed by practical minds. As one Massachusetts Institute of Technology journal said, reviewing Forrester's book: "In its essentially poetic relation to truth, metaphor can accommodate ambiguity and contradictions inherent in the human condition that invalidate scientific laws. Even in science (consider phlogiston, the ether, the Bohr atom as examples) a metaphor does not have to be true to yield illuminating insights and indicate new directions towards understanding, which can survive an ultimate rejection of the metaphoric framework."

What Forrester's particular metaphor suggests, as set out in *Urban Dynamics*, falls into three parts. First, that it is perfectly possible for a city to sicken and die. Once the under-employed attain political dominance, and vote for themselves improved welfare services that can only be paid for by higher taxes on the already declining productive sector – both individual and corporate – then the producers will ultimately be driven away. Second, that "attractiveness" is a key concept. "For any class of person, conditions in the area must be approximately equal in attractiveness to conditions elsewhere. As an example, conditions in a city for people of the lowest economic class must not be substantially better or worse than the conditions of other parts of the country from which there is free mobility. If the city is more attractive, inward migration will occur until it is overloaded. Unable to cope with the influx, the city falls to the lowest attractiveness level with which it communicates." Third, that the best hope for the health of any city lies within itself. Metropolitan life is such an intricately interwoven fabric, and its internal checks and balances so firmly integrated into its texture, that it will resist and counteract all but the most violent forms of interference. But like the human body, it is full of self-corrective devices and renewal mechanisms. Often the reason "corrective" policies fail so badly is precisely because they swamp and undermine these in-built antibodies.

In this, perhaps, lies the best hope for the almost unimaginably vast agglomerations predicted for the twenty-first century. But, as this book will show, there are many enormous problems, here and now, for which benign neglect could never be a politically acceptable solution. The difficulty is to make sure that the man-made solutions underpin, rather than erode, the city's natural regenerative powers.

SECTION II

The Crisis of Affluence

Then the vision of an enormous town presented itself, of a monstrous town more populous than some continents and in its manmade might as if indifferent to heaven's frowns and smiles; a cruel devourer of the world's light. There was room enough there to place any story, depth enough there for any passion, variety enough there for any setting, darkness enough to bury five millions of lives.

JOSEPH CONRAD,
Author's note to *The Secret Agent*

CHAPTER 5

The City and the Ring

The first requisite to happiness is that a man
be born in a famous city.
EURIPIDES, Encomium on Alcibiades

The symptoms of disorder – the poverty-in-affluence, the break-down in public services, the inner-city decay, or the cultural deprivation of sprawling lower-income suburbs – affront that pride in the great city which has traditionally been associated with the growth of the Western world's prosperity. Planners, politicians and economists, even while acknowledging the crisis in the cities of the rich, tend to articulate a conviction that it is absurd that we do not implement solutions, and in some sense morally culpable that we cannot say with any certainty what they are.

Professor Natalie Becker, of New York's Columbia University, opened the planning seminar at Oxford with the challenge: "I have never seen a solution to an urban problem." Discussing the contemporary situation in the United States, in a tone which combined moral outrage with qualified despair, she reflected that "with over $100,000 million expended annually on housing and housing-related items, and over thirty years of federal housing subsidies, which were to have provided housing for low income families, we have built only about 10 per cent of the nation's needs." She looked for explanation not to Jay Forrester, but to the erosion in the Old American pioneering spirit. "I am asking why, in a nation that set a goal and reached the moon, that set a goal and harnessed nuclear energy, can we not set a goal and accomplish it, where for example a decent house for every citizen is at issue? We must conclude that such a talented nation does not lack the technology, nor the resources. What it lacks is the commitment."

Stephen Spender, in a wry reference to Spiro Agnew's

announcement when touring South-East Asia in 1971, that it is "characteristic of Americans to believe that all problems can be solved", reflects on what he sees as a New World tendency to favour "question-and-answer procedures" whereby "the language of the past, a language of mysteries and rituals, would be translated into the present, a language of diagnosis and cures". The dangers of assuming that identification of the problem takes you half-way to the solution were described in the preceding chapter. Yet the metropolitan sprawls of the developed world urgently demand, even as they elude, a language of diagnosis.

The choice of language, however, implies some structure of approach. Whether we view the problem in terms of governmental structures, population pressures, the creation of employment in the cities' transition from an industrial to a service-based economy, or participative democracy, each category calls into being its own vocabulary. To take the question of governmental structures: Professor William Robson points out in *Great Cities of the World* that only five or six metropolitan regions in the world have seriously tried to set up governmental schemes capable of meeting their "present and future needs in regard to organisation, services, finance, co-ordination, planning or democratic control and even in these exceptional areas the measures taken are barely adequate".

The implications of that failure are particularly serious in the cities of the developed world, with their complex economic interrelations and the patina of social and cultural habits they have acquired. Existing structures – the city's resources and mechanisms for control – are being stretched by the growth of the suburb, the outward reach of the metropolis and the dimming of the distinction between urban and rural. But how are we to resolve the question of city government? Committed as we may be to bringing structure into line with needs, are we to use in doing so the language of economics or of demography? It is not, of course, that these languages exclude each other, but that a primary angle of approach gives us terms in which to resolve the disparate elements. So long, that is, as language does not degenerate into formula. The trouble with the very notion of "goal" is that it suggests the singular.

The mega-region, which nowadays includes not only the metropolis and its ring of outer suburbs, but an amorphous and

Walking tall in the precarious passageways of a Lima tenement. For millions, this is "city lights".

New York, the richest city in the world, erupts in violence (top) while Calcutta, probably the poorest, is more or less crime-free.

extensive extra-urban commuting area, puts immense strain not just on the services but on the identity of the city. Planning battles rage between the advocates of centralised control and integrated metropolitan government, and "regionalists" who argue for decentralisation and the encouragement of local organisational initiative. The chaotic overlapping of rival administrative territories remains the daily reality. And underlying these arguments – and this is where the languages of politics and sociology assert their strongest claims – is the urgency of creating or preserving that most elusive element, the quality of human interchange. Between suburban scatter and metropolitan congestion, complains Lewis Mumford, "as an agent of human interaction, as a stage for the social drama, the city is rapidly sinking out of sight".

Yet paradoxically, while its identity is being called into question, the city concentrates more and more of the developed world's population and increasingly dominates its activities. We may question the very meaning of urbanisation; but many of the great political questions which engage Western society are essentially those of its cities. The scale of urbanisation generated a certain mood of excitement and even exhilaration in the early Sixties. Writers like Constantinos Doxiadis and Jean Gottmann were even seriously discussing the development of the single, world-covering city, which they called Ecumenopolis. Already, almost 75 per cent of Americans live in an urban environment; a megalopolis stretching from Boston to Washington is not an impossibility. Tokyo's metropolitan region, fanning out in a radius of fifty kilometres from its Central Station, will contain 33 million by 1985. Two-fifths of the French and the British, more than half the Japanese and 56 per cent of Americans live in cities of over 100,000.

The "exploding cities" of São Paulo and Calcutta are growing faster than the great cities of the West; yet the magnitude of the changes, in functions and in sheer size, even of those relatively stable cities outstrips the planners' controlling formulae. In the United States and Japan, the number of million-cities has more than doubled since 1950, and between 1950 and 1970 the number of people living in such cities increased in the United States from 37·9 million to 77·7 million, and in Japan from 10·4 million to 26·4 million. Over the same period, Italy's entire population increase of 7 million was absorbed into urban areas, and more

3

than 6 million were added to its major cities. In France, the rural population actually declined by 2·6 million, as its city population virtually doubled and two new million-cities – Lyons and Marseilles – grew to rival the long-dominant Paris region, in which a fifth of all Frenchmen now live.

Some of these cities were, of course, near the million mark in 1950; the step over the magic line does not necessarily mean that their problems become qualitatively more difficult. All, however, relatively stretched for funds to provide adequate services, have resources which make possible standards of urban welfare beyond the dreams of the newer cities of the Third World. Yet the sense of defeat in creating a reasonably habitable environment increases as opportunities multiply and the city's organisms become more complex. While the planner may continue to talk about matching city organisation to the new dimensions of metropolitan spread, almost as though it were a question of the same order as "setting a goal and reaching the moon", metropolitan life becomes ever less susceptible to the language of conventional analysis. On the contrary, as Kingsley Davis remarks, technology itself complicates matters in two ways: "it allows continued participation in city life even when one's residence is miles away, and it encourages dispersal by increasing the noise, congestion and pollution at the centre".

Because of this, although the problem of organisational lag behind the growth of a city is common to the cities of rich and poor alike, suburbanisation is a more acute problem in countries with a high standard of living. The transport expert, Wilfred Owen, in a paper for the Brookings Institution, refers to the gap between the "immobile and the mobile nations". The miles of new roads and streets added annually to European and American networks at a still-accelerating pace link their cities and, too often, cut a swathe of freeways through them. The end result of this increased accessibility to the central areas is that the metropolitan rings are growing faster than the city centres.

The pattern of spread takes two forms. If the cities of America tend to emulate Detroit, once described as "a fat white doughnut with a black hole in the middle", the cities of Western Europe rather concentrate their affluence at the centre, pushing the lower-income groups into a featureless no-man's land of ribbon development interspersed with blankly concrete, cheaply constructed high-rise housing. Inner Paris has a fairly stable population of 2·8 million, and a metropolitan area – much of it hideously planned – of over 9 million. The centres of all the major United States cities grew between 1960 and 1968 by only 400,000 people – well under 1 per cent, while the suburban rings swelled from 54·6 million to 69·9 million. The underlying social and economic patterns differ radically on both sides of the Atlantic. But the sheer geographical spread of the cities is much the same.

Revolutions in communications and transport have accelerated what Mumford contemptuously calls "suburban scatter", and the phenomenon is here to stay. According to Kingsley Davis, "although local and national controls may dampen the centrifugal movement, the pressures are such that the movement tends to occur anyway in one form or another. . .". The organisational problem implicit in "scatter" is compounded by what Daniel Bell, in *The Coming of Post-Industrial Society*, describes as a "tightened social framework", a greater degree of social interdependence. Less able to insulate his private world, the city-dweller lives with what Bell calls "a change of scale – the spread of cities, the growth of organisational size, the widening of the political arena – which has made individuals feel more helpless within larger entities". Poverty, noise or pollution are not more embittering ingredients in the breakdown of "affluent" urban society than the citizen's sense that the urban environment is beyond his control.

J. K. Galbraith, tracing for the conference the lineage from the industrial city to the present polymorphous metropolis, viewed the suburbs, "the Camp", as a stage along the route. "From the earliest days of the Industrial City there was a strong desire by the few who could afford it to escape its smoke and grime and even more its unlovely landscape. So with the Industrial City came the suburb. With the reconstitution of a mercantile class and the appearance of the new managerial élite, the growth of the suburbs gained greatly in momentum . . . these settlements had no central function – they did not rule, sell or make. They were places where people found space." The transport revolution has linked them with the city to form the metropolis, but essentially they still neither "rule, sell or make". They do, however, enormously complicate the problems of metropolitan government. And, trapped between central office block (more office buildings have

been constructed in New York since the end of the Second World
War than in the whole of the rest of the United States, and more
than a third of the top 500 American corporations have their
headquarters there) and the middle-class dormitories increasingly
distant from it, the transient urban population of the city itself
is being eroded in morale and deprived of amenities.

Those who move into the suburbs, in most American cities,
are the prosperous and, predominantly, the white populations. In
Europe, by contrast, city centres are still heavily populated with
those who are neither tired of London nor, as Dr Johnson would
have it, tired of life. Social mixture is more assured in the city
proper than in the suburbs. The key to the United States out-
migration was, according to Galbraith, the movement of immigrant and rural-urban migrant communities into the cities. "As
the acculturation of the recent rural migrants proceeds, we should
expect," he says, "a return of population from the camps to the
central city. Marx spoke accurately if untactfully of the idiocy of
rural life. Grass is not a substitute for cultural amenity. The
suburban movement was the response of the older city dwellers
to the poverty and indiscipline of the new arrivals. As that shock
effect loses its relevance, the superior quality of city life will
naturally assert itself."

But "the superior quality of city life" has been vitiated by
poverty and transience. New York's central city population has
remained steady at 7·8 million over the past twenty years, as
Senator Roy Goodman, Chairman of the Committee on Housing
and Urban Development, New York State, reminded the Oxford
conference. But during that time about 1·8 million of the white
middle class have moved into the suburbs, and "approximately
1·8 million of deeply underprivileged migrants have come into
the city. . . . The result is that the city's total population can be
broken down to about 61 per cent white, 25 per cent black and
12 per cent Puerto Rican. The fact that the city has been able to
absorb that incredible change of composition and still be a city
is in itself quite extraordinary."

Downtown Detroit, reports Stephen Aris, the *Sunday Times*
New York correspondent, is even further from becoming an
irresistible attraction to the wealthy inhabitants of Hunter's
Ridge and the other condominiums and suburbs that ring the
city at a respectful distance. Detroit, which now has a black

majority and in 1973 elected its first black mayor, Coleman Young, on a straight racial ticket, has been losing population to the suburbs ever since the first serious race riots in 1948. Then, reports Aris, "Detroit had a population of 1·8 million, of whom only 20 per cent were black; by 1960 the population was down to 1·6 million, of whom 37 per cent were black. In the following ten years another 100,000 people left the city, raising the black percentage to 44. Over the past three years something like 40,000 people have been streaming away from the city. . . . 'It's a severe strain,' Detroit's chief planner, Charles Blessing, observes mildly, 'to have a quarter of one's customers leaving.' "

Galbraith may yet be right. The latest United States government statistics show crime falling in many large cities and rising in the suburbs. Rural-urban migration from the South is falling, and in most cities the numbers of the poor are stabilising. Late in 1973, the *New York Times* asked New Yorkers whether they thought the city would be a better place to live in ten to fifteen years' time – and 38 per cent thought it would, and 26 per cent expected the situation to stay the same. Over half praised its physical beauty, 74 per cent its cultural life and 67 per cent its job opportunities. Citing the figures, Goodman claimed that this was "hardly the profile of a city which has lost hope".

With many of its affluent tax-paying citizens working in the city (and using its amenities) as day-trippers only, the central city struggles to finance a gigantic social welfare and services burden on inadequate revenues. Opinion is still sharply divided as to whether the "whiting" or "re-whiting" of American cities is likely to bring relief or simply fiercer competition on the housing, services and schooling front. But the "great return" would add to revenue, and it is hard to quarrel with "rehabbing" as a fashion when in stringently rent-controlled New York, "between 1950 and 1970, some 90,000 units were abandoned. Just that, abandoned. Abandonment is the result of a complex of cascading causes. . . . A landlord is unable to maintain an apartment house and pay taxes. He fails to deliver proper services to the tenants. They move out. Now vandals move in. . . . Other residents move out. . . . So the cycle continues, and a neighbourhood deteriorates." The heralded return of the middle classes might put heavy initial strains on services and force up the price of central city housing. But nothing is worse than sustained exodus.

CHAPTER 6

Governing the Metropolis

Life in the modern city has become a symbol
of the fact that man can become adapted to
starless skies, treeless avenues, shapeless
buildings, tasteless bread, joyless celebrations.

RENÉ DUBOS

The cities of the West suffer a double time-sense. On the one
hand, their societies are attuned to "problem-solving". They
expect answers: the bigger the question, the more all-embracing
must be the solution. They are societies geared to accelerating
change. They recognise that the cities will require more complex
mechanisms to guide them, and expect that these will be forth-
coming. On the other, there is an awareness that the great cities
have not become adjusted to a fundamental shift of function:
the displacement of diminishing manufacturing capacity by the
service industries. The evident disarray of too many urban
schemes and the lack of convincing diagnostic outlines would
seem to suggest that neither planners nor economists have
successfully mounted that particular tiger. Against impatience
to arrive at particular salves or solutions, planners themselves
balance the sense that time, in the absence of certainties, may
sort the muddles out. This makes for the mixture of frustration
and anger in professional talk and, among ordinary city-dwellers,
for a refusal of commitment to many levels of urban organisation.

The growth of the service industries affects the future of the
metropolis partly because productivity tends to grow more slowly
in this sector than in manufacturing. In New York, manufacturing still counted in 1972 for 19 per cent of the 3·5 million jobs
available, but the number had dropped since the early Sixties by
26 per cent – and by 1974 New York had lost a quarter of a
million manufacturing jobs in three years. In the ten years leading
to 1972, the proportion of posts in service industries had reached

22 per cent of the total, representing a 22 per cent increase in the number available; and government jobs now occupied 16 per cent of the market, having climbed by 31 per cent. The problem of reduced productivity is integral to the transfer to post-industrial society, writes Bell, and it "comes to a head in the cities, whose budgets have doubled and tripled in the last decades (apart from welfare) because the bulk of municipal services – education, hospitals, police, social services – falls into the non-progressive sector of the economy. . . . Yet it is productivity which allows the social pie to expand." This process puts considerable strain on the condition that the American planner, Jane Jacobs, and Jay Forrester attach to growth and urban health – the city's ability to add new productive work to old.

To the problems common to most cities – migration, the costs of services and the maintenance of "minimum standards", whatever each country may hold them to be, the outmoded structures of governmental machinery – to these, and a dozen other crises in law and order, education and social mobility, the cities of the rich add another. Their very affluence requires more regulative techniques, in line with the greater number of amenities. Higher standards mean more ambitious public planning. What in the industrial city of the nineteenth century was fought out in terms of economics, in government and on the shop floor, has broadened to embrace a wider section of society in what has been called the "participative revolution". Yet never has there been sharper concern about "alienation", about the individual's inability to influence decisions which affect his daily urban life. This is fundamentally a political question; and it goes to the heart of the metropolitan crisis.

Confidence in the functioning of a city is not always a predictable thing. At Oxford, Simon Jenkins, a British journalist specialising in planning problems, was moved to an unaccustomed panegyric. London, he said, had faced all of the problems of the exploding cities of the developing world: faced them and largely overcome them in the last century. "I know," he said, "that when foreigners visit London they are infuriated by the smugness with which Londoners present the city to other people, taking them round all their successes. The fact of the matter is . . . London has managed to solve many of its problems. . . . Two aspects are of interest, the first being the importance of public sanitation

policies. . . . The second is the importance of public finance –
getting the balance of taxation right between town and country
and between different portions of the town. . . . And linked to
this is the importance of the constitutional structure of local
government."

Undoubtedly the points were important; and London has a
good record on all three. Yet, the following month, the government raised in parliament the question of organising a conference
to look into London's urban problems; and in June the Home
Secretary was requested to support an urban commission "to
study how stress, poverty and racial tension in inner city areas
should be tackled". The Chairman of the City Poverty Committee urged action on the basis that government programmes had
totally failed, and that the growing difficulties in the inner cities
might lead to collapse of essential services and increasing tensions
between minority groups. A report issued in mid-1974 by Britain's
Community Relations Commission expressed in strong terms
anxieties about the increasing alienation from the community of
second-generation West Indian migrant youth, and pointed out
that unemployment among black school-leavers tended to run at
roughly double the rate of that among their white contemporaries.

These indications that London cannot guarantee quite the best
of all possible worlds do not invalidate Jenkins's optimism. London, carefully regulated within its two-tier structure and thirty-
two Boroughs, is by most standards of the government of great
cities remarkably free from friction. Yet the breakdown in essential
services is no frivolous chimera. Speculation in property, and the
huge metropolitan office building programme, have driven out
of the city its basic workforce. Professor Robson expressed a
widely held view at Oxford when he said that "the pool of rather
lower paid semi-skilled or unskilled labour on which the public
services depend – particularly London Transport and the local
authorities – for their less skilled work has simply been reduced
to a point where it has become almost impossible for the post
office, for the police forces, for London Transport, for the local
authorities to recruit that kind of labour."

Sheer size tends to daunt the planners and their political
masters. Senator Goodman emphasised that "to understand New
York City's problems, we must grasp the hugeness of everything
in it. We are eight million people in the City limits, surrounded

by an additional twelve million in one metropolitan area. We employ nearly 400,000 public workers. We have 31,000 police officers in our police department. . . . Our 1·1 million school-children are taught by 57,000 teachers; and more than 37,000 people operate our transit system. We clean more than 6,000 miles of streets. The City's operating budget is now over $10,000 million. . . . Dealing with metropolitan problems is difficult enough in any metropolitan area. In the New York area, there are special considerations. These include the division of the region among three states each with different priorities and different approaches to providing services, and the presence of more than 1,400 local governments."

Many of the problems with which city governments must theoretically deal do not come under their sole aegis. In very few is there working machinery to deal with questions that spill over local borders: in New York, about three million enter the city each day to work; Tokyo jams in 1·3 million and hopes soon to rival New York. In neither is there a unified regional transit system. In Tokyo, the situation is absurd. Commuters struggle into the city via one of the nine privately owned railway systems (three belonging to department stores), the seven privately owned bus companies, or the single publicly owned subway system, which hires retired wrestlers as "pushers" to ensure maximum utilisation at rush-hours.

The inner city rarely has adequate powers to deal with pollu-tion, solid waste disposal or its public housing programmes. Tokyo, which has an operating budget about a third of the size of New York's and which has increased its population since the war from 3·5 million to nearly 12 million, concentrated on economic revival and plain survival after half its housing stock, and almost all its metropolitan industry, was destroyed by American firebombs. In the process, more than 80,000 factories were constructed, assuring the city's economic pre-eminence – and severe doses of photochemical smog. As Professor Robson described it, "all the social functions of a great city were neglected, both in terms of capital investment and of human resources". Less than 40 per cent of the special ward area – the most highly developed part of Tokyo – has sewerage facilities. And, although Tokyo now builds 120,000 dwelling units a year (double New York's average), the housing shortage is estimated at

3*

well over half a million. "Whole families are crowded into rooms of just under ten square metres . . . at least 30 per cent of the population is acutely dissatisfied with the housing situation."

Is government of cities like Tokyo on the edge of breakdown? Robson has grave doubts about Tokyo's future. Its government, he found, is confident that it will be able to transport three million people into the special ward area each day by 1985; he is convinced that this is impossible, that at present levels "the misery of the daily journey to work has already reached a peak: if it is not relieved and if the housing situation is not improved, the political stability of the regime may be clearly called into question . . . The National Government and the National Diet seem unaware where these daily pressures are likely to lead." If Tokyo, a very wealthy community even by some West European standards, courts these risks, it puts in acute form the question of the governability of megalopolis.

The astonishing fact about Tokyo is that it remains an exceptionally law-abiding city, in which the major outbursts of violence are from students (and in which, after almost all major demos, even the most militant usually leave on time to catch the crush-trains to their suburban homes). If the pressures on Tokyo threaten "political stability", what of New York, where 34 per cent of people questioned in a Manhattan survey had been subjected to some form of criminal attack and where housing comes fifth on the list of New Yorkers' greatest worries? And what of Detroit, proverbial heartland of unease and violence?

One of the principal reasons cited by Mumford and others for the flight to the suburbs throughout industrial America is the congestion in the central city. That criterion cannot apply to half-deserted, derelict Detroit. Detroiters are retreating from the turmoil of the central city, and Stephen Aris found that "many planners see in Detroit's present plight the grim future of the modern industrial city, not only in America but elsewhere in the world". They see, then, what Mumford in his scathing *New Yorker* assessment of Jane Jacobs's remedies for the cities, called "the increasing pathology of the whole mode of life in the great metropolis, a pathology that is directly proportionate to its growth, its purposeless materialism, its congestion, and its insensate disorder". Yet the void is more frightening still.

It is easier to analyse the components of breakdown than to

discover the underlying causes. Detroit, in common with New York although not to the same extent, has absorbed vast migrations from rural areas. It was the site in 1967 of the most serious of America's race riots, in which forty-three people died and more than $15 million worth of property went up in flames. In 1973, it had the highest murder rate in the United States, one a year for every 1,806 inhabitants. Its public school system, catering for a 75 per cent black population, is on the edge of bankruptcy. There are more abandoned and derelict houses in this city than in any other in America. Worst of all, with the exception of the thirty-two-acre complex called Detroit Renaissance, being erected with strong backing from Henry Ford and other industrialists, there is, Aris discovered, "no new commercial development in downtown Detroit". Nor is there likely to be until the middle classes' faith in the city is restored.

Earlier prosperity has left some traces: the median income for Detroit's blacks is $2,640 above the average for American black families. Against this, 40 per cent are living on wages below the Federal poverty line, 30 per cent live in substandard housing. In 1974, unemployment came to 10 per cent, double the national average. The decay in the inner city lies at the root of its crime, and its fear of crime. And worse damage than was ever inflicted in the 1967 riots was visited on the housing stock by the Federal Housing Authority's scheme to restore pride in house ownership by underwriting a massive house-purchase scheme. The scheme, left to private enterprise to implement, developed into a wholesale swindle which affected, according to one estimate, 120,000 people and may have been responsible for the destruction or abandonment of 10 per cent of the city's accommodation. Even today, houses are being pulled down faster than they are being built.

Detroit is a city whose decline can be checked only by immense inflows of resources. Industry is there, in the suburbs, where revenue doubled in the Sixties, while declining in real terms in the city proper. Ford's "Renaissance" project is designed "to draw people and firms back into the city", he says. If money can do the trick, the project ought to work: by the time it is finished in 1985, the investment will exceed $500 million. But the huge and costly freeways built in the past decade have not had that effect: all they have done is to turn 65 per cent of the downtown areas into roads, flyovers and parking lots, and facilitate access from the suburbs. In any case, it is debatable whether the most elaborate and costly scheme can achieve anything without some diminution of racial polarisations. This, after all, is the city where the joke that delighted patrolmen whom Stephen Aris accompanied one night concerned a presidential announcement: "My fellow Americans, I have some bad news and some good news. First, the bad news: Martians have landed. Now the good news: they kill niggers and piss gasoline."

It is in this context that the concern of New Yorkers, and of metropolitan America's millions of white suburban dwellers, about crime should be seen – in the context of transience, racial tension and social unrest. Nearly half New York's residents are of foreign birth or the children of foreign-born residents. A fifth are black. New York has seen eight major migrations; to cope with the latest, from Puerto Rico, 1,200 of the city's police are now learning Spanish. The shifts in ethnic population have affected the city's services across the board, from education and housing to welfare costs. (One out of seven New Yorkers receives some form of public assistance: the story of the small girl who told the social worker that she wanted to "draw" when she grew up, and who turned out to have in mind the drawing of welfare cheques, may be apocryphal, but is certainly symbolic of the extent of the problem.)

New Yorkers are obsessed, with reason, by violent crime. Yet the crime statistics, for what they are worth, place New York below eighteen other American cities. The point is still that crimes of violence are disproportionately high, and that what there is was found by one task force to be borne chiefly "by the poor, the minorities, the elderly, and other New Yorkers who are least able to sustain the damage inflicted". Housing and education are more acute questions, but not more disturbing ones. They do not kill, nor, visibly, do they maim.

But public education in New York, said Goodman, demonstrates the real difficulty of assimilating migrants with non-urban backgrounds, different languages and cultures, in the predominantly poor and working-class city centre. "The problem of integrating schools has not been solved. A disheartening percentage of students do not have basic reading skills. . . . The drop-out rate among black and Puerto Rican students is over

50 per cent ... 65 per cent of the public school population is comprised of minority group children, while a majority of teaching staffs is white." Most disconcerting of all, several of the schools have become unsafe and have to be patrolled by security guards.

Reviewing the difficulties of providing services and amenities for the city, Senator Goodman described its "economic posture: greater needs for more services, a shrinking middle-level work force, a shrinking tax base, inflation, and astronomically growing budgets". The combination of these pressures, he recognised, raised basic questions about the government of New York, and of most metropolitan cities: "At what levels do the various governmental functions, services and powers properly belong? What should the city's functions be? ... A better approach to regionalism must come, otherwise problems of poor transportation, deteriorating air and water quality, imbalance of economic resources, and absence of rational planning on a regional scale will continue to plague us." But the definition of a "better approach to regionalism" remains pretty foggy. For specific problems in metropolitan government, efficiency and prosperity will do much; to the city's central dilemma – the dilemma of "who decides, who allocates what?" – they provide an incomplete, even irrelevant, response. And nowadays many cities, even of the rich, are finding both efficiency and prosperity increasingly hard to come by.

CHAPTER 7

The Planner and the Community

> This owner, that landlord never dies they say.
> Other steps into his shoes when he gets his
> notice to quit. They buy the place up with
> gold and still they have all the gold. Swindle
> in it somewhere. Piled up in cities, worn away
> age after age. Pyramids in sand. Slaves.
> Chinese wall. Babylon. Big stones left. Round
> towers. Rest rubble, sprawling suburbs, jerry-
> built, Kerwan's mushroom house, built of
> breeze. Shelter from the night.
>   No one is anything . . .
>
> JAMES JOYCE, *Ulysses*

The planning controversy is central to the political question of "who governs". Barbara Ward, in the keynote speech to the conference, which ends this book, asks: "Is it necessary to endure mega-regions which are so separate, so spread, so thin in the suburbs, so neglected in the centres, so overloaded in their office districts, so given over to all the strains of mass commuting that they become the focus of rejection, *anomie* – and even violence?" With Lewis Mumford and some of the most respected planners, she argues for decentralisation and regional policies. Yet we should perhaps look more carefully at society's definition of intolerable ills. If we take congestion as an example, we should then ask ourselves why people jam Times Square every New Year's Eve, or Trafalgar Square every sunny weekend. If we dedicate our wealth to eliminating slums, we should remember that some inhabit them from choice.

Jane Jacobs confidently challenges the notion that sheer size must mean atomisation and disorder. "To limit the size of great cities as is often advocated, because of the acute problems arising from size, is profoundly reactionary. Cities magnify an economy's practical problems, but they can also solve them by means of new technology." The question, to her as to Shirley Williams, leading British Labour politician, is partly, as Mrs Williams said at Oxford, "how to marry modern architecture with a sense of community . . . the new brutalism of our architecture and of its conflict with human values and, if you like, human angularity, discrepancies, curiosities, opposites, is something to which we must turn our minds and to which we have turned our minds insufficiently". Both would argue that the existing areas of inner cities must be revitalised. But the question then is, how to "let the human spirit grow in the interstices between the engineering".

The consequences of major planning projects without a clear anticipation of long-term consequences were examined in the section on city models. The major federal programmes of slum clearance resulted in large-scale dislocation and rebuilding of an often shoddy standard. In the name of such programmes, Mumford asserts, "many quarters of Greater New York that would still have been decently habitable with a modest expenditure of capital have been razed, and their inhabitants . . . booted out, to settle in even slummier quarters". Small physical improvements in rehousing schemes have been offset, in this view, by worse social conditions and the atomising of the community – and by "further social stratification – segregation, actually – of people by their income levels".

The history of the grand federal plan to aid the cities of the United States, where the battle between the proponents of "engineering" and those of "the interstices" is most bitter, is not encouraging. Mumford, testifying before the Ribicoff Committee on Government Expenditure in 1967, reminded the committee that the federal housing project had horrified its backers, as "the financial-bureaucratic process and the bulldozer mind had wiped out our concepts for a better urban community, and produced those nightmares of urban anonymity and human desolation that dominate the skyline". Repeating the argument for planning on a regional scale, he insisted that Senator Ribicoff's plans for restoring neighbourhoods as the basic human environment, and for creating "the technology of Metropolis", were totally incompatible. His advice was not to invest on the grand scale, but to "experiment with small measures and small units, until you have time to prepare better plans".

The urban distortions to which Mumford referred have been brilliantly criticised by Jane Jacobs and glumly listed by every variety of sociologist. They are visible in almost every major city, in Europe as in the United States. They have accelerated an erosion in public confidence in plans to ease the city's housing and planning problems. They were created on a large scale. In East Harlem, $300 million was spent during the 1950s on public housing and related construction. More than 1,300 commercial enterprises were demolished, Jane Jacobs asserts, to make way for housing projects. Since 1950, after expenditure roughly equal to $1,500 a head, rates of unemployment, under-employment, welfare and even of housing have, in her opinion, worsened. Of the programme of Urban Renewal, Scott Greer complained in 1965 that "at a cost of more than $3,000 million, the Urban Renewal Agency has succeeded in materially reducing the supply of low cost housing in American cities".

The main weight of federal programmes was directed to mobility – both mass transit and the construction of national expressway systems – to the provision of Federal Housing Authority (FHA) mortgages and to urban renewal programmes. The first two assisted, if anything, the suburban drift – by making it easier to get there, and by favouring the purchase of *new* homes – which were mostly built in the neatly zoned suburbs where land was cheaper. The third, whose principal aim was to attract middle-class residents back into the city, may be working – but at what cost to the poorest city residents it is difficult to compute. There seemed to many planners an absurd inconsistency behind planning which produced highways and FHA schemes which paid the middle-class resident to move out of the city, and urban renewal and mass transit schemes encouraging him to move back in.

"If there is no administration, there is no freedom," suggested Professor Joseph Rykwert at Oxford. Of all the cities' problems, nothing has perhaps proved less responsive than the housing situation, whether administrative effort has been concentrated on new building or on restoration of existing stock. Land prices have exacerbated the problem. In Paris, in London, the cost of apartments now entails mortgages whose repayment costs a very high proportion of the post-tax income of even the middle-class buyers. In New York, said Goodman, "a new, conventionally

Three dimensions of density: These London row houses and the estate which looms over them (top) house the same numbers per acre as St Francis Square, San Francisco (below) – a humane exception to the planning rule.

The dynamiting of Pruitt Igoe, St Louis: only a few years earlier, this crime-plagued, derelict project was an award-winning model of lowcost housing. Replacement cost, $60 million.

London squatters patch up "permanent" housing. Their Peruvian counterpart's "invasion shack" (top) will last as long as he wants.

financed two-bedroom apartment in a six-storey elevator building
... must rent at over $400 a month. With rent equivalent to
25 per cent to 30 per cent of income, the family must earn
$16,000 to $19,000 a year. Only about 7 per cent of the city's
families earn annual incomes of $15,000 and over." Public
subsidy is obviously one remedy, but to have much impact it
would have to be on an enormous scale.

In any case, how should the subsidies be used, and who should
have a say in policy? Middle-class "rehabbing" in the United
States has come under sustained criticism; certainly, "gut
rehabilitation", in the Americans' graphic if ungraceful phrase, is
enormously expensive, and there is considerable bitterness over
the allocation of generous loans to relatively affluent families,
when help for lower income families for similar purposes would
be impracticable on anything but an outright grant basis. At
Oxford, the planning imperatives underlying "rehabbing" and
the integrated neighbourhood, versus the rights of the less
articulate segments of society, were the subject of strong dis-
agreement between Professor Becker and Senator Goodman.
Natalie Becker argued that rehabbing might look fine to an outsider, but that it reduced the stock of low-cost housing, involved
the dislocation of established communities, however deprived,
and despoiled the poor of their birthright, the crumbling houses
the middle classes left decades ago for the suburbs. Goodman
viewed the rehabilitation of neighbourhoods as an essential
ingredient in a policy of re-creating mixed income communities
in the city centre. If the tax-paying, energetic and innovating
classes did not move back into the cities, he argued, they would
lose any sense of commitment to it – without this, there would be
no birthright but decay and squalor for the poor to lay claim to.

In any argument pitting the "whole society" claim against the
disruptions involved in conversion and rehabilitation, the temptation to put the planner in one scale and the people who have to
live with his plans in another is great, given the high economic
and social costs which have accompanied relocation of low income
communities. Natalie Becker traced the failure "to reach our
goals in almost every aspect of our urban problems" – the existence of large pockets of poverty, and the increase in the disparity
between incomes at a time when expectations are rising – to some
degree of political failure of will. In the United States, she found,

"powerlessness is the general rule and the cause of its current trauma". Lack of responsiveness to this dilemma implied faulty planning; the planners should "ask themselves fundamental questions about power and its meaning before rushing to the drawing board".

The solutions they might find would, she argued, lie in consensus politics as a basis for urban planning. Yet she conceded that a wide consensus would in practice be unobtainable. The point was still that a "desirable community" could not by definition issue from technical expertise, because of an inherent conflict of interest between planner and planee: "solutions are less important than the processes by which we arrive at them".

Daniel Bell sees the "contradictory impulses towards equality and bureaucracy" as characteristic of the social tensions of Western post-industrial society, to a point where desire for "greater participation in the decision-making of organisations that control individual lives . . . and the increasing technical requirements of knowledge . . . form one of the axes of social conflict". When the processes of consultation are far from reaching the level of satisfactory dialogue, how are the cities to be revitalised with the consent of the citizens concerned? One way, according to Natalie Becker, is for the planners to abandon some cherished goals. "Perhaps we should give up the idea of re-colonising New York City with the solid fun-loving, culture-loving and tax-paying middle class. Perhaps the cities must remain what they are now – way stations for low income groups on their way up." That would be preferable, in her view, to "the destruction of low-rent housing and the construction of new housing for those who can best afford it". But here "up" still implies "out" – a sorry formula under which "creatively to reconcile the diverse interests in the urban centres, in such a way as to help those who most need it", if only because of the question mark it leaves over "diversity".

Is the mixed-income population an evil? Slum clearance has produced, in Europe as in the United States, some disastrous housing projects and the fragmentation of dilapidated but well-knit neighbourhoods. But part of the problem in wholesale clearance is that it frequently has not attempted a social mix. In New York, the proponents of the "balanced community" favour a cautious ratio of 70 per cent middle or upper income groups to

30 per cent poor, with the balance tipping under the 30 per cent rather than over. There is in such re-jigging considerable loss of low-income housing. But what are the alternatives?

Nearly 70 per cent of New York's housing is over forty years old; costs of upkeep have for years been prohibitive, and have contributed to the rate of abandonment of old houses and apartment blocks. With a dozen separate agencies concerned in the city's housing problems, and the economics as intractable as they are, confusion is bound to be a distinguishing characteristic of public intervention. Construction, overwhelmingly through public programmes, has in the last five years just about equalled the number of buildings abandoned, plus the "units required to meet new family formation". But the Federal Government has abandoned its commitment to housing support; and, as Goodman observed, the building rate has now dropped from 60,000 units a year to 14,000. This, together with the replacement of residential stock by office buildings as New York converts from a manufacturing to a service economy, spells crisis. "It is obviously very difficult indeed to protect the rights of the lower class when new construction occurs," Goodman conceded; but he continued, "I would ask what is the option if we do not build the new buildings? . . . the city will have no self-renewal, no regeneration and will eventually become one massive slum."

Goodman is committed to the struggle "to keep upper and middle classes in the cities. . . . There can only be vigour in a city when it has population balance and provides the opportunity for people of all income levels to live together in some degree of harmony." Against this, Natalie Becker argues that to split the poor up is to deprive them of whatever political power they have got together. They may also, quite simply, value what they have as an environment. Boston Urban Renewal Administration asked a Brandeis research unit in the Sixties to canvass a middle-income black neighbourhood. The respondents were offered better housing, at prices they could afford, in white areas. Only 13 per cent took up the offer; the community valued the proportion of income released for other purposes as a result of renting the cheapest living space in the city – more important, it was used to itself as a community, and declined to be uprooted.

Ralph Ellison, arguing that urban improvements without relocation were what Harlem residents wanted, told a Federal

Committee in 1966: "it isn't the desire to run to the suburbs or to invade 'white' neighbourhoods that is the main concern with my people in Harlem. They would just like to have a more human life there. A slum like Harlem isn't just a place of decay. It is also a form of historical and social memory." At Oxford, a young black architect and planner, Joseph Black, echoed the same resistance to the mixed neighbourhood. Objecting that "the housing bodies very often deny people the opportunity of living in their former neighbourhoods", he insisted that Harlem's future must be based on better use of the existing fabric, a fabric enriched with improved housing, more efficient control of crime, improvement of community facilities and job opportunities within the area.

But the homogeneous community presents difficulties. The American architect Oscar Newman, although a strong critic of low-cost housing policies, had this to say about crime and the neighbourhood: "The size of a public housing project is the strongest *physical* indicator of the crime rate. The strongest indicator of all is the social characteristics of the residents. The lower the income, the higher the crime rate, regardless of the form of the housing or where it is located. That is not very encouraging. . . . Residents in communities surrounding public housing projects are concerned; most people living in the projects are fearful. Low-income people are very vulnerable. They live among a population with over three times the criminal records of the average; they don't command police protection and they feel they cannot make demands on authority or each other. . . . Concentrating them together, or allowing them to be concentrated, is an effort which is short-lived. The public housing projects we built in America ten and fifteen years ago are falling into disuse, they are uninhabitable."

Newman's argument is supported by evidence from city areas throughout the developed world. He points out that good housing left behind by middle-class families in their move to the suburbs provided an excellent stop-gap for lower income groups in the States – for a time. Then schools deteriorate, more middle-income families move out, parks and amenities previously maintained out of taxes run down. Shops are taken over by the blight of poor areas. They provide shoddy produce at inflated prices. Job opportunities vanish. The black, moderate income families who moved in, he points out, didn't think they were moving into a slum, but into an area which they hoped would provide better schools and amenities: "they didn't want to see that area turned into a ghetto, and the hard earned savings they invested in a house, vanish". The pattern is recognisable in Birmingham, in Milan, in any city with a high degree of social mobility and cultural or social diversity.

How are the divided cities of the rich and the poor to be integrated? By listening, Newman says, to the middle classes, learning what they will accept as a successful mixed community. "You can say, damn the middle-income people, but the point is that if you say that, the middle-income people will move away, out to the suburbs. What else is the mad development of suburban America all about? It is the flight from low-income population . . . at incredible cost."

It is more attractive for the liberal, advocate planner to say, forget the technocrats and listen to the poor; evidently the planners have dispensed with anything more than token consultation for too long, and too many buildings demonstrate it. But it may make more sense to say that the understanding of middle-income needs offers the best chance of creating "a workable, walkable city" and a secure neighbourhood – and thus the best way to help the lower-income groups. Crime comes top of the list of a Harlem-dweller's dissatisfactions with the city, just as it does for a Park Avenue duplex-owner.

The point that Newman is making is important because it argues that, if you want to prevent the vicious slum-creating cycle from forming, you have got to see to it that people who can afford to move elsewhere will stay by choice. Today's middle classes were not always middle class: cities generate what sociologists call "upward mobility". The phrase has an ominous ring – because it suggests not just improved circumstances, but a tendency to go where you can enjoy them in the company of your peers. In doing so, in leaving a district, you leave a space for somebody on a lower rung of the ladder to move in. Jane Jacobs defines as a "perpetual slum", a district which people desert when they can, "and in the meantime dream of getting out". The more this is the case, the less likely are patches of affluence to exert a sufficiently powerful regenerative influence.

Slums have a tendency to spread; and as they do, the costs of breaking the cycle increase on a multiplier principle. A homogeneous district of low-income people is doomed partly because it is not a stable district in any sense other than that of income bracket. A low-cost housing project will run into difficulties precisely because the "means test" administered by authority operates to keep it poor. Slums are more than the sum of their housing. In the rehabilitation programme, a gamble has been taken on minimising the sense of defeat. Unless a diverse neighbourhood can be created, where "upward mobility" has a chance to work within a geographical area, a cycle of "downward mobility" is all too likely to be created. The stabilisation of moderate income neighbourhoods may be the essential part of the rehabilitation process; but unless the city can offer loans, job opportunities and incentives to encourage the more prosperous to stay faithful to their neighbourhoods, then "rehabbing" will continue to mean the return of the affluent from the suburbs under programmes which imply the displacement of the poor to clean up a neighbourhood. Shirley Williams recalled one American sceptic's description of this process: "the replacement of a black man by a tree".

But the first signs that the arguments do not have to be so sharply polarised are emerging in the United States. This is an entirely new development, and immensely encouraging. It also has interesting parallels with the discovery of the virtues of self-help housing in the cities of the poor.

What has been happening is that tenants of housing in a desperately deteriorated state, because the landlord has either abandoned the building altogether or is in the process of doing so, have taken matters into their own hands. Faced with breakdowns in the elevators, in the heating and hot water, with leaking roofs and smashed entrance doors, they have banded together to use informally collected "rent equivalents" and used the money for emergency repairs. From this first step, grounded in desperation, they have formed *de facto* co-operatives and set about rehabilitation of the buildings. Some of these tenants' co-operatives have now obtained legal title to their building.

The advantages are evident: when new building is inadequate to the city's housing needs, and "gut rehabilitation" prohibitively expensive, this form of piecemeal "rehabbing", with the tenants

still in residence, on a scale tailored to their needs as they recognise them, could save from demolition housing which is often
fairly sound. And this form of "rehabbing" works out at less than
$10,000 a unit, making possible monthly charges of only $30 a
room, even in New York.

The notion of tenant ownership and tenant management has
been considered for some years as a possible device for preserving
older housing and easing shortages in American cities. Up to now,
assumptions about the managerial, constructional and operational
skills which would be required have generated scepticism as to
the feasibility of such plans for congested, low-income areas. But
in the autumn of 1973, a startling report by Robert Kolodny, an
urban planner at Columbia University, was published. Called
Self Help in the Inner City, it charted the development – mostly
since 1970 – of a movement of tenants to protect their own
interests in housing which landlord, city and housing experts had
given up as hopeless.

Kolodny located 136 projects involving tenant co-operatives in
New York City by mid-1973. Only twelve were then completed,
with the title in the tenants' possession; but he reported rapidly
growing interest. Expert attention had been focused on preven-
tive measures to stop neighbourhoods deteriorating further. But
Kolodny found less tenant interest where conditions had not yet
reached bottom; and tenant commitment is the *sine qua non* of
success in what is a spontaneous effort "prompted above all by
desperate housing circumstances". Three-quarters of the projects
were found in the most troubled areas in the city, in acutely
"distressed" properties; much of the activity stemmed from
unconventional tenant co-operation with the aim of gaining some
control over their living conditions. In 75 per cent of the projects, the tenants took a leading role in the whole process of
rehabilitation, often supplying labour themselves in a form of
"sweat equity" which cut costs. Buildings where outside sponsors
were particularly active tended to be the least successful; only
through retaining the initiative, Kolodny found, were tenants
able to make the break from "tenant psychology", to see themselves as "the owner of something substantial, a novel experience
for minority households that have become involved in conversion
efforts". The risk for any sympathetic outside authority which
might get interested in such schemes is that it will all too easily

be taken for a surrogate landlord, with tenant commitment dropping accordingly.

The incidence of self-help has largely been confined to New York, although there are projects in Boston, Washington and Detroit. Behind the movement, Kolodny found no theory about the virtues of ownership or determination to prove that the lower-income families could go it alone. "That pride in ownership, satisfactions growing out of co-operation and feelings of security in tenure can follow conversion is not the issue," he comments. In most early instances, the tenants had no idea that others were following the same course. It was simply that something had to be done. Nor was this low-cost conversion, in all its informality, burdened by artificial homogeneity. Kolodny found that income disparities within a project were around $10,000 a year between households. Certainly, the tenant co-operatives were over-whelmingly composed of minority groups, either black or Puerto Rican: given the neighbourhoods, this was to be expected. Tenant leaders tended to be found in the more "upwardly mobile" families; but this was not necessarily true – one particularly competent co-operative leader was a mother on welfare (almost a third of households were headed by females without partners and with several children). Projects contained every form of household and age group, including a large proportion of families with five or more members.

The emergence of this movement offers one solid prospect for breaking out of the slum circle without the necessity of relocation and wholesale demolition. But tenants can only go so far unaided. Despite the dangers of paternalism, Kolodny points out that large-scale development along these lines would require an extensive supporting organisation of expert guidance, together with readily available seed financing, loan facilities and thinning out of red tape to enable tenants to make easier claims to title. The costs to the public have proved to be much lower than in any other form of slum regeneration. By working backwards from rent and maintenance costs and assessing the tenants' ability to pay, sale prices and loans could be calculated realistically. Hidden subsidies in the form of cheap loans and expert assistance would be needed; but the tenants would repay the loans. Experience here suggests the beginnings of a workable form of dialogue between "planee" and planner, with the "planee" often the initiator.

In developing world cities, under immense migratory pressure and lacking funds, such public intervention must necessarily be limited and self-help a natural response. Planners in the West, looking at the decaying brownstones and Victorian terrace houses which are the unlovely legacy of industrial growth, have yet to come to terms with the truth that new housing is not and cannot be adequate to need. Western planners, preoccupied with creating a new sense of urban community – call it by whatever name – in the carefully planned blocks that have swept away the untenantable tenements, have perhaps too readily assumed that better sanitation would create a climate of confidence. Kolodny's findings suggest that the sense of being in control of one's own living circumstances, however reluctantly this control is assumed, is a hopeful answer both to the shortage of housing and to the transience which goes with the degenerating slum. It is not the only answer, as he emphasises; but it is worth acting on at a time when affluent societies are spending huge sums on research to find ways of re-creating the village instinct, the community spirit, of which the cities of the West have so much less than the migrants to the shanty towns and the *favelas* of the Third World.

CHAPTER 8

The Defensible City

Any city, however small, is in fact divided into
two, one the city of the poor, the other of the
rich; they are at war with one another.

PLATO, *The Republic*

The great French architect, Le Corbusier, saw in his elegant
skyscrapers with broad expanses between them the antidote to the
high-density slum – the "city in a park". But in practice, the
realisation of this vision has produced what Lewis Mumford
acidly but more accurately has called "the city in a parking lot".
High-rise no longer seems a complete and satisfying answer to
the manifest lack of light and space characteristic of nineteenth-
century working-class housing.

Nothing, it turned out, bred claustrophobia more surely than
the hermetically sealed apartment block of concrete and glass
with green acres sprawled, empty, beneath. Space in its human
dimension – the interstices which encourage interchange – had
been sacrificed to mere emptiness.

Not that planners, then or now, thought of the grand spaces
they created as empty. In Macao, the magnificent old Praia
Grande, with its plane trees and low pastel houses fusing the
architectures of Portugal and China, is being torn down as fast as
funds can be raised. Round the multi-storey blocks which will
tragically replace it, the architects' placards proudly display
drawings recalling the Fifties and the Festival of Britain.
Animated pencil-skirted and finger-waving groups in the style of
early Dior walk the concrete pathways (carefully avoiding the
grass), and the saplings, which will replace the old trees now
shading stuccoed doorways, are spaced so that they will provide
interlocking shade a hundred years hence – after the demise of
the buildings they are landscaped to enhance. An hour's journey
away, the great high-density rehousing estates of Hong Kong

offer an unheeded warning – even though the earliest resettlement estates, built in the Fifties, are already being gutted within as a cheaper alternative to demolition. The architect's drawing offers only "such a vision of the street as the street hardly understands".

Much high-density housing in fact turns its back on the street altogether, cutting itself off from surrounding neighbourhoods in a way which has proved more than merely symbolic. The results have, with few exceptions, turned out to be not merely boring but unworkable. In England, concern about the increase of vandalism and crime in such projects led in May 1974 to parliamentary requests for a ministerial pledge that no more such projects would be started. The pledge was not forthcoming – for the reason that, although no new projects of the kind were going on to the drawing board, a backlog of approved high-rise developments had accumulated. In Paris and other major French cities, the policy of tearing down slum areas and replacing them with enormous high-rise complexes has been reversed in the last two years, following the realisation that what was being created was a completely alienated population which resorted, as one jaundiced writer describes it, to "crime, multiple rape and other such amusements".

The temptations were obvious: there was a chronic shortage in all industrial cities of decent housing, and restoration work was yielding an increasingly poor return on investment by comparison with starting from scratch. Also, planning is expensive, so much so that the processes of site selection and getting designs approved by the appropriate authority are a substantial overhead. Consultation procedures add to the cost. Architects found however that these overheads were roughly the same for a small housing project as for a mammoth; the way was set for multi-unit projects.

The mounting evidence, from social workers and case studies, that what people hate, they desecrate, prompted an American architect, Oscar Newman, to set up a research team to study "how people use the physical habitat that has been designed for them or which they build for themselves". "We were looking," said Newman at Oxford, "for the mechanisms which operate to give them certain opportunities and controls, or conversely to find the mechanisms in the physical design of habitat that prevent them from assuming certain of their capacities and potentials."

Research into many kinds of urban housing established for New-man a set of ground rules relating architectural design to security and stability; he has called them "defensible space".

Starting with the fact that the American votes with his feet, as soon as he can afford it, for the single family house with its own land, Newman took a close look at what he calls the "marking mechanisms" which people set up round their homes. How could these little gardens, flower pots, picket fences and such like be reconciled with the densities inevitable in city life, where the high cost of land must be split among as many families as possible?

The most drastic step in increasing density of occupancy, he found, is the splitting of houses into apartments so that parts of the interior space become public in nature – a step which archi-tects took without thinking when converting large houses into multi-family units. Even with moderate-size conversions, the result was the erosion of personal privacy, choice and commit-ment. Collective space, the responsibility of no single family, risked on principle becoming a no-man's-land. Yet, "not having thought about it," he says, "we then pushed ahead and went on to produce the densities and environments we have now, which in New York reach up to 230 units to the acre". The no-man's-land became a waste-land – worse still, at times a battle-ground.

The problem, Newman insists, is not essentially density. Some walk-up projects achieve very high densities and work better than high-rises of equivalent density. The elevated buildings of the low income housing programme in the United States were erected as a rule at the same density as the slums they superseded. "The purpose behind the high-rise programme was noble: in effect to replace the slums and to rehouse in the same space exactly those families that lived there. They have been rehoused in elevated buildings, with a lot of ground around them for chil-dren to play and people to sit. There is air and light; but unfor-tunately the idea has produced a set of problems . . . problems so critical that they are beginning to tear out the very fabric of this programme and the very fabric of the housing."

One of the most notorious images of the wreck of good inten-tions is Pruitt Igoe. A gigantic, award-winning scheme on the outskirts of St Louis, this complex was built on the premise that people need light and open space, and insulation from the street system. "There is internal vehicular circulation, but no through circulation; there is parking provision; grounds are free, and all the building space faces south to catch the sunlight." Only forty-seven families to the acre, because it was built high, all of the acreage was common ground. Each building was shared by 150 families.

But despite its good intentions, Pruitt Igoe rapidly began to decay. Windows were smashed, play equipment wrecked, and quickly the criminals and drug pushers moved in. It never achieved full occupancy. Soon, people began to desert it, and empty apartments became hideouts for criminals on the run. During the last five years the vacancy rate exceeded 75 per cent. Finally the immense losses due to maintenance and repair were cut by a simple expedient: the entire project was dynamited.

What had gone wrong? The trouble, says Newman, was that the environment, inside and out, belonged to no one. "With all the interior circulation space, totally anonymous, no one was really in a position to identify who lived there – to distinguish stranger from resident. There was no way for mechanisms to evolve where people could agree to a common acceptable use of space; there was no juxtaposition of this space with the dwelling unit proper. People who lived in this sort of massive development lived in their apartments only and were frightened of everything else." Their withdrawal aggravated conditions and reality became worse than their forebodings.

Newman argues that this wilderness is not inherent to high density housing; other projects, built at the same density, and inhabited by the same kinds of low-income families, still have long waiting lists. Typically, they are no more than three storeys high, with the grounds split up and assigned to small groups of residents; communal space overlooked by, and close to, the dwelling units. Families feel safe, because they can tell neighbour from stranger, because they can see where their car is parked, because they are near enough to the ground to yell from the window at Johnny to come off that swing.

He contrasts two housing projects in New York: Brownsville, a cluster of three- and six-storey walk-ups, and Van Dyke, a high-rise building in a large paved area. Across the street from each other and inhabited by the same kinds of family, each has seventy-two dwelling units to the acre. Both are in a high crime area. In Van Dyke, 120 families share an entrance and eight to ten a corridor; the interior of the building has become intolerably unsafe. "People usually call each other and walk through the building in groups"; mothers will not let their children go down to the play area alone. The open space on the grounds is empty, an object of fear. By contrast in Brownsville, entries are used by six to twelve families; no more than three share each open corridor, and residents feel the communal space is theirs: "within that space they will challenge people that they do not know." The grounds are better maintained and intensively used; cars are parked on the street alongside. Newman finds that the closeness of the street alone makes the project safer, and the project in turn spreads an umbrella over the street. People leaving Van Dyke cross to the Brownsville side of the street to walk, "entering a zone, or a penumbra, of safety".

Nothing dictates that high-rise buildings need be the pattern of high-density housing, except that architects like building them. They are structurally challenging, they evoke an image of modernity – of a new and total society. They are also tidy – at least until residents move in. If people find the communal space hard to use, impossible to linger in, the way is open for vandalism. English high-rise estates are comparatively crime-free; but the next ten years will show whether the children now covering the passages with graffiti – in more ways than one, Newman warns, the "writing on the wall" – will turn to more dramatic amusements. Estates need not be fenced off from the community to prevent vandalism: most of it in any case comes from within. There need be nothing to stop neighbourhood children coming in to use the play equipment – provided that the play equipment evidently "belongs" to an identifiable group of people.

The city in the parking lot is the city without order. Buildings and areas of this kind, says Newman, "will be destroyed – they have been destroyed. They will be vandalised, they will become unliveable. They are contrary to the way we have evolved our habitat, contrary to the entire rules system. The concept of territory is basic to the home environment and we have forgotten it."

Nor do these developments make economic sense. In most instances they cost more to build per dwelling unit; and, because grounds and interior corridors cannot be allotted to residents, they must be maintained at public expense. They also become crime-ridden and derelict. Newman's team took one such project, an area of row houses, and assigned 90 per cent of the grounds to the tenant. If, they reasoned, tenants would assume responsibility for upkeep of their "own" area, they would exert control over space which was previously plagued by street gangs. "Two years later," Newman reports, "with no inducements, no provision of shrubs, no provision of grass, the place was transformed by the residents themselves. The place became safer, because the residents were able to take control and to define a set of rules for the use of grounds. We all live in a world with sets of rules. Poor people have the same right to develop personal prerogatives; they are no more communally minded than middle-income people." The investment by the local authority paid off in decreased maintenance costs, in a dramatically lowered crime rate, and above all because an area heading the way of Pruitt Igoe became a working entity in which people were glad to live.

Societies which share the same values and goals, which live, as in the Chinese village, as part of an extended family, are less dependent on the physical environment, Newman suggests. In cities of the rich men live differently; they live as individuals, and as strangers. "We don't share common life-styles, concerns or pursuits with our neighbours. We don't necessarily want to. We have a fabric of friendship that extends through the city. . . . We can however admit that there are certain things we need in common: a building which is not vandalised, grounds which are safe and cared for; play space for our children which is safe and easily supervised. These we share, and that is what 'defensible space' is about."

Interestingly, a recent experiment in tenant management indicates that personal commitment may possibly be as important as humane design. The Darst project, again in St Louis, which embodies all the evils of size and high-rise and large open spaces which Newman views with such justified distrust, is staging a remarkable recovery under tenant management. Scheduled for abandonment in the near future, it was turned over to the tenants on a research team's advice, following a rent strike. Vandalism has been reduced; the tenants themselves have obtained the eviction of drug-pedlars living there; a skating rink proudly occupies the space in the centre of the project formerly designated as a parking lot, and is intensively used. Occupancy rates are up: tenants actively question strangers, despite the size of the buildings (tenants' meetings result in much wider acquaintance within the block); and the complex is ripe for tenant ownership rather than demolition.

Newman's message is that the architect must stop building for an abstract Mr Average User and think seriously about what people do when they live in a place. If he fails, the occupants will either devise their own rules or they will retreat behind apartment doors, effectively in a stage of siege. The encouragement of the proprietary instinct which Newman regards as essential is the same principle as that behind self-help schemes in the shanty towns of the developing world. This instinct can, as the project in St Louis showed, be developed in more unpromising physical circumstances than his examples might suggest. Against boredom and ugliness and the stereotyped environment, therefore, there seem to be three forms of response open to the individual: the construction of one's personal island; self-help in the creation of a communal order; and systematic revolt against the general condition.

In the last instance, which is also generally the last resort, the individual joins one of the many subcultures of the city. And in a collection of subcultures, the most violent tend to be dominant. The citizen's protest is a process we do not well understand in its multiple forms. But as politics and planning become more divorced from the neighbourhood community, social conflicts increase, and responses follow other rules than those the planner envisages. The distinction between systematic revolt and human waywardness is one we are only beginning to learn to make.

CHAPTER 9

The Citizen's Protest

Trust the People.
MAO TSE-TUNG

The market economy is easier to measure than the degree of integration in a city's social and cultural life. From *West Side Story* to *Cotton Comes to Harlem*, the "efficiency" of the city is mocked in the behaviour of those for whom its role as productive centre and market place is irrelevant. Since the city depends on those who perpetuate its ability to supply goods and services, those outside the economic logic of the city are viewed as dangerous forces, making for instability, which must be integrated. Fortunately for the diversity of city life, integration is not an automatic by-product of education and a welfare cheque.

The pressures on the individual to harmonise with the purposes of metropolitan life – and the degree to which perplexity is a constant feature of the effort – were illustrated in the following advertisement in *The Times* in June 1974. Nicely juxtaposed to the crossword, it read:

Are You a
LOSER

in the concrete jungle?

Has your bag been pinched, your car stolen, your house or flat burgled?

Do you fall for confidence swindles, bright lights, gambling?

Do you lose your way in cities, fear crowds, flying, the Underground?

If you answer "yes" to any of these questions, or have suffered any other mishap in a city, you need

SURVIVAL IN THE CITY

The publishers were advertising a "really practical" handbook for the evasion of crises, a "guide to security, safety and confidence in a big city, showing you how to act, what to guard against, how to deal with each situation – above all, how to change your attitudes and come out a Winner". It is a poignant image of the extent to which the city has, as one architect expresses it, "ceased to be a place and become a condition" – a condition which implies continuous human adjustment and interaction. It suggests a level of alienation which reduces the condition of city dweller to a form of abstract gamesmanship. At the same time, it has the look of a Victorian manual for self-improvement and success in life – only not in terms of the individual's character and qualities, but of the physical realities of the life confronting him. The magic solution is presented in the context of the very complication and foreignness of the city as object.

What patterns of action in the city express the individual's need to adapt the impersonal to his own use? Which of them contains the elements of alienation and revolt? In his essay, *Megalopolis as Anti-City*, Lewis Mumford argues that the sheer size of the city subtracts from its "organic social complexity", creating a mechanical conformity in urban life "quite as deadening as the social conformity of the tradition-bound village". Atomised parts subtract from the cultural fertility of the whole, in a "random scattering" of strangers. In such a vision of the modern city, "belonging" has little place.

But the same propensity to the creation of social order which characterises the shanty town and makes self-help a workable system for the rural–urban migrant operates equally in the ghetto, in Soho, and among "les petites lumières de Mesnilmontant". For Professor Glean Chase, of New York's Pratt Institute, what is needed to come to terms with the crisis in the cities, is a theory of the "unintended uses" of the city as artefact.

Bureaucracy, he said at Oxford, creates systems and laws designed to rationalise the distribution of goods and services; the "intended user" is the user who adopts the rules which mediate between individual and city, whose purposes accord with its economic and social goals. "Unintended uses," argues Chase, are "a form of urban cavemanship . . . we see the modern city dweller discovering the city and transforming specific objects into cultural objects." The urban caveman's use of the city is based on expedience; it can take the private form of the man dossing on the park bench, or the rationalised outlet of groups like Shelter. He can opt for personal island or systematic revolt. Almost inevitably, Chase maintains, his "interests and social actions are considered by the society as outside its on-going logic, and appear to challenge the very foundations of the autonomous reproduction of metropolitan orders and myths".

The urban caveman is an increasingly common feature of the affluent city – whether lumped into such descriptive categories as urban poor, black, or drop-out, he is an entity whose purposes bureaucracy is not well fitted to understand. But the subcultures in the post-industrial city, like the shanty dwellers in the developing world, have their own modes of order and often create self-regulating mechanisms. The Harlem mugger who returns the intruder's bag with just enough money left to get home is acting more consciously "within the rules" than the intruder.

Chase emphasises the importance of understanding the "unintended user's contributions to urban order" – if only, he urges, because this is a potentially revolutionary aspect of the city's structure. The general organization of urban life must develop more sensitivity to the arbitrariness of human uses for the city as object, or that arbitrariness will coalesce into revolt. It is in these terms, he argues, that the life styles of the ghetto must be understood and given breathing space.

At the other end of the scale of the relationship between individual and society, Japan, while industrialising on a scale which has brought it into third place in the world's economy, has played most successfully on the notion of a closely-knit community to muffle clashes of interest. The Japanese word for pollution, kogai, means public hazard. And to some of its left-wing sociologists and scientists, the most formidable kogai Japan has had to contend with is the stultification of individual expression by a strongly authoritarian social system wholeheartedly committed to industrial power.

In the post-war fight for prosperity, the great majority of Japanese were skilfully conditioned to believe that the greater the expansion of industry, the better and more rewarding would be their daily lives. The reality, as Professor Robson indicated at Oxford, is "acute dissatisfaction and hardship" in certain crucial areas of metropolitan life. If houses are chronically scarce in

Tokyo, it is largely because, as he says, "there has been no attempt by the National government (and no power is possessed by the Tokyo metropolitan government) to restrain speculation which has made land in Tokyo . . . now something like 10,000 times higher in price than it was before the war" – a rate about double that of the increase in the wages of the city's lower paid workers.

In place of houses and social services, roads and harbour construction were sold to the public as "social input" or "regional development". Those who drew attention to the problems of the social classes which did not demonstrably benefit from such "social inputs" were told that these problems were simply a natural antagonism between the economy and society, between production and consumption. Because the industrialisation of Japan had taken place in the nineteenth century under the impetus of the Meiji Restoration, conflict between the entrepreneurs and their feudal predecessors had been minimal; there was no element of a bourgeois revolution in the switch from feudalism.

Japan lacked the social mechanisms in which popular awareness of individual rights flourishes. As pollution accompanied industrialisation (the first celebrated case of copper poisoning, from the Ashio mines, emerged in the early 1880s), the victims were strongly conditioned against protest. After the Second World War, as heavy industry was concentrated increasingly in the major cities, drawing workers into urban centres which became intolerably congested, what struck foreign visitors was the contrast between the evident pressures on the Japanese city dweller and the high level of tolerance he seemed to have evolved. In a paper presented at a symposium on environmental disruption in 1970, Mr Sonoda, a left-wing sociologist, offered a curious definition of the city: "a state of accumulation and concentration of population according to character as influenced by enterprise or capital on the basis of the law of approach between consumers and manufacturers". In other words, the *raison d'être* of the city lies in economic exploitation.

To political and economic pressures, the Japanese industrial structure added another factor which discouraged personal protest. Workers for large companies tend to remain with them throughout their working life. A gap is created between them and

workers in small firms; and the system, reinforced by the institution of the workers' dormitory, encourages an innate conservatism
and fanatical corporate loyalty. Workers at Japan Nitrogen Co.,
which was poisoning both people and marine life with methyl-
mercury waste from its plant at Minamata, even fought the fisher-
men who came to the plant through the autumn of 1959 to
protest at their own financial ruin and the danger of the plant's
operations to Minamata's inhabitants.

But the fight for the victims of Minamata disease – the victims
themselves did not sue the company for ten years after it was
first detected, another example of socio-economic conditioning –
marked a new development in the people's relationship with the
government. Ui Jun, a public health engineer at Tokyo University, mobilised for the first time a public outcry about pollution.
The long process of complaint coincided in Japan with a gradual
loss of confidence in the mechanisms of representative democracy, fortified by the consistent stonewalling of the government
over compensation for victims of Minamata disease; of Itai-Itai,
the cadmium poisoning case in Toyama, whose potential victims
number over 1,000; and of Yokkaichi asthma. Anti-*kogai* groups
were formed and became the central nucleus of a growing civic
movement.

Japan's anti-pollution laws are on paper the strongest in the
world; but Ui and his co-campaigners claim that they are strong
on paper only, and are all instituted for the purpose of deflecting
and relaxing the pressure of public opinion. All redress depends
on the National government, which holds the vast proportion of
powers allocated in other countries to local authorities, just as it
appropriates 70 per cent or more of regional or municipal tax
revenues. The government remained unresponsive.

The Sixties in Japan saw the birth of a group of popular movements essentially Japanese in character which expressed the
strong grassroots trend towards "direct democracy". Ui claimed
at Oxford that such a movement is the only way to break the
collusion between business and government; in a country where
public opinion is not geared to organised protest, perhaps only
the widespread recognition of the individual's helplessness before
kogai could have created it.

What is needed, says Ui, is nothing less than some kind of
"religious reformation", the abandonment of "a system of values

based on the monetary unit". Ui offered evening lectures to the public (although his career has not prospered as a result of his outspokenness: he is still only an instructor at Tokyo University, and its administrative rules do not allow him to lecture to students) to alert them to the issue. With the entrance fees, which those who disagreed with the lecture could claim back, and other funds, victims of Minamata disease were sent to the Stockholm Conference on the Human Environment in 1972 – in turn reinforcing the movement in Japan.

Ui's aim is to break the monopoly of what he sees as the twentieth-century version of the reactionary monks of medieval times. Scientists, he says, "support the rule of the strong in our society.... They maintain a monopoly on knowledge by the use of difficult technical language – as medieval monks used sacred texts. We have computers instead of gongs and pipes, magnificent university buildings instead of temples. The power of the hierarchy is the same. The task of those of us who know something about industry and science is to fill the gap between the experts and the weak and the poor – by abandoning the privileges of the experts, and by marshalling our knowledge in their service." Once the poor have the facts, Ui asserts, they will choose wisely. "The weak are moderate."

The growth of popular protest is centrally important – even though the voice of the citizen is still faint in densely populated, business-orientated Japan. For the fundamental demand behind the calls for a liveable environment is "for greater powers of self-government and the decentralisation of the decision-making process", even though Ui may have been over-optimistic to expect that "If a majority finds in favour of the same demands, the entire economic system, the values of capitalism, will have to be rethought. Daily life will have to be restructured on more egalitarian lines."

Slow as protest has been to make itself felt in a country which suffers from *kogai* to an intolerable extent, it may finally be reaching even the corporate establishment. At Oxford, Professor Robson emphasised that "Japanese industrialists are much more prepared to change than you would expect in a country where the main concentration of investment and the great preponderance of effort has been in the direction of successful capitalistic growth". He cited an issue of the Mitsubishi house magazine, which stated that the Japanese economy must now move away from heavy industry, from steel and petrochemicals, and turn to "the so-called knowledge-based industries, the computer industries". Mitsubishi's stated aim probably owed more to sound business sense than to public-spiritedness. The move into "knowledge-based industries" in Japan was in full swing by the mid-seventies. Pollutant and, incidentally, energy-intensive industries were increasingly shifted overseas, to centres of primary production. In Japan itself, expenditure on pollution control was absorbing around 2 per cent of GNP by the early Seventies, contamination of the air by sulphur oxides and carbon monoxide had been halved, and a whole industry had grown up around anti-pollution systems.

This remarkable turnabout may mean that the Japan of the Sixties, in which even sewerage was a luxury enjoyed by around 20 per cent of households, becomes the garden-city country of the Eighties; Japan has achieved greater miracles, once seized of an idea. If so, the habit of popular protest, so hesitantly established, will focus on other claims for individual welfare.

CHAPTER 10

Oliver Twist in Utopia

In the next forty years we must rebuild the
entire urban United States

LYNDON B. JOHNSON,
My Hope for America

When President Johnson introduced "the Great Society" he was, as Daniel Bell remarks, echoing Adam Smith, for whom one of the three prime duties of the sovereign was carrying out certain "public works" which would further the common good. The sovereign filled out an area of activity for which "the profit could never repay the expense to any individual or number of individuals, though it may frequently do much more than repay it to a great society".

The extent to which modern metropolitan life must be organised in terms of these communal goods – sewerage, education, public transport, health services – has both politicised the government of cities and diminished the importance of the sum of individual goods in the whole. The development of the public sector is more overwhelming in the affluent societies, if only because they demand more communally purchased ingredients for the "good life". Because the individual cannot apply to these the same yardsticks of satisfaction and relative cost that he can use for his personal economic choices, he increasingly feels alienated from decisions that intimately affect his daily well-being. The "they" of the industrial era were a simple object of hostility, the "bosses". In the technological age, the individual feels disquieting uncertainty as to who is taking which of the multiple decisions in the ever growing public field, and as to the criteria "they" adopt. The more we emphasise the "social rights" of the members of "the Great Society", the more we enlarge the area of public, communal choice, and the more complicated the making of decisions becomes. Apathy and alienation, two recognised social problems of the cities, are related to the extent to which public investment programmes necessarily are conceived in terms which most individuals can neither understand nor influence.

As the crises in the cities – organisational, social, economic – seem to call for inter-related solutions, the pursuit of social justice and economic well-being involves more complex measurement of social indicators and an ever greater degree of political involvement. The most acute challenge, if the cities are to be humane communities, is to strike a balance between the "human angularities" of the people who live in them and the planned environment; to encourage the private voice within the context of far-reaching public commitment.

To say this is to beg the question of what that public commitment entails. Is it to be, as Sir Karl Popper states the problem, a commitment to patch together, to make improvements piecemeal, in recognition that perfection is not a practical pursuit? The piecemeal approach, as Popper expresses it, is that people should not "be made unhappy where it can be avoided. . . . The piecemeal engineer will, accordingly, adopt the method of searching for, and fighting against, the greatest and most urgent evils of society, rather than searching for, and fighting for, its greatest ultimate good."

But when the urban situation calls for radical action, and the contradictions in the piecemeal approach are all too painful, the temptation to conceive solutions as a whole is compelling. Plato's image of the just city presupposed that each man's character and his function were perfectly adjusted to the general well-being. A psychological justice, attuned to both natural hierarchy and common aims, assured personal content and social harmony. Into this scheme, the intricacies of social engineering were subsumed. But such a justice was conceived in terms which were wholly political and not economic. Underlying all, was the sense that a relating of all of the parts was possible. The attractions of the *tabula rasa* present themselves to the modern planner in a different, egalitarian form. But the idea of the "just city", in whatever guise, haunts the megalopolis of the twentieth century just as it fascinated the city-statesman. Popper's concern, in *The Open Society and Its Enemies*, with the dangerous implications of such a vision is essentially, and deliberately, modern. It seems

4*

so feeble not to have an overall design, not to be able to construct a city in which the parts do fit the whole. What else do the urgent calls for "social justice" and the "participation revolution" reflect? In face of the complexity of the technical choices before us, we return to the identification of the problem in visionary terms. The risk, for ideologue and model-builder alike, is that the emphasis on a whole-cloth, politically ideal solution of the physical and social malformations of the cities has as its *doppelganger* our old friend, the Utopian formula. The planner's dilemma is that of Socrates's draughtsmen: "they will take as their canvas a city and the characters of men, and they will, first of all, make their canvas clean. They will not start work on a city nor on an individual (nor will they draw up laws) unless they are given a clean canvas or have cleaned it themselves."

It would be disturbingly easy to rephrase this formula, as Popper emphasises, in terms of some of the standard requirements of modern city planning: the need for the parts to fit the whole, that we should "know where we are going", that to help us we must develop more accurate "predictive techniques", that we should mobilise our "political will" to enable the construction of a "blueprint" for the "great society". The attractions of the "Utopian" approach are increased by the empirical necessity of catering for increasingly large and complex urban entities. The greater the expectations and aspirations of the members of the urban society, the stronger the need for integrated plans to meet them.

Natalie Becker quoted with approval the Beatles' complaint that "the nowhere planner is making nowhere plans for nobody", and went on to identify the planner's "greater task . . . to help rebuild a civilization with meaning, with belief in man and in community and in the possibility of social justice". The difficulty is still the reconciliation between the (somewhat sweeping) social vision and the processes of consultation which she advocates. Who decides, and on what scale, is the central political debate.

From the failures of capitalism to provide "the things and services that cities most require", J. K. Galbraith argued at Oxford that "perhaps the most urgent need for improved urban existence is to accept that the modern city is, by its nature, a socialist enterprise. . . . But this necessity is related to a yet further requirement. That is to see, far more clearly than at present, the essentially social character of the city as a whole."

In the days when the city was an extension of the ruler's household, Galbraith reasoned, no line "separated private from public tasks. It seems likely that what would now be regarded as public tasks absorbed a major share of the aggregate of public and private income." Having lost sight of this, and assuming that the city annexes revenue on which "the private household has a major claim" to carry out its public tasks, we have a situation in which there is a conflict between services and goods supplied out of private income and those the city provides; houses are cleaner than streets, televisions more numerous than adequate schools – and the products of capitalism, the motor car and the plastic bag, add to the city's public tasks. So long as the private claims to revenue take precedence over the public, he argued, we shall suffer the legacy of the industrial city in all its physical and social ugliness.

"Conceivably in the future, if the city is to be pleasant, healthy, otherwise agreeable and culturally and intellectually rewarding, public expenditures will have to be higher than private expenditures ... the concept of a civic household will have to be recaptured. . . . This is not a matter of ideological preference, it is a circumstance given by the intensely social character of the modern metropolis." Acceptance of this reality, for Galbraith, is the clue not just to clean streets and adequate housing, but to the "art and design" of the city.

Here his proposals carry the most radical implications. "Dresden and Leningrad," he said, "were faithful to a central conception, a common style. It was enforced as the architect enforces a common conception for a whole house. This concept can be good or bad. But one rule can be laid down as final: whether good or bad, it will be better than when there is no governing order at all. As a legacy of classical liberalism there is, one suspects, a special unwillingness to socialise design, to specify overall architectural styles to which the subordinate units must conform. There is no place where the substitution of social for classical liberal expression is more urgent."

The builders of Dresden and Leningrad, however, hardly had in view the city as "a socialist enterprise". They were not concerned with citizens' well-being in our sense of the word; they were concerned with visual effects, and public grandeur. So was Mussolini; his Rome was simply a working out of the same idea, in worse taste. It cannot always be assumed that "good or bad, it will be better than where there is no governing order at all" – if by no order, the random natural growth of cities is meant. Galbraith's distaste for the higgledy-piggledy of the modern city is understandable, even if there is no obvious correlation between an aim "to socialise design" and the workable, liveable city. Yet London is the model of the piecemeal city, thrown together (despite the Great Fire) to fulfil changing functions and needs. The result is a city of villages (with occasional terrible grey regions, in Jane Jacobs's sense of grey); it works none the worse for its patent lack of overall architectural style. It could even be argued that if we were now to embark on rational planning, the city as designed object, to the image of which "the subordinate units must conform", the undertaking might imply a planning process in which the individual citizen was given scant consideration. Obviously the great planned cities of the past, geared to functions that were very much simpler and almost exclusively public, worked in ways that the post-industrial metropolis, with the high values it places on personal amenities, may not.

To "make their canvas clean", Galbraith's disciples of the "socialised design" would need to exercise far-reaching controls; they would, after all, be cutting from the whole cloth, rather than patching the ugliest tears in the urban fabric. Galbraith recognised that they would find "the key to this order in the control of land. I continue to be puzzled as to why, when socialists gather to celebrate their faith, they give so little attention to the socialisation of urban land. For no other form of property is the case so strong. It is the commanding height on which, more than anything else, the quality of future urban development depends."

Galbraith harks back, in his examples, to the city as a work of art. In the jumble of plans and conflicting interests of the affluent metropolis, the positing of Utopias – visual or functional – is probably as useful a way as any of reminding us that we might break a great many eggs only to find (as Lenin did in the Twenties) that they will not necessarily make an edible omelette. Or, at the least, to find that people have intractably dissimilar ideas as to what makes an omelette edible.

In focusing on the question of land ownership, Galbraith none

the less picked out one of the most persistent themes to recur at
the Oxford conference. The control of land was urged both by the
advocates of the piecemeal and by the proponents of the "greater
task"; by those whose attention was directed to the cities of the
developing world, and by those who perceive the congestion of
the post-industrial metropolis as the most threatening legacy of
free enterprise uncontrolled by social engineering. The basic
fact, that land is far too expensive in Tokyo, Central London,
New York and almost every industrial metropolis for most
citizens to be able to afford commercial rents, was put forward as
a strong case for public ownership, without necessarily implying
a sweeping plan "to socialise design". The inflated values of land
in the central city pose many of the questions about the relationship of public controls to individual aspirations and idiosyncracies
which any city government must seek to resolve.

One symptom of the contradictions in the cities of the rich is
the essential paradox that the very desire to control or destroy the
property speculator in the name of the public good could, in the
developed economy, jeopardise those vast savings funds which,
through banks and insurance companies, have been invested in
property. The irony is that these institutions are in turn the
guarantors of the pensions and life insurance schemes of the
stable middle classes. The heart of the paradox is that the very
forces which prevent a middle-class citizen from buying his house
in the cities of Western Europe and Tokyo, in Manhattan or
Chicago's North Side, are those on which his security depends.
Again, as Newman said, you can say, damn the middle classes.
But only if you have measured the consequences (if you *can*
measure them with any accuracy), and are satisfied with the
alternative approach.

The management of the "organised complexity" of the modern
city involves a complicated system of what Bell calls the "claims,
grants and contracts" which modify the meaning of property.
Savings may be replaced by social insurance, and property be
largely determined by "social rights"; the central question remains the difficulty of juggling aspirations. The most whole-
hearted commitment to social welfare cannot assure correct
choices along the road to achieving it. The planner, like Zeno's
arrow, will always be half-way to the goal.

Nor can he be certain that the straight course is the best

one. Expenditure on school places may produce a generation of bored drop-outs; freeways may encourage car ownership and increase the congestion they were constructed to ease. So far, predictive skills have proved inadequate to the multi-form, open-ended requirements of the affluent society. The creation of the "good life" involves, even for the richest city, a balancing act in which the factors of equilibrium keep shifting.

The cities' very stresses are created and exaggerated by expectations: in measuring, in Bell's phrase, "relative differences of preferences at relative cost", the new scarcities of affluence present themselves. Introducing *Poverty Report 1974*, the British sociologist, Michael Young, argues that increasing affluence implies "a permanently floating poverty line". Somebody is always at the bottom of the heap – and there is the aggravating factor that increased prosperity makes the poor somehow still poorer. "It is more of a deprivation to be without a car when most people have one and public transport becomes worse, or without a telephone when so many do have one and can corner attention and information for themselves by using it," he suggests. Affluence itself may create deprivations perhaps more bitter than those of poverty. To be without a flush lavatory in a Hong Kong shanty town means little or nothing when the possession of a flush lavatory in a high-rise resettlement estate would mean giving up your vegetable patch – and when none of your friends attaches much importance to a flush lavatory anyway.

This relativity is at the heart of planners' problems in evaluating schemes to provide communal goods and services. The political choices which govern social engineering operate against a background of shifting – and always rising – aspirations. And the complex inter-weaving of multiple choices tends to distance the individual from the governing processes. The *anomie* and dis-affection of the city-dweller stems from a sense that affluence ought to mean the Caucus Race, where everybody wins and all may have prizes. It is exaggerated by the evidently imperfect correlation between the assertions of social rights and the techno-cratic machinery which pledges their fulfilment. The so-called "participation revolution" is just one vehicle for the individual's demand that this gap should be filled. Utopian results are expected on the instant, but paradoxically only if they are achieved by responsive governments willing to adjust goals. The crisis in the cities of the rich calls for improved skills in inter-weaving the different areas of government, greater ability in feeding the question-and-answer process through the computer, fuller use and understanding of the relevant aids to long-term planning. But responsiveness to the multiplicity of demands and changing social needs implies the piecemeal approach rather than the overall blueprint. The singularities of personal desire not to respond to question-and-answer formulae, even if the answers could be given with certainty for the city as a whole. The cities of the rich, bound by few of the resource limitations which affect the developing world, must to some extent play the politics of disillusion even more bitterly once deprivation in absolute terms is no longer at issue.

SECTION III

The Cities of the Poor

> The city may be a crucible for social change, but not many developing countries can afford the necessary investment to turn the new urban dweller into a productive asset.
>
> APRODICIO LAQUIAN,
> *Town Drift*

CHAPTER 11

Makeshift for the Millions

The restrictions placed by poverty upon
urban design always come as a shock to
Western-trained observers.
RICHARD L. MEIER, *India's Urban Future*

The cities of the West creak and groan with the strains of deliver-
ing affluence for all, but at least we are, as Lévi-Strauss has said,
"accustomed to associate our highest values, both material and
spiritual, with urban life". He was drawing a stark contrast with
India, where he had registered, with shock, what he called "the
urban phenomenon, reduced to its ultimate expression . . . filth,
chaos, promiscuity, congestion: ruins, huts, mud, dirt: dung,
urine, pus, humours, secretions and running sores: all the things
against which we expect urban life to give us organised protection,
all the things we hate and guard against at such great cost. . .".
It is, in its way, a romanticised picture, in the completeness of its
revulsion suggesting the nineteenth-century traveller rather than
the modern sociologist. But it aptly reflects the sense of outrage
with which the rich world confronts the cities of the poor.

"Piped water reaches the dwelling lots of only about a quarter
of the urban population in the developing countries; half the
population has almost no access to piped water at all. The situation for sewerage is worse. Roads are increasingly inadequate.
Public transport, on which the majority of urban population must
rely . . . is increasingly inadequate and becomes more and more
difficult to maintain at an even tolerable level." So Harold
Dunkerley, the World Bank's senior adviser on transport and
urban projects, exposed the bones of the situation at Oxford.
Resources are not available to accommodate the needs of the
cities' present population, never mind additions; conditions must
almost certainly worsen before they improve.

If London's transport problems defeat goodwill and expertise, what are the prospects for the cities of the Third World, which are not, like London, steadily decreasing in population (from 8 million to 7·3 million between 1963 and 1973) but well on the way to doubling within a decade? The most farsighted political vision, the most skilful manipulation of resources, the most imaginative and flexible planning, will mitigate but not avert "the prospect of urban population increasingly outdistancing the urban services and housing available". The urban population of the developing world will more than quadruple by the year 2000. And the nature of that growth is intensely disquieting: the World Bank reports that many major cities are "experiencing shanty-town population growth in excess of 20 per cent a year and a doubling of slum and shantytown population within the next four to six years is now in prospect". Since these settlements already contain over a third of the populations of many cities – often over one-half in Africa – they will be the dominant form of city life in many countries before 1980.

Even for those who view the city as the focus and hope for development in the Third World, research understandably has concentrated on the problems rather than the potential offered by such explosive growth. Whether the arguments centre on promoting balanced national development by concentrating on rural programmes, or on the urgencies of integrating the urban poor into the civic structure, they are tinged with a sense that the cities are distortions, tragic parodies of the urban ideal. As José Arthur Rios, surveying Rio de Janeiro in the late Sixties, expressed it: "Rio is the product of a vast maladjustment. Its growth is unparalleled by any other city in the nation. The tendency has been to enslave the whole country to this abnormal growth, like a tumour which drains all the energies of the body. Its high life is fed upon by the misery and backwardness of the rural population. Its army of civil servants lives on taxes levied throughout the country."

Rio at the time was something of a special case. Rios calculated that 45 per cent of Guanabara state's total expenditure was absorbed by salaries and wages for the state bureaucracy. The extraordinary progress made by Brazil's National Housing Bank had yet to make its impact not just on housing but on urban prosperity as a whole. But worldwide, the speed with which the "vast maladjustment" of city life is taking place has swelled the population of cities like Lagos – which increased from 250,000 to 1·5 million in two decades – far more rapidly than either resources or skills to meet basic needs.

Throughout the Third World, as Dunkerley says, "the level of savings which these countries are able to mobilise" to absorb the additions to their population, "or even the basic incomes which their inhabitants possess, are very much less than London's in the nineteenth century, or London's in the eighteenth century, or London's in the seventeenth century". Attempts to curb metropolitan growth by rechannelling migration to secondary urban centres will most likely fail, since half the expansion in primary city population is due to natural increase among the people already there. Throughout the developing world, population is increasing at rates never reached by the West. In any case, a reduction, by whatever method, of the growth rates of major cities like Bangkok or Mexico City would make only marginal differences to their absolute size, and none at all to the dimensions of the problems confronting them over the next decades.

Despite the common elements in the cities of rich and poor – congestion, pollution, land speculation – the difficulties of the poorer cities, so often described in medical metaphors by words like "cancerous", "pathological", "pustular", even "bubonic", are of a new order. Professor Buu Hoan sees "a different kind of sickness, of different scale and intensity, requiring a different type of diagnosis". At the centre of the diagnostic problem is the tension between growth and income levels, a tension which has led the urban demographer, Terry McGee, to characterise the development of the city in Asia as "pseudo-urbanisation".

In many developing countries, national *per capita* income is still less than US$200 a year. And this, as Buu Hoan points out, takes no account of gross inequities of income distribution. Even taking the *per capita* figure on its own, the picture is discouraging. "If," said Dunkerley, "we take a typical city in a developing country growing at 6 per cent to 7 per cent a year, this means there is one new addition to the population each year for every fifteen people who are there in the beginning. If, again, we take a typical, perhaps rather high, figure of $300 per head income of population and say that 20 per cent of this is saved, or $60, this means that for every fifteen people savings will amount to $900 a year. If all of this went to equip additions to the population, you would have

$900 to accommodate an individual's *lifetime needs* of capital for housing, transport, work places, water, electricity and everything else. In actual fact, all the savings are not going in that direction. The figure which will be available is going to be much smaller. In Jakarta the municipal revenue is working out at something like $5–$7 a year, to cover all operating costs as well as new investments."

The World Bank puts typical net savings even lower than Dunkerley's deliberately optimistic estimate. It suggests 10 per cent to 15 per cent of income, working out at "below $25 a year for the majority of countries . . . and below $15 for many". This results in an allocation of $500 to $800 a head for new arrivals, assuming all savings could be channelled in their direction, and that the population grows at only 3 per cent a year. In Bombay, even before the oil crisis, municipal revenues in fact worked out at roughly $330 per additional head.

Costs of a "lifetime's needs" obviously vary so considerably as to be barely comparable. But according to the World Bank, the bill might read roughly as follows: water supply and sewerage, $200 a head; conventional low income housing, from $1,000 to over $2,000 a family "for construction costs alone" (implying, conservatively, little over $200 a head); capital costs of primary schooling, around $450 per place; and *per capita* costs of providing a traditional type of job running from $100 to over $400. Totally excluding transport, health, electricity, police and fire brigade, garbage collection and other services, not to mention all the amenities which make cities more than clusters of shacks, together with all secondary and tertiary education, the lowest possible outlay would still add up to nearly $1,000. And, Dunkerley added, equipping a work place in more capital-intensive industry may require investment upwards of $5,000.

Even if all net savings were available for such needs, they would fail to meet the case. In practice, the natural desire for higher living standards, the necessity of replacing existing equipment, and the fact that so few of the current population are provided for means, even on this minimum scale, an ever-mounting backlog. In South-East Asia, which has a low rate of urbanisation compared, say, with Latin America, around 70 per cent of families simply cannot pay for conventional minimum standard housing. Public housing schemes may be deliberately tailored to low-income groups and offer both subsidies and concessional mortgage interest rates. But they cannot hope, even in successful instances such as Jamaica, to reach the bottom 20 per cent or more of families.

"There is," says Dunkerley restrainedly, "something very wrong here.... At present levels of cost the improvements or extensions to urban services can inevitably reach only a small proportion of the urban populations.... This is the lesson of most government and most international agency aid programmes of the last two decades. For the great majority of the developing countries we cannot evade the choice between maintaining present standards and benefits for the few, or designing much more economic minimum standards in order to reach a much wider spectrum of society."

But in cities which are largely without essential services, even the most radically economical schemes would far outweigh available funds. Rasheed Gbadamosi, Commissioner for Economic Development and Establishment in Lagos, described at Oxford the situation as Lagos was transformed from a port and administrative base for the British colonial government to the capital of a new nation. The colonial residential district is tidy enough: the British built solid, well-spaced houses with a disregard for local conditions which even stretched to equipping them with fireplaces. But narrow roads, adequate to a colonial trading centre, do not fill the bill for a city which is nowadays not only highly industrial but the hub of Nigeria's oil refining and exporting. For this the infrastructure is, to say the least, incomplete.

As in Jakarta, there is no underground drainage system: "The British administration relied chiefly on open drains to carry wastes into the lagoon and on to the ocean. The post-colonial government has not built any underground drainage or sewerage systems. Even in the new urban areas and planned developments we still rely on the open-drainage system. There is no storm water drainage at all, and Lagos is in the tropical rain forest belt." The cost of proper sewers was estimated in the 1920s at about £5 million; about ten years ago, the same programme would have required £100 million. Nothing was done. The cost today of putting in the first phase alone is in the region of £150 million.

Street congestion is appalling, as it is in many developing cities (in South-East Asia, 5 per cent to 10 per cent of urban land is

devoted to streets and roads, against an average of 20 per cent to
30 per cent in Western European cities); but a scheme to build a
freeway round Lagos would cost about three times the annual
budget for Lagos State, just for the first section.

Gbadamosi described how he presided over a meeting to discuss development plans for Lagos in 1975–80. "They produced
an estimate amounting to about £1,000 million for a plan to save
the city of Lagos – sewerage, transportation, rapid transit, the lot.
I sat politely through the meeting and let the Ministry defend all
its projects. At the end I said 'Yes. On a rule of thumb, I will
take three of your projects and let you have the resources; and put
a token of about £10 each on all the others subject to either
international or Federal Government assistance.' "

Nor, Gbadamosi argued, is international aid necessarily the
answer. First, it cannot begin to correspond in scope to the
demand for funds. Secondly, it can create problems while it is
solving others. He cited the case of Eko Bridge, the elaborate new
four-lane artery with arching flyovers which now links Lagos
with the rest of the country. Its construction in any case entailed
formidable problems of relocation and urban renewal. "These,
understandably perhaps, were not the main preoccupations of
the consultants for the project, mainly Italians and Germans.
They proved extremely – even ruthlessly – efficient in drawing
up plans for roads and flyovers." Lesser details, such as the fate of
those whose dwellings were in the way of progress, were left to
local officials. What happens too often with foreign-assisted
development, Gbadamosi pointed out, is that consultants fly in,
draw up the alignments, return home and work out the final plan
from there. "Before you know it, bulldozers are at work. Local
needs and local consultation tend to be missed out in the process."

Part of the trouble is that co-ordination of development plans
within the ministries of the recipient countries may be rudimentary: Gbadamosi argued strongly that international assistance
was most needed not on specific construction projects, but to
help developing countries establish efficient administrative
mechanisms – to undertake the "institution building" which the
World Bank finds worryingly incomplete in most of the Third
World.

Despite scarcity of resources both financial and managerial,
the chaos of the cities would seem to demand all-embracing

strategies. Yet, as the World Bank's 1972 paper on urbanisation emphasised, ambitious planning schemes for urban growth are full of pitfalls: "the provision of more and better highways provides by itself no more than temporary alleviation . . . metros or urban railways tend to have their major impact in diverting passengers from buses . . . 'low-cost housing' tends inexorably to provide shelter for the medium rich . . . comprehensive urban plans have tended to be unrealistic in terms of resources and implementation capacity, and out-of-date by the time they are completed".

Yet the very rapidity of growth of these cities creates its own opportunities: the rapid urbanisation of new land, the smallness of the industrial base in most instances, and the still-limited number of private cars offer planners the kind of clean-sheet opportunity that Western colleagues would give their eye-teeth for. But the emphasis must be on flexibility. The World Bank argues that, provided relatively short-term solutions are accepted, explicitly linked to individual projects and immediately available resources, *ad hoc* decision-making need not wait on the realisation of that fantasy, the comprehensive urban model. You may not be able to find the funds or the predictive certainties for a complete urban freeway system (even assuming that you want one), but a good deal can be done with strategically sited traffic lights.

Unfortunately, expedients which make better use of existing resources often lack political appeal. Para-transit systems such as *betjaks* – bicycle taxis – tend to be actively discouraged, even in cities where they fulfil a useful role in providing some form of employment and supply transport to people who would otherwise have to walk. Ambitious planners trained in terms of modern high-technology often ignore or despise the advantages of the makeshift, but often these are considerable. Standards can be tailored much more closely to local conditions – provided somebody is prepared to take the rap for breakdowns in services when these have been "built in" to the system provided. Electric power, which eats up a sixth of public investment in many countries, is a case in point. Simpler systems certainly increase risks of supply failure, but enable services to be extended to many more people. And a 10 per cent saving in costs, the World Bank estimates, would save the developing countries $1,000 million a year by the

1980s at projected rates of investment. Water-supply costs vary between countries, by a factor of 30; but it is possible to restructure charges to middle-income householders who often consume nine times as much as those who have to rely on communal standpipes, but pay less than 2 per cent of their income for the service, whereas the standpipe user may pay 10 per cent of his. It is often feasible to expand piped-water networks quite cheaply, if you accept a relatively low standard. But cheaper services need not be shabbily constructed; indeed, "to build a good cheap system requires almost as much sophistication" as a conventional one, "including a design effort which is very rarely given to it". The trouble, warns Dunkerley, is that the planned risks necessarily involved are often unacceptable to the local authority, to the consulting team, and even to international agencies' technical experts.

The same reluctance has affected the housing sector, to which typically over 10 per cent of the Third World's total private and public investment is directed, despite general recognition that conventional minimum-cost housing cannot be made universally available and alternatives must be found. Even where the usefulness of harnessing self-help and savings potential through the "site and services" approach is recognised, the unquestionable desire to incorporate "officially acceptable" roads and sewers can still push costs beyond the practical level. It takes imagination and even courage sometimes to argue that cesspools can be successfully used in certain soil conditions, that sewerage systems running under footpaths instead of roads are considerably cheaper, and space and rights of way can be quite easily reserved for future upgrading even where funds are not available to provide immediate urban services for new sites.

Recent work suggests that the basic minimum figure of $1,000 to $2,000 per conventional housing unit can be substantially cut, using the "second-best" line of attack. Some schemes for "site and services" developments, including rudimentary water, sewerage and roads, with further space reserved for social facilities, work out at between $300 and $600 a unit. This is still wildly beyond Jakarta's municipal budget allocation of $5 to $7 a head, even allowing for the (somewhat limited) local savings potential; but it is a marked reduction, and use of local materials can often reduce costs further. Also – and this is very important – self-help building creates jobs in the tertiary sector, since most of it is done on an informal system of contracting out. Temporary structures, finally, suit a dynamically developing city, since – as the developed world has learned – many urban problems derive from houses and infrastructures usually built to last for too long.

If urban growth is to be orderly and reasonably cheap, argue the international agencies, most cities need to strengthen their powers to control land-use, and to streamline procedures for acquiring land from private ownership. Security of tenure, in their view, is an absolute prerequisite for successful "site and services" development, whether or not the land is sold to the occupier or let on long lease with the possibility of eventual ownership. Also urgent in almost all developing countries is the need to modernise and enforce urban land taxation systems. Properly applied, such action not only cuts down land hoarding, but also generates considerable development income.

Professor Hoan, discussing means whereby cities could generate income out of the development process, comments: "The phenomenon of capital gain on land which changes from agricultural to urban usages, and the fact that this unearned gain can in principle be turned to public account without hindering the productive process, has long been recognised. But very few South-East Asian countries have taken adequate measures to capitalise their potential for financing urban services." On conservative estimates of urban expansion, capital gains taxation of this kind would yield large enough dividends, he argues, for planners to "discover abundant incentives to devise or perfect fiscal mechanisms for capturing a larger fraction of these gains in order to finance further urbanisation at no cost to the hinterlands".

The necessity for such policies is demonstrated by the fact that, even where urban services as a whole are provided on a rigorous minimum-cost basis, the cities of the developing world will still fail, if everything is done on a cheese-paring basis, to shake off the gruesomely pathological adjectives which stick to them. Cities need more than the bare minimum if they are to qualify as other than mere workers' dormitories. "It is neither practical nor economic, to provide minimum facilities for the labour force alone," says Buu Hoan. "A city, if it is to be viable, should be able to attract foreign investors and hold national professional managerial groups. A socially diversified community is a characteristic, if not an aim, of any urban development. The issue is how to charge the privileged few for the services they require at rates that are at least equal to the social and economic costs involved."

Unhappily, the principle of "full-user charges" to industry, and to the middle-income car owner or the rich property speculator, for instance, is easier to allow than to practise in most current political climates. Even to limit road construction to essential arteries, leaving footpaths where these will serve as cross-streets, is a difficult proposition to put to the politician in Jakarta who knows that only 1·3 per cent of his city is serviced by all-weather roads, compared with 10 per cent in Singapore. To cut expenditure on roads, or to tighten up urban land taxation, might be equivalent to putting a secure noose round his political neck.

But planning without land control, and without income generated from measures like these, is almost impossible. Purchase mechanisms may be essential to ensure close proximity of employment areas to planned residential sites, so as to reduce transport costs both in terms of consumer and of infrastructure requirements. According to Dunkerley, "relatively little has so far been achieved in this direction or even mooted, but the opportunities are great in most of these cities [where] the present area will . . . in twenty years' time be only a quarter or a fifth of the total area."

The lack of amenities in most of the poorer developing cities is what strikes Western observers. It does not deter the immigrant, who has put up with worse in his village. He is drawn to the city by employment and by facilities which are an improvement on the countryside's. A recent survey of one of the earlier forms of "site and services" development, Jamaica's Tower Hill, asked locals what they liked least about their homes. Interestingly, none mentioned their actual houses. Crime worried some, crowded schools several; but the primary concern was with lack of employment, or costs of travelling to and from the place of work. Imaginative fostering of self-help housing has to include community development of educational facilities and employment opportunities if it is to be successful. "Such projects," Dunkerley emphasises, "need very careful planning. They are not easy to prepare, if they are to succeed."

Also, they need to be prepared – and if necessary altered – by people who remember that they are dealing with human beings, not just with statistics, official bodies and bits of paper. Ichsan, the *betjak* rider in Jakarta, is hounded by endless official bodies. There are too many *betjaks* in Jakarta, connecting slum with slum. As the *Sunday Times* reporter Philip Norman found, "the Indonesian national pastime is to form a sub-committee, then to abbreviate the initial letters of its name. Above the *betjak*-driver's unworldly head BAPPENAS, PPNI, YTKI and the multitudinous other bodies derived for his discipline circle like harpies. He may be challenged at any moment to produce his authority to reside in Jakarta. . . . Returning to his hut, he may find it beaten flat by police. He will be taken by truck and dumped outside the city boundaries; compelled to begin again that pilgrimage" back to the same form of life. But for Ichsan and countless others, the city is still the place of opportunity.

The skilfulness with which most of the Ichsans slot themselves into the city structures; the fact that when Norman asked Ichsan what he thought about when riding the *betjak*, he replied: "Making money"; the stability of the squatter communities; all these suggest that if the cities could succeed in the area of job creation by actively encouraging the tertiary sector, the productive forces stimulated would go some way to alleviating the chronic restraints on resources. To assist the Ichsans and "marginals" to break out of the low income – low opportunity circle implies, above all, the recognition that a selection of priorities – planning – must reinforce whatever self-help can do to alleviate misery. But many critics, like John Turner and Dr Bryan Roberts, the authors of the next chapter, believe that this approach is self-defeating – that planning and the establishment of priorities can only stultify the massive but largely unappreciated power of people to work out their own salvation.

CHAPTER 12

The Self-help Society

by John F. C. Turner and Bryan Roberts

To tell men that they cannot help themselves
is to fling them into recklessness and despair.

J. A. FROUDE,
Short Studies in Great Subjects

To look at the "exploding cities" of the Third World from the
perspective of the urban poor is to see them empirically, to argue
not from theories but from the experience of living and working
among them. Our aim has been to understand how people cope
with their rapidly changing environment, and how it is that so
many manage to build so much with so little. Practical observa-
tions and insights suggest that shared material development
depends on the capability of ordinary people and, therefore, on
their access to tools. Conventional accounts unimaginatively
view urban problems as consequences of an unassimilated influx
of incapable people at the margins of society who are a drag on
modernisation. This should be challenged, as should the notion
that urban problems can be solved through the supply of goods
and services by commercial corporations or governments guided
by professional experts.

To those that still believe commercial organisations and public
institutions both can and should house low-income people
according to norms designed by the élite, it will seem that we are
advocating a return to *laissez faire*. This is not what we are saying
at all. From our experience we see that rapid and effective improvements in the material and social condition of urban life
depend on the liberation of the people's own vastly underrated
capabilities. If people who are illiterate and who often live in
appalling conditions can make a reasonable and often imaginative
job of coping with their circumstances, then more rapid and more

effective change depends on their freedom to do what they are capable and willing to do for themselves. In the field of housing, which dominates the growth of cities, this demands the mutual trust of local owners and builders and central planners, along with the corresponding separation of responsibilities and powers which makes this mutual understanding possible.

It is difficult to give a brief but balanced outline of "cities the poor build", because the variety of urban settlements and housing types built independently of government authorities and large-scale commercial enterprise almost covers the range of contemporary residential environments. In the *ranchos* or squatter settlements of Caracas, for instance, blocks of flats have been built illegally; other *ranchos* in the same city consist of wretched shacks huddled in ravines draining raw sewage from their surroundings. There are huge areas of Manila packed with a mixture of shacks and quite comfortable houses, and there are equally vast squatter settlements in Lima, in which nearly all the houses, mostly unfinished, are of brick and reinforced concrete on regular plots and streets. Other *barriadas* of Lima, like those of Ankara and Seoul, are inhabited by tens of thousands of the urban poor, the very poor, and the relatively well off. In many African towns it is practically impossible for the casual observer to see where the older villages leave off and the newer squatter settlements take over. And in many other cities, including Buenos Aires, Bogotà, and Mexico City, there are vast areas of houses built by low-income people who are not squatters, but purchasers of plots in illegal subdivisions created by unauthorised landowners and developers. In the exploding cities of rapidly urbanising countries these squatter settlements or illegal developments generally form between one- and two-thirds of the present built-up areas of the larger cities, and most of these are growing at twice the rate of the cities as a whole – at between 10 per cent and 15 per cent per annum.

The scale of these areas settled and built up by the poor, the huge markets they represent for building materials, tools, and labour and, at least potentially, for financial credit, together with the fact that their populations form large proportions of the labour force and the electorate, invalidates any attempt to isolate "cities the poor build" from those they build only as wage labourers.

In order to explain how low-income people commonly build,

and what their methods and the dwelling environments do for them and for society as a whole, two cases can be briefly described. They represent no more than fragments of the whole spectrum, although both demonstrate ordinary people's capabilities and potential, and explain how local building and housing action can be an effective vehicle for social and economic change. One is an evolutionary, or progressively built, extended family house in Barcelona; the other the rooming houses of Dar-es-Salaam. They are instances of owner-builders using a wide variety of resources in order to provide their families with shelter. Both are built and managed in ways that support and accelerate the fulfilment of the family members' lives and expectations while contributing to social and economic development.

Many of the neighbourhoods of contemporary Barcelona have been built by their inhabitants, although some have now been replaced by public housing, incurring costs and personal losses of the kinds described below. One house in a settlement that has not been and, it is to be hoped, will not be eradicated, has evolved over the past generation. Its owner migrated from the south of Spain to Barcelona after the Civil War and set up a shack as a squatter on a river bank. First, he expanded the shack into a small, concrete apartment at the bottom of the bank. He worked as an apprentice bricklayer and began to build a second floor; the first floor he rented out to get extra cash. On the second floor he installed a bar which his wife tended; the family lived behind the bar. Then he built a third floor which he has finally completed in the last few years. This third floor is an extremely well built and well appointed apartment in which each of the four children has his own bedroom. The second floor is now to be rented out and the bottom floor is used as the official neighbourhood centre, with games rooms and a legal advice service.

Most of the neighbourhoods of Dar-es-Salaam have been built up by owner-occupiers, most of whom have built *swahili* houses. These are usually four- or six-room structures of mango poles, cane wattle and mud daub, with corrugated steel roofs. The traditional *swahili* house does not lend itself to building by stages and the structure, at least, must be built at one go. It is cheap and relatively easy to build, however, and if the owner-builder (who buys the *use* of the land rather than its freehold) can raise the modest capital needed for the land fee, the materials, and the

skilled *fundi* he contracts for the framing, he can recover
the investment in a few years by living in one room and renting
the rest. Many *swahili* owner-builder-landlords earn a living in this
way; very modestly, to be sure, and often earning less than any
of their tenants. As in the case of the Barcelona owner-builder,
living and building at a much higher material standard in a far
wealthier society, the Tanzanians of Dar-es-Salaam also add to
their incomes while building for themselves; both provide a
widely distributed and competitive supply of low-rental accommodation for those uninterested in or unable to build or buy their
own homes.

These two superficially different cases show how ordinary
people use resources and opportunities available to them with
imagination and initiative – when they have access to the necessary resources, and when they are free to act for themselves.
Anyone who can see beyond the surface differences between the
many forms of dwelling places people build for themselves is
bound to be struck by the often astonishing economy of housing
built and managed locally, or from the bottom up, in comparison
with top-down, mass housing, supplied by large organisations and
central agencies. Contrary to what we have been brought up to
believe, where labour is an economy's chief asset, show how large-
scale production actually reduces productivity in low-income
housing. The assumed "economies of scale" are obtained at the
expense of reduced access to resources local owners and builders
would otherwise use themselves, and of the inhibition of personal
and community initiative.

We must be careful to avoid over-emphasising the self-help
owner-builder as the same principles apply to many forms of
local enterprise, whether co-operative or commercial. In its
personal, owner-builder form, local control over housing is
maximised and the clearest case is made, whether the data used
are from the richest or the poorest countries of the world. Owner-
builders of new, single-family permanent homes in the United
States built over one and a half million houses during the 1960s,
for instance; the average reduction of construction costs of these
standard or better-than-standard structures was nearly one-
third compared with similar units built by the average general
contractor. This represents a much bigger saving, of course, when
borrowing charges are taken into account. Although their

Third World counterparts rarely use mortgage loans, as these threaten their security of tenure and so undermine a primary motive for investment in housing, they make similarly large savings by building incrementally out of current incomes, and by assuming precisely the same responsibilities.

Whether owner-builders have high, middle, or low incomes by their own local standards, the rich North American, the moderate-income Spaniard, the low-income South Americans (referred to below), or the very low-income Africans, all use resources that no large organisation can employ. Owner-builders of all income levels, and in all places where they are free to build, employ diverse resources, including small quantities of exceptionally cheap materials, equipment and help that can be borrowed from friends and relatives. They can make full use of small, individual sites, as well as all their own management and manual skills and spare time. A current study in Mexico has identified no fewer than twenty-two local easily obtainable resources commonly used by owner-builders in the metropolitan area. The savings made by the owner-builders generally far outstrip any opportunity costs (any sacrifices or losses, such as overtime or a second job, which investment of time in construction involves). The average equity earned by a sample of suburban owner-builders in the United States was over $9 per hour worked, equivalent to an income well above the national median. The same advantage holds for owner-builders of permanent dwellings in the squatter settlements of Lima.

Only when building is on a small scale can full use be made of local conditions and resources, and these individually small but collectively vast resources far outweigh those that are possessed and directly controlled by large commercial or state enterprises. If they are not used, actual production and improvement in housing will be far short of the potential. Many resources, such as the initiative and spare time of the people themselves, will be lost altogether; others, such as their additional savings capacity, may be wasted or misused.

A parenthetic comment on the common objection that building small creates costly and low-density urban sprawl is needed here. Taking space first: well-designed layouts with single-family plots of up to 160 square metres provide net densities at least equal to those achieved in typical walk-up multi-family schemes – and even in high-rise blocks, unless they are crammed together. The land cost, therefore, is no greater. Secondly, small sites demand less in the way of capital and operating costs. Capital investment of the kind required for high-rise development is impossible for low-budget economies on anything like the required scale. Unlike conventional housing developments, small sites geared to gradual development can be occupied years in advance of completion. For the low-income family, they thus avoid heavy dependence on credit which most could not raise – and would anyway, in an unstable economy, shun because of the inflated costs-in-use and the risks of foreclosure.

Objections to locally-controlled housing, and especially to owner-building, are further reduced by the social side of the comparative cost-benefit account.

Small-scale buildings, developed in response to family circumstances rather than planning imperatives, provide a social flexibility which may be as important to poor families as any economic benefits. The Spanish evolutionary house, which is typical of many houses in Istanbul, Seoul, and Valparaiso, and the Tanzanian rooming-house, which uses a principle by which large areas of Boston and Montreal were built, are both active supports for the realisation of their owners' and users' expectations. The fact that the way in which a house is sponsored, built and managed can be as important as the material product, and the fact that both the procedure and the product can act as vehicles or impediments to the realisation of people's expectations, are ignored in conventional housing analysis. This recognises only the passive physical function of shelter and treats the occupant as an inactive consumer.

As many recent studies confirm, cities with the fine grain created by local entrepreneurship in housing give lower-income people, especially, a vastly greater opportunity to match the places they live, the dwellings they live in, and the tenure they have secured with their sensitive and changing priorities. Before Mexico City was partly ruined for lower-income people by often well-meant but ill-advised "improvements" or modernisations of housing standards, rent controls, and ambitious housing projects (in addition to the common sin of omitting to control urban land prices through proper taxation), the city worked rather well for the mass of the people. The many builders and owners of low-cost tenements provided temporarily or permanently poor families with cheap accommodation where there were high concentrations of low-income jobs, as well as markets with the lowest prices. The availability of cheap plots on the periphery provided opportunities for all those with relatively steady jobs and sufficient savings and income to build, or start building, their own and larger homes for their growing families. Many also had opportunities to take in lodgers or set up their own businesses, as in the Spanish case. Just when they most needed it, families could consolidate their social and economic status and insure themselves against the worst effects of economic or social disruption.

When governments decide for people and impose their own institutional "solutions" to "problems" officially perceived and defined, the frequently very efficient and socially effective settlements that the people build for themselves are still-born or, worse still, destroyed before their potential can be fully realised. By no means all squatter settlements have the potential for development of the kind illustrated by the Barcelona family, of course, but even when physically dangerous slums are eradicated, the displaced inhabitants are often worse off as a result. Massive and forced transfers of the poor from inner-city slums and shanty towns to greatly improved dwellings on the urban periphery generally impoverish the poor.

The downtown, high-income Zona Sul of Rio de Janeiro is tidier now that most of the *favelas* have been cleared away, and real estate values have risen rapidly. But most of the construction workers, domestics, and many other service workers who lived there must now spend hours each day travelling to and from work that was once on their doorsteps. Most must pay between a quarter and a third of their reduced family incomes in order to keep up with their house payments and maintain their tenure. Before, they had neither amortisation payments nor commuter travel costs to pay, and many families earned more as the wives and older children could find work nearby. Now, even the head of the family can no longer take a second job without living away from his own family. It is hardly surprising that a majority in three relocation projects, just investigated, are three months or more behind with their house payments. In Barcelona, too, the inhabitants of public housing projects replacing squatter settlements which had high potentials for improvement complain of their high cost, poor standards, and poor services.

Whether we are looking at informal economic activities or local housing, it is evidently their flexibility and adaptability to local and personal needs and opportunities that make them so effective and necessary for economic and social development. At the altitude from which high-income observers view the city, most low-income areas seem disorganised, threatening to the kind of order symbolised by their own residential neighbourhoods, or by the designs of professional planners and architects. But shanty-town life is often better organised than it appears – just as Western cities' highly structured, or at least regimented, estates may be chaotic in social and economic reality. A common first reaction of upper-income visitors to shanty towns, or even to progressively developing owner-built settlements, is shock and surprise that anyone could survive in such places, either physically or mentally. But on getting to know the people and their environments, they nearly always turn out to be highly organised and stable communities of ordinary and generally admirable people. The very subtle and complex arrangement of the many physical and social elements is a vital factor that enables the poor to cope with the often severe problems and great risks of living out the urban and population explosion in an unstable economy.

It is clear that the "cities the poor build", and their "informal" economies, order themselves differently from those that are planned and administered by central agencies. The more tradi-tional systems controlled from the bottom up, employed by the mass of the people of the world's exploding cities, are based on lateral information and decision networks that are totally different from the vertical and hierarchic organisation of large-scale works and services. When these centralised systems are used to house the poor, their scale and the limitations of manage-ment rule out the essential variety and flexibility of housing options; even if the planners were sensitive to and could have access to the fine-grain information on which local housing decisions are made, it would be administratively impossible to use it. Housing can only be supplied from the top down in large lumps. Big developers and central government agencies create coarse-grained cities; the first to suffer from the tensions and frictions, which increase in proportion to the grain, are, of course, the poor. Whether the coarsening tendency of modern cities is deliberately fostered, as in Rio de Janeiro, or just allowed to happen by default, as in Mexico City, the low-income majority have progressively fewer options and find it harder to live where they need to, in dwellings they can afford, and with tolerably secure tenure. The more they become subject to a diminishing number of standardised sets of housing services, the fewer matches can be made with individual priorities.

The greater the mismatches between households' priorities (for location, forms of shelter and of tenure) and the housing they obtain, the more reluctant they become to save for and invest in their housing, to care for it, or even to pay for it. As the maintenance of buildings and installations depends mainly on the users, and as the recovery of investments made by third parties also depends on the users' will, the substitution of locally-controlled housing by centrally-planned and administered housing is doubly uneconomic and counter-productive. Not only does centralisation and standardisation reduce the range of resources normally employed, by eliminating owner-builders, local co-operators and small enterprises, but it also reduces the potential returns on the investments made. And not only are dwellings more expensive when built by large organisations, and therefore smaller or fewer in number to begin with, but those that are built tend to deteriorate faster.

Traditional, disaggregated, and locally-controlled housing systems derive from facts ignored by bureaucratic centralisation: that a person's will to act depends on satisfactions experienced or confidently expected; and that a person's tolerance for mismatches of personal priorities and housing conditions increases proportionately with his or her responsibility for the decisions made or, even, for the management of housing supplied by others. By turning the traditional activity of housing into a commercialised or institutionalised commodity, and therefore denying personal responsibility and grossly limiting choice, modern urban-industrial societies have greatly increased the material costs of housing, and have therefore reduced its availability and quality, especially for the poor.

While this argument applies to the *assembly* of essential housing services (to decisions with regard to location, shelter forms and tenancy) it is clearly inapplicable to the very different levels of action required to make the local assembly of housing services possible. Only central government can guarantee local access to land, technology (materials, tools and skills) and finance or, at least, their equitable distribution. These are the *elements* from which all housing services and their components are assembled. Some housing components, such as road and public transportation, water and drainage, electricity and telephone networks, can only be partly built or installed and managed by local organisations, and not at all by individual households. While local groups should have the option to do whatever they can do for themselves, these capabilities must not be used to exploit those that are poorer and therefore more likely to help themselves where they can save substantial sums of money for other purposes. If their initiative is merely used to reduce their share of public services, if they are used to subsidise the relatively wealthy, the self-helpers will not get the proper benefit and gross injustice will be done. Especially in this intermediate *component* level of action, it is essential that the highly variable boundary between local and central responsibilities be established justly and according to the equally variable local conditions.

The following instance from Guatemala illustrates the policy issue raised here. Problems began to emerge in the squatter settlements of the capital city when the government intervened. In the first place, the government became interested for the wrong reasons; the authorities were concerned with the settlements as focuses of crime and political unrest – characteristics that are now widely recognised as equally or more commonly concentrated in other areas of low-income cities. The government's primary motive was to obtain more information about the squatter settlements and populations in order to control them. Government-sponsored committees were set up to help the official agencies "solve" the officially defined "problems" of the settlements. Instead of the neighbours organising their own neighbourhood, the city government tried to do it for them. Municipal workers started to install a new drainage system. They did it inefficiently and at greater cost than the one already started by the neighbours themselves, many of whom were construction workers. The local community combined a number of building skills with their own information and social network, enabling them to obtain materials, tools, transport, and technical aid. The government's intervention disrupted the neighbourhood and destroyed this highly effective informal self-help organisation. Seeing the government doing those things badly which they were prepared to do for themselves, the neighbours lost the incentive to work and the development cycle was broken.

If the government of Guatemala had been more responsive to popular needs, it might have acted in the very effective ways in which recent Peruvian government agencies and those in Allende's Chile, have done. Instead of trying to substitute their own plans for what the people can and wish to do for themselves, more appropriately and more cheaply than the government can do for them, central authorities can support local housing action groups in two essential ways: by making basic resources available, or by providing infrastructure services that individuals cannot provide for themselves. Since 1961 Peruvian national agencies have been consolidating the *de facto* tenure of the *pueblos jovenes* (literally, the "young towns", as the once pejoratively named *barriadas* were renamed by the populist military administration). By legalising land tenure and, more recently, by making state-owned land available for new settlements as demands arise, the Peruvians have shown how local housing action can be effectively supported and channelled. A further development is taking place in Lima: the installation of utilities in response to local demands demonstrated by the willingness and capability of neighbours to carry out some of the work themselves. In a somewhat cruder way, the Allende government of Chile supported urban land takeovers by highly organised groups of squatters. These demonstrated the extraordinary potential of self-determining communities, such as Nueva Habana in Santiago, which was abruptly turned over to a commercial developer soon after the 1973 coup.

Although these cases are mostly taken from countries and cities where poverty levels are less desperate than many in Asia, for instance, the issues raised and the problems stated are as applicable in principle to the poorest city in India as they are to the wealthiest in Scandinavia. Whether it is for the personal benefit of the family, or in the national and international interest, the functional improvement of housing, or the improvement of what housing processes and houses and their installations do for people, depends on who decides, and on who does what for whom. This issue of authority underlies both problems of economy and justice

– anyway in housing, where increased effectiveness and a wider sharing of resources and improvements go hand-in-hand. The issue and these problems only become clear, however, when the different levels of action and authority are recognised. Only then can we identify the problems implicit in any particular stand on the basic decision-making issue.

This chapter has focused on the problem of identifying the boundary between personal and neighbourhood, and municipal and central government authority over housing services and their components and elements. The implication is that the higher authorities and the larger, supra-local organisations should not carry out housing schemes at all. The assembly of components – of sites, services, and the building of dwellings – must be left to local enterprise, and must be done in small units. The provision of many components, however, depends on municipal or central agencies, although most may be shared. Access to the basic elements and resources, on the other hand, can only be ensured by central government action, whether by direct socialisation or effective controls over commercial uses and transactions. Central planning and local control are complementary in this view, which argues that all government housing action should strive to increase local control. Its own part should be restricted to settling and maintaining performance standards – taking responsibility only for those parts of the infrastructure beyond the powers of local groups to handle.

CHAPTER 13

Limits to *Laissez-faire*

The earthly city is generally divided against
itself by litigation, by wars, by battles, the
pursuit of victories that bring death with them
or are at best doomed to death.

ST AUGUSTINE, *The City of God*

The doctrine of self-help is deeply attractive. It appeals to everyone's belief in human ability, neighbourliness, ambition and good
sense as solvents for the most intractable difficulties. It also, less
nobly, encourages people to believe that there is nothing much to
worry about, that the less interference there is with natural forces
the better, and that everything will sort itself out in the long run.
This is almost certainly not true – or will come true only after
unimaginable and largely avoidable human distress.

Such distress is already endemic in large parts of most of the
cities so far discussed in this book. For every upwardly-thrusting,
self-improving *favela* or *barong-barong*, well on its way to official
recognition, legitimate tenure, and an international shanty-town-
of-the-year award, there are ten still in the initial stages of tar-
paper, squalor, and amoebic dysentery. As the World Bank
reports, such settlements, which already represent the major part
of many cities in terms of living conditions and urban pattern,
vary widely in type, social structure and degree of poverty. But
"they are in large part characterised by absence of even minimal
standards of housing, water supply, sewerage, streets and social
facilities". Calcutta, with two-thirds of all families reportedly
living in one room, represents conditions "only slightly more
drastic" than many other places in Asia, Africa and Latin
America. The World Health Organisation estimated in 1970 that
only a quarter of the urban population in such cities has access to
domestic water supplies, either in the house or its courtyard, and
only a further 25 per cent can even get water from a public stand-

pipe. Drainage standards are worse, and deteriorating by the month, as the backlog of uncompleted maintenance work builds up.

Even this only represents the current situation. For many cities the minimum expectation is that both population and area will treble over the next twenty years. In much less than that, the newly colonised sections will be larger than the whole of the present occupied space. In many ways this represents an enormous opportunity – for rational planning, for escaping the pressure of soaring city centre land costs, for integrated disposition of housing, work and transportation. But it will all be thrown away if the whole process of urban development remains a game of unregulated catch-as-catch-can.

The real problems, it is not over-simplifying to suggest, occur at the interfaces, the frontier where the needs and desires of the individual confront the requirements of the community-at-large, who is of course the individual in society. This frontier can be drawn almost anywhere – in Britain it is necessary to seek planning permission for a garden shed; in Lima a substantially self-governing and self-providing community of 100,000 people can establish itself over a four-year period, with minimal linkage to the city's basic services. But in the end relations have to be organised across the border, and it is the nature and form of those relations that set the limits to *laissez-faire*.

The point is sharply illustrated by Charles Correa, the Bombay architect and planner, when he says that India, of all places, has no real low-cost housing problem. Certainly there is an officially-estimated shortage of 12 million homes in the country's urban areas, and no conceivable hope that these could be built to conventional Western standards. But the simple houses, built from brick, set in mud mortar, and roofed with country tiles, which exist by the hundreds of thousands in districts like Udipi in Mysore, can be put up for around 1,200 Rupees per 100 square-foot room – including the cost of shared toilets. That is the equivalent of £65 or $150. "Thus, we find that there *exist* in this country, in fact there have *always existed* in this country, solutions at a price which the people can afford. In other words, we do not really have a problem of *low-cost housing*; what exists is a problem of *land-use planning*. To put the question precisely: can we pack these individual units close enough together, so that land is not wasted? And in such a manner that the other three factors in the equation, viz. the service and social infrastructure, and the transport facilities, do not become inefficient and expensive."

Correa is in no way antipathetic to the concept of self-help. Still less is he an uncritical lackey of the official planners, whose high-rise efforts, he says, have largely created the situation where the city's new immigrants are thrown out destitute on the pavements, and where there is less than a quarter of an acre of green space per thousand inhabitants (London has seven acres per thousand), including the grass on the traffic islands.

But he argues vehemently for a powerful injection of forethought and organisation if the self-help home-builders are to have any hope of integrating their efforts into a workable city-scale community.

Take, for example, the crucial factor of mass transportation – the means by which the majority of people get to work and move around in most developing world cities. Efficient transport is essentially a linear function. You need to pick up people, in economic numbers, and take them where they want to go, with as few interchanges as possible. There is virtually no way now in which an efficient bus, or train, or subway system could be imposed on the diffused sprawl of a Los Angeles. But must every one of the new million-cities go the same way? Must they all imitate Lagos, where the cross-town journey, that could be walked in twenty-five minutes fifteen years ago, now takes a hellish couple of hours to drive? But they inevitably will, if the shape of these cities, for the next hundred years, is to be set by the random invasions of the squatters.

This is the thinking which underpins the "site and services" policies, now being fostered by the World Bank and by many of the more enlightened local and national administrations. These, it is hoped, will successfully harness the high motivation, the ingenuity and the energy of the do-it-yourself man to the more complex requirements of a healthy urban environment. Sixty two-room shacks per acre, which is roughly the density Cerrao envisages for his mud-house estates, are likely to create nothing but chaos, filth and social problems, if they are scattered higgledy-piggledy over an illicitly-acquired field or ravine side. But set out in relatively neat rows, organised into squares, with genuine streets between, however elementary, and basic facilities for drainage, piped water, electricity, and perhaps a nursery school, they already form a very different sort of unit in the city's structure. In an array of such rows, only 2,000 feet square, it would be possible to accommodate some 27,000 people, with their own shops, and none of them more than three or four minutes' walk from a centrally placed bus-stop. This is already sufficient to support an economic bus service, and a chain of several such developments, suitably sited, would soon justify a parallel link into the local rapid-transit system, whatever that happens to be. With that sort of mobility, wide job-choices become open, even to the poorest, and thus one of the primary aims of urban planning has been achieved. But so too have several others. By rational siting, the unit costs of supplying water, sewerage, power and other basic services are sharply reduced. Schools and shops can be placed to give maximum convenience and efficiency. The houses themselves, being essentially self-built, are varied in appearance, flexible enough in construction to grow with the owner's income and size of family, built of whatever cheap material happens to be available, and run up very fast. But because they will only last a fraction of the 100-year life-span of a conventional house, they leave open the widest possibilities of redevelopment – possibly on a communal, or co-operative basis – as and when the country's economic prospects improve. And perhaps most important of all, the people are integrated fully into the city's life, ready to contribute, through their taxes, savings and service charges to the financing of further improvement; not living marginally, illicitly and often parasitically on the fringe.

The World Bank is now sponsoring ten such "site and services" programmes around the world. The earliest of them, at Dakar, in West Africa, aims at family units costing around $300 (excluding land). This compares with $4,000 per family unit, which was found to be the average for sixteen conventional public housing developments in the city. The Bank's projects are deliberately experimental at the moment, encompassing a wide variety of space allocations, financial assistance, provision of utilities, types of tenure, construction standards, and participation of private enterprise, but its officials are already convinced that the approach holds out a good deal of promise.

Just how much promise, and how big a contribution such projects can make to housing the next billion city-dwellers, depends very much of course on the availability and price of land. One consequence of the decades of uncontrolled shanty town growth is that most developing world cities have a remarkably high proportion of unused space. Land is either intensively built-up, squatted on, or held for speculation – as is understandable, when, according to Harry Cole at Oxford, one site on the edge of Rio has increased in price by 2,400 per cent, from one cruzeiro a square metre to twenty-five, in the past two years. In downtown Rio, and on the coast at Copacabana and Ipanema, fifteen- and eighteen-fold increases are commonplace over the same period. Yet at the same time, half the usable land in urban São Paulo is still unoccupied, and two-thirds of all the registered sites in Rio. In Goiana, north of Recife, which is only just joining the ranks of the exploding cities, there are, almost unbelievably, 100,000 households and 700,000 vacant lots.

To capitalise on this situation, Brazil launched in the early 1970s an ambitious new campaign, under the name Intraurbs, which means town-within-a-town. Work was started in Recife, in Salvador, and in São Paulo, on trying to design and develop these large open spaces within the existing urban complex. The hope, said Cole, was to "offer a balanced community in terms of rational industrial and commercial sites, environment and housing, utilities and amenities". Such ideas depend for their success on clearly understanding and subtly manipulating the very intricate social, economic and political interrelationships that make up a city. Many authorities, including the World Bank, are openly sceptical about the possibility of such fine-tuning, but Brazil has probably gone as far as any Third World country in its efforts at scientific control of the urban flood. Its policies and policy makers have recently run into quite a lot of trouble. But if they ultimately succeed they will have many lessons to teach other governments – including some in the supposedly-developed West.

The most powerful instrument in Brazil's now formidable array of planning and development mechanisms is the National Housing Bank (BNH), founded in 1964, when half the country's 16 million houses were unfit for habitation and inflation was making money virtually meaningless for the bulk of the population – 80 per cent of whom were living below subsistence levels anyway. In these dire circumstances, the small but growing industrial sector offered the only possible source of funds, and it was by forced savings – 8 per cent of every employer's payroll compulsorily deposited, and earning interest only after the third year – that the country started to power its economic take-off.

Dr Mario Trindade, the Bank's first President, reckoned from the beginning that housing finance would only pull its full weight in solving Brazil's problems if it was treated, not in isolation, but as part of a "system of systems", fully integrated with planning, research, education, employment and the whole matrix of national economic activity, urban, rural, and infrastructural. Each he said, must act like a micro-circuit in a television set: complex in itself, but only producing results when it is working smoothly with all the others.

Proceeding along these lines, BNH in its first ten years was responsible for building a million new houses out of a total of 3 million erected during the same period and, through its PLANASA programme, embarked on a huge scheme which, by 1985, should be supplying 85 per cent of Brazil's city population with water and sewerage. Trindade and his colleagues always looked at housing in two very different ways. Partly, they acted as a building society, lending to credit-worthy borrowers, and redeploying the interest and repayments as they came due. But at the same time they viewed housing as one of the essential components of the town and the nation, from which the human resources of the country would sally forth to produce real wealth for the community as a whole. As one of the group put it, "Healthy families, rich or poor, living in healthy homes, in active communities or towns, have a much greater potential for contributing to local wealth (and in summation, national wealth) than sick, neglected, deprived, non-tax-paying families (of whom there are still far too many throughout the world today)".

Brazil's conscious and concentrated efforts to relieve such misery have unfortunately produced rather ambiguous results so far. Among its good effects, the house-building programme has stimulated the local construction industry to the point where, in the early 1970s, it was creating 500,000 new jobs a year. At least 30,000 of these recruits were then able to benefit from state-encouraged education, literacy and craft-training courses. The general boost to economic activity, in which the operations of BNH and its many associated agencies have played a large part, increased the number of Brazil's income-tax payers tenfold, from the mere one million of 1964, while their average contribution to the national revenue rose from an exiguous 12 cruzieros to 170. At the same time, personal savings, almost non-existent in 1964, were healthy enough a decade later to have contributed nearly £500 million to BNH's various loan funds. But on the housing and location front, which is, after all, the main object of the Bank's endeavours, things have turned out rather less happily.

The million houses built – 60 per cent of them, by law, reserved for the poor – certainly represent a substantial achievement. But for the people who have to live in them, there are distinct drawbacks. The dwellings, by Brazilian earning standards, are expensive; some of their amenities are costly to run and maintain, even when they are not in excess of the owner's real needs; and above all, transport costs to the peripheral estates and tower blocks can be cripplingly high. One teacher, temporarily transferred from South to North Rio, found she was spending her entire weekly salary on bus fares. In 1973, in a wave of mounting discontent, BNH's mortgage holders started to go into arrears on a massive scale. Many gave up payment altogether, and more than half were three months or more behind. The Brazilian authorities smile tightly, and declare they are prepared to live with the situation. But no one pretends that this was precisely the way things were planned.

It is this sort of experience which makes so many people engaged with the practical results of urbanisation so suspicious of, and antipathetic to, official attitude that smacks of "paternalism". José Arthur Rios from Rio, Ramiro Cardona from Bogotà, Elizabeth Jelin from Buenos Aires, all spoke feelingly at Oxford of the danger that too much of the wrong kind of bureaucratic "encouragement" and "assistance" will merely stifle the best features of the self-help movement and cut its heart out.

As Rios put it: "In Rio, we have built up tremendous systems of financing housing for every class. These systems become too costly and too complicated for the lower strata of society. This is a general problem which has been occurring all over the world. Systems of solving problems from State central agencies become too difficult, too complex, too unmanageable for paupers – particularly in countries where paupers are also illiterate, and

Makeshift cities: roadbuilding using rubbish as fill, Salvador Bahia, Brazil; and (top) *betjak* mobility, Jakarta.

From shack to city in less than a decade – self-help housing in Bogotà, Colombia. The house on the left (facing page, bottom) replaced the earlier shelter; drains

and water were installed (top right) and by the 1970s the area, Policarpa Salavarieta, was a flourishing, if only quasi-legal, suburb.

Hong Kong's per capita income is ten times Calcutta's (left) – but it still hasn't completely cut out the daily water queue.

when they come from traditional, I would even say archaic societies. There is no common scale of values shared by the State bureaucracy or technocracy and the poor, and so it becomes more and more difficult to insert the pauper into the new technological urban structure. This is a very serious problem and I can see it very clearly in my own country and in the neighbouring Latin American countries. The absorption of these communities into the general context of urban societies becomes more and more difficult, since the State technocracy and bureaucracy do not accept the values and the cultural patterns of archaic societies. When there is any relation, it becomes one of dependence, of subordination. The technocratic élite look on the paupers as dependent, as born dependent. They don't see them exactly as independent human beings who also have their values, their centres of decision, their own system of leadership. The result is a very curious situation with political and social effects, an aspiration for charismatic leadership, a close dependence on a state minority, a sort of frame which can be mildly termed anti-democratic."

Rios disapproves wholeheartedly of the National Housing Bank attempts to rehouse the shanty town dwellers in distant suburbs and high-rise blocks. He offers a qualified welcome, though, for a more recent, and more modest scheme, the Community Development Company (CODESCO), which uses BNH funds to help the *favelados*' own efforts to improve their surroundings. CODESCO offers them the building materials, to be paid for over 20–25 years, and they then build, or rebuild, or add on to their own designs. "This is, in my opinion, the most sophisticated solution we have found for the housing problems of the poor in Rio, but it is not enough. I think even this so-called democratic solution still carries a tinge of paternalism. It is very nice to have people building their own house according to their own design, and helping them only by laying out the structure of the neighbourhood, the community. But the scheme still depends on some action, on some motivation from the upper technocratic strata. . . . As a general solution, from a world-wide point of view, I think this is not enough; we have to be more ingenious in finding new solutions."

In similar vein, Dr Ramiro Cardona, Director of Colombia's Regional and Urban Planning Corporation, recalled the change that took place when the United Nations chose to call an international conference on squatter settlements, which was held in Bogotà. As recently as 1966, squatters, carrying their pathetic paper houses, one man to each corner, had had to run through a hail of police bullets and batons to invade a site on the outskirts of that city. But by the beginning of the 1970s, when the conference was held, "the idea was gaining ground that the inhabitants of the squatter settlements were not criminals. Their evolution, in any case, had been so rapid that in many, many cases standards in the official housing programme, after ten years, were lower than those prevailing in the shanty towns." At the United Nations Conference, it emerged that most of the developing countries were thinking in the same way. They were recognising that the squatter settlements might be a solution to urban development, a solution for the poor. In 1972 the President legalised all seizures of land in Colombia. A new blueprint for reform was presented to the Congress and it suddenly became fashionable to view the squatter settlements as an excellent thing. No longer were the people described as criminal, or even 'marginal' – the new way of describing the settlements was as 'new towns' or 'young neighbourhoods'.

"It is at this point that I begin to get a little anxious about the evolution. However much I recognise that the change of attitude is very important, and that the squatter settlement achieves a lot of things that the urban reformers were not able to effect – for instance, obtaining land for the mass of the people – 'legalisation' poses problems. With the creation of the 'stayer' types and their families, not only do I fear, but I actually see a lot of people working hard, in Peru for instance, to develop the idea of the evolution of the squatter settlement. The danger, if they persist, is this: governments will again start to avoid their responsibilities. They say to these groups: 'Fine, Yours is a great pioneering success. Just go ahead.' So we start to build two kinds of cities, the cities of the squatters, and, well, normal cities.

"The second thing which concerns me is that, as we face the danger that governments will again shirk their responsibilities, the actual evolution of these squatter settlements will in future slow down. We have some evidence that migration was, and is, a selective process: not simply by age and sex, but by education and drive. We know for instance that in Colombia the more educated, higher-income people have been moving to cities as well as the poor. However, it has recently emerged that people moving into Bogotá are less educated, and poorer, than those who came twenty years ago. Those who arrive now may not be so lucky – or so well equipped. Among other obstacles, they will find that grabbing a corner of a traffic-island won't be so simple. In the original squatter situation, the threat of police action was the strongest incentive to build a house and stay in one place. The migrant knew that if he and his friends formed a neighbourhood, they would have more chance of being able to stay there. But once the settlement is legalised, the expansion both of the individual unit and the neighbourhood will slow down."

This is the dilemma now faced by governments and city authorities all over the world. How to harness people's natural talent and inclination for pulling themselves up by their own bootstraps, while not at the same time discouraging them and alienating them in the very process of providing them with those supports and services they cannot produce for themselves. The rate at which any single city, or town, or community can proceed with its own development, unaided, is dependent entirely on the rate at which it can raise funds from its own resources. As soon as its ambitions and aspirations outstrip these, the shadow of "paternalism" creeps in. Yet for most cities, even in a relatively rich country like Brazil, there is no alternative. As Harry Cole says, "in Recife in 1967, the *per capita* revenue of the local government was about $38 per person per year. This year we have redone the calculations. We found out that now it is only about $20 per person per year. This is a pattern that is happening in most of the towns outside the larger *municipios* and capitals." Yet as local taxes grow ever more difficult to collect, so demands for new and more sophisticated facilities expand, "especially for the fleet of new cars that are sort of slipping into our towns".

Transport, in fact, even more than housing and services, presents perhaps the toughest single problem, both for the "planners" and the "individualists". As Wilfred Owen, of the Brookings Institution, wrote in a penetrating report on "Automobiles and Cities: strategies for the Developing Countries", for the OECD and the World Bank, "in planless cities ... the haphazard location and arrangement of urban activities, the poor environment, and the lack of physical relationship between housing, jobs and services mean that they [the inhabitants] must rely on travel to compensate for disorder". Yet it is precisely the shortage of resources to provide such facilities that multiplies the hellishness of city life, both for those with and those without motor cars (which remain as much the symbol of success in the Third World as elsewhere). Such is the chaos in many existing built-up metropolitan areas that probably no proper solution is possible until funds become available for wholesale redevelopment. For new urban growth areas, however, there is still some hope – but only if the solution of transport problems is facilitated by appropriate community-design. "The most effective attack on urban congestion," says Owen forthrightly, "may be an attack on accidental cities."

At the moment, one of the biggest problems of the accidental city is that it is becoming accidentally and unwantedly full of motor cars. It is easy to forget, while pondering the proliferation of the poor, that the ranks of the not-so-poor have been swelling significantly too in the developing world. Asia, Africa and South America between them had 17 million cars in 1970 and about 25 million by 1975. In the year 2000, the figure (subject of course to the price and availability of petrol) is expected to be over 100 million. The World Bank expects to see 2 million in São Paulo by 1990, and even more worryingly 1·5 million in Buenos Aires, which will be only quarter the size. Even little Dar-es-Salaam, where 70 per cent of the people currently walk to work, is confidently expected to have 50,000 private motor vehicles by the 1980s, with roads, garages, social divisions and traffic jams to match. Already, Mexico City has more cars than, say, Philadelphia. As Owen says, "motorisation, urbanisation and affluence go together, and the world is becoming larger and more urban, and its cities more affluent". Also, unfortunately, more congested, more polluted, and more unpleasant for the very poor, who "operate outside the mechanised transport system or do not travel at all".

As the World Bank's cold statistics tell you, 3·8 per cent of Indonesia's population is huddled in Jakarta, but also 37 per cent of that vast archipelago's motor cars. Most of them, it seems to the visitor, are perpetually driving up and down Jalan Thamrin, the great thoroughfare with the savings banks and the skyscrapers and the foreign hotels, from which all native transport has been banned during daylight hours. As Philip Norman has written: "In Jalan Thamrin is proclaimed the city's coming renaissance. Along Jalan Thamrin now the traffic may go, un-hampered by anything whatever. Of all human activity in Jakarta, few sights are more affecting than that of some citizen attempting to cross over this prestigious artery. The chains of cars lash out of the mountainous horizon, endlessly shrieking, circling endlessly, their design spanning four decades of colonial occupation. It is as if, by eliminating people here, someone hopes to redress the burden of the slums. So, eventually, one crosses, dissuading destruction with the fingers of one hand."

In a sprawling, accidental, low-density city like New Delhi it is always best to be individually mobile, whether by car, bicycle, or, as Charles Cerrao says, by jet-propelled roller-skate. In fact, with Delhi's even grid-pattern of streets, a car is quite useful, as you can always by-pass a traffic jam by going round the other three sides of the square. That is why the decision-makers of India, almost all of whom travel in private cars, tend to think Delhi is a "better" city than Bombay, where everyone travels by bus or train. But in fact, for the ordinary citizen Bombay is a far more "usable" place. He can buy a month-long railway pass, valid for an unlimited number of journeys between Andheri in the north and Churchgate, 22 kilometres to the south, in the Fort area, for as little as Rs8.55 (45p). Bombay has one of the most economical mass-transit systems in the world, and the reason is almost entirely a matter of density and shape. It is a linear city, based on two parallel transport corridors – the Western and Central suburban railway lines – with six million people strung out on either side. Like the people of Bogotá, another long thin city with good public transport, the Bombayans make heavy use of the services, taking roughly three times as many trips a week as the passengers of the notorious Delhi bus corporation. And significantly the commuters of the Colombian capital, although they are richer and twice as heavily motorised, travel twice as frequently again.

It is weight and evenness of usage, plus flexibility for future expansion, which characterises a good, economical transport network. Roads, rivers, railways, bridges and bus-routes dictate the form of a city's growth more aggressively than almost any other group of factors, and it is only too easy, by wrong choices, to impose a straitjacket or a tourniquet. Correa, however, in his plans for developing Bombay, is working in quite a different way – not a frozen master plan, but the definition of a series of growth options. "Because of the organic – almost biological – nature of urban growth, it is counter-productive to postulate only preconceived fixed patterns. What is needed is a flexible structural plan which indicates probable nodal points; these nodal points, of course, being primarily determined by the interchanges on the mass transport systems. Human settlements have always tended to locate at transport junctions, on a scale directly proportionate to the importance of the junction. Thus a natural hierarchy of nodal points develops, culminating in the city centre."

A bus in mixed traffic is economical up to about 6,000–7,000 passenger trips a day. When traffic thickens and speeds drop below 30 mph, special buses running on reserved tracks should take over, with higher loads; and beyond 20,000–24,000 daily trips it is time to start thinking about an electric train, on two or more tracks. On this basis, Correa has devised three new linear transportation spines, radiating out from Bombay's central business district like a pin-wheel, and linking at their outer ends into the regional and national railway net. The basic objective is to open up the whole of the greater city area, while at the same time keeping densities in the residential parts at near-optimum levels for the economic provision of services, and avoiding the kind of "escalating pressures which distort and finally destroy our cities". First a series of residential and mixed employment-residential sectors grow out along a secondary, preferably meandering bus route. Then as traffic and activity grows, a primary train track links several of the more important sectors, thus further enhancing their potential. If all goes well, further secondary lines and developments can be spun off in parallel – in Bombay's case, possibly away from the sea and closer to the hills. And if this in turn prospers, there is still room for a second rail link, with opportunities for new social amenities and facilities for the growing population.

Thinking of this kind goes a long way to bridge the gulf between planners and people. It treats large-scale investment projects, such as transport systems, not as separate entities but as "part of an intricate feedback" involving all aspects of practical city management. When consultant planners were told by the Bombay authorities in the 1960s to draw up a new transport solution, treating existing land use patterns as "fixed", they came up with precisely the conventional series of freeways, tunnels and flyovers which would have both crippled the city's finances and dwarfed the human scale of the inhabitants it was supposed to serve. But changing the land-use pattern, along Correa's lines, could "drastically alter desire lines (and hence traffic flow) at a mere fraction of the cost. Land-use patterns, desire lines, transport systems and land values are inextricably interconnected – properly understood they could provide the planning authorities with the tools necessary to deal with the urban growth ahead."

But somehow, dealt with it must be. It will not deal with itself. As Wilfred Owen says, "Transportation should not be used exclusively to support congestion but to move away from congestion and help build communities that work." Such communities are unlikely to come about by a lucky fluke. They require hard thinking, careful co-ordination and a great deal of sympathetic and imaginative insight into people's real needs. Even then, of course, they can go badly wrong, with disruption, waste and bitterness all round. But the effort has to be made. At the end of the day it is even worse for governments to shirk their responsibilities, as Cardona fears, than to accept them and make the inevitable mistakes. At least from mistakes it is possible to learn.

CHAPTER 14

Jobs for Idle Hands

It is the intrusion of Western values that has
led to a situation in which the traditional
leisureliness of the peasantry becomes the
joblessness of under-development.

JACQUES BERQUE, *Le Village*

In Sri Lanka, at the start of the 1970s, urban unemployment rates
for young people between sixteen and twenty, with the equivalent of an English "O" level education, stood at a staggering 90
per cent. And even by the age of twenty-four, only one in four
of them stood any reasonable chance of finding a job.

Such figures, though uniquely high, illustrate a state of affairs
duplicated throughout the towns and cities of the developing
world. Solid, secure, well paid, regular work is hard to come by,
particularly for the young, the literate, and the aspiring. Even at
the levels of mere subsistence, the gap between slowly expanding
labour demand and spiralling labour supply widens every year.

In the most exhaustive survey so far carried out, for the International Labour Office, Paul Bairoch found that out of thirty-four
Third World countries, one-third had urban unemployment
rates above 15 per cent and almost two-thirds more than 8 per
cent. These rates are based, however, on the tight definition,
agreed by the 1954 International Conference of Labour Statisticians, which characterises an unemployed person as one who is
without a job and is seeking work for pay and profit. If those
"available" for work (but who have decided after long and bitter
experience that it is pointless to "seek" it) are included, then one
recent OECD Development Centre study suggested that the rates
might well be doubled.

In the developing countries as a whole, Bairoch calculates,
urban unemployment, which ran between six and eight million
in 1950, had risen to between 20 and 24 million by 1970. This

colossal waste of human resources stems very largely from the sheer pace of world population growth. During the nineteenth century, the proliferating industrial enterprises of Europe and North America were able to absorb anything between 40 per cent and 100 per cent of the additional active labour produced by natural increase and the switch from agriculture. But in the Third World, although *per capita* annual growth rates are substantially higher than anything achieved by France, Britain or the United States a century ago, the equivalent absorption rate has been tiny, while the absolute numbers involved have multiplied tenfold.

Bairoch estimates that between 1950 and 1960, the active rural population in Asia, Africa and Latin America increased by approximately 81 million. At the same time, only 14 million new jobs were created in manufacturing industry, and of these half were required to absorb the additional children of workers already established in this sector. Thus less than 10 per cent of the rural surplus – a prime component of the world-wide drift to the towns – could find work in the most dynamic areas of the economy. Admittedly, this was a considerable improvement on the previous thirty years, when manufacturing in the developing countries was unable to employ fully even its own workers' children. There was possibly a small improvement, too, in the 1960s – in the sense that the rural-absorption rate seems to have gone up from 10 per cent to 11 per cent. But the gap remains one of the most formidable obstacles to healthy growth in the world's new cities. It is all the more depressing to realise that, had population growth in the developing nations somehow remained at the 0·6 per cent annual rates typical of Industrial Revolutionary Europe, their current patterns of output and productivity expansion would have provided jobs for over 70 per cent of the would-be workers leaving the land in the last two decades.

Between 1920 and 1970, however, the Third World's cohort of farmers, peasants and agricultural labourers virtually doubled, from 240 million to 450 million (leaving out China). Half of this increase took place in the last twenty years, while the amount of land in cultivation only went up by a quarter, so *per capita* acreage, which in Asia is already minute compared to pre-industrial Europe (1·1 hectares in Indonesia, 1·9 in India, as against 5 or 7 when Manchester and Lyons reached their take-off point) remains under very severe pressure. Optimum levels of rural occupation, in most developing nations, were left behind decades, if not a full century, ago. It is no accident that Chile, Argentina, South Korea and Sri Lanka are virtually the only countries where average city incomes are less than twice those prevalent in the countryside, and the discrepancies soar as high as 410 per cent in Mexico, 530 per cent in Venezuela, 630 per cent in Thailand, and 1,460 per cent in Gabon.

Thus, in crude terms, the push-pull mechanism continues to operate: growing pressure on scarce rural resources, and the magnet of better things in the town. But, as usual, the averages are highly misleading. As Buu Hoan said in Oxford, "around a third of South-East Asian city populations must be considered as living at subsistence levels that are not unlike agricultural subsistence levels". Such families, in addition, are tending to grow much faster than city populations as a whole – on average between 6 per cent and 12 per cent a year. And although the widely expressed fears that they will form a powder-keg of political unrest have so far been unrealised, they can hardly help but to contribute substantially to the spreading pool of urban unemployment.

Such unemployment, it is increasingly argued, is of a type and on a scale which vitiates any comparison with the situation in the developed nations. There, for the past thirty years at any rate, unemployment has been for the most part cyclical, relatively short in duration, moderately well cushioned by welfare payments, and rarely exceeding 5 per cent (except in special cases like Ulster or during particularly sharp but usually short economic recessions). In the developing world, on the other hand, unemployment tends to be structural in nature, resulting more from the form of economic organisation than from temporary trade fluctuations, and generally occurs at very much higher rates. Buu Hoan quotes 12 per cent as typical in South-East Asia and 30 per cent in some major African cities, while Bairoch bears this out with figures ranging from 11·6 per cent in Ghana and Malaysia to 26·6 per cent in Algeria.

Migrants, as already mentioned, frequently account for 50 per cent or so of the growth in city populations, but in themselves they do not contribute dramatically to the unemployment figures. In fact, there is considerable evidence that new arrivals find work with relative speed and ease – either because they waited for friends or relations to line up the opening before they decided to take the plunge, or because they were prepared to take virtually any offer that came along. The real difficulties are faced by their children – and particularly those who have climbed a few steps up the educational ladder. Almost without exception, from Thailand to Zaire, and from Trinidad to the Philippines, unemployment figures for the 15–24 age bracket show urban unemployment rates double or more than double those of the active population as a whole. The shift from school desk to work bench, is, as Bairoch dryly quotes, "a hazardous journey". And for none is it more hazardous than those who have completed some form of secondary schooling (anywhere between six and eleven years of training). Their chances of getting appropriate, or indeed any work, are only half as good as those who dropped out at the primary level (one to five years) and only two-fifths as favourable as the outright illiterates.

With cut-throat competition for the relatively few high-skill, high-technology, high-wage industrial jobs and for the more attractive posts in government, banking and modern-sector commerce, a very large part of the employed work-force is inevitably forced into the vast grey area of "tertiary" services – tiny-scale shopkeeping, catering, transportation and so forth – which marks, as clearly as any single indicator, the difference between the developed and the developing city. It is on this sector, inevitably, that the main responsibility for employing the swelling army of new urban workers will devolve over the next two or three crucial decades. Yet in the nature of things, relatively little is understood, let alone agreed, about its economic significance or expansion-capacity. Can its self-help ingenuities be relied upon, as people like Turner and Roberts believe, to provide an income-generating safety net, even when the "accidental cities" of Asia and South America swell to 10 or 20 million people apiece? Is there a case for judiciously bolstering and encouraging such enterprises – even if this means reversing most current official policy, which is all for modernity, tidiness, and sweeping the pedicabs and the fried-prawn stalls off the streets as fast as possible? Or is the "tertiary economy" just a sentimentalist's lost cause, for which swift and efficient strangulation would be the kindest fate?

A vivid description of a bazaar system, and its often startling ability to absorb quantities of additional labour (even if only at near-subsistence levels) comes from Clifford Geertz, in his work on Indonesia. "Like Javanese agriculture," he says, "Javanese trading is highly labour-intensive, and perhaps the best, if slightly caricatured image for it is that of a long line of men passing bricks from hand to hand over some greatly extended distances to build slowly, brick by brick, a large wall." Such a system is charac-terised by sliding price scales, a complex balance of carefully managed credit relationships as goods pass from middleman to middleman, and an extensive fractionalisation of risks, as each trader along the chain generates a claim to his own particular fragment of profit margin. Rather like rice cultivation, another intricately structured form of Javanese economic activity, it involves great tenacity in preserving the basic pattern, much elaboration and ornateness in the methods applied, a high degree of technical hair-splitting in the interest of division of labour, and almost unending virtuosity in the invention of new sub-specialisations.

The strength of such a set-up is in many ways remarkable. Its techniques and philosophies are perpetuated by heads of house-holds as they introduce new members of their family to the system, but at the same time it is very easy to introduce more labour from outside these traditional family groups. It can be expanded rapidly in line with population increase – as exemplified by the phenomenal multiplication of Singapore's open-air food vendors in recent years. Every evening the city's central car park is taken over by hundreds of tiny stall-keepers, each preparing his own particular speciality, while the customers wander round with plates and choose whatever combination they fancy: a development which has precisely paralleled the build-up of Singapore's central business district. And this too is very important, for the bazaar retains strong and intricate links, both upward and downward, with the rest of the economy. It has many ties with the countryside, whose products it largely processes and distributes, and with which it frequently interchanges seasonal and other forms of occasional labour. At the same time, it main-tains complex relations with the capitalist sector – partly as provider of jobbing and sub-contracting services, and partly as beneficiary from such downward-filtering items as servants' wages, employment on the odd one-off prestige project, and even sometimes welfare payments.

By and large, though, welfare benefits tend to play an ambiguous and even corrosive part in the pattern of urban employment. Frequently the providers of major capital investment in a developing country are required to adhere to minimum wage laws and also to pay a very substantial social security surcharge. Given the poorly-trained and often unreliable nature of labour in many such countries, this means that, despite generally low hourly or daily wages, total labour costs per unit of output can still work out at a substantial sum. At the same time, the tax concessions, special exchange rates, subsidised interest charges and other devices used to attract the investment in the first place often make capital relatively cheap, and reinforce the already powerful bias towards labour-saving which is embodied in most modern technology.

In face of this, it would seem all the more important that the bazaar or tertiary sectors should be given maximum encouragement to perform their very efficient cushioning function in rapidly-developing urban societies. In fact, though, in far too many countries the economic, spiritual, political and educational pressures are all the other way. The dangers were only too efficiently blue-printed in the Cuba of the 1950s, where all the small, inefficient, untidy sources of non-modern employment were systematically squeezed out: a process which undoubtedly contributed to the success of the Castro revolution. Similar developments in Jamaica and Puerto Rico have only been defused, for a time, by extensive emigration – an alternative that is increasingly unavailable in most parts of the late twentieth-century world. Elsewhere the process has gone less far, but in most of the world's great cities the activities of the "informal" sector are at best tolerated and ignored, and in many individual cases actively discouraged – even though they often account for more than half the total livelihood of the population.

Roberts, in particular, argues that this is wholly wrong. To illustrate the potential of the informal economy, he cites the case of a lottery ticket salesman in Guatemala. "He used the gross return from the sale of the lottery tickets to travel once a month to the Mexican border and purchase cheap contraband material. He sold this material at a profit in Guatemala City, repaid the money owing the lottery and used the remainder as income and to subsidise further activities. These activities included selling refreshments on the streets and in cinemas, a small shoe work-ship, and door-to-door selling of household goods. In these activities he employed some five other people at what was a reasonable wage for the working population of the city. This man was, in effect, making use illicitly of dormant capital, by providing himself with loans that banks or government would not risk granting him. Such activities may not be desirable in the long run, but we must recognise that this man was performing a service to other people and to the city in which he was living."

This sort of enterprise, Roberts and Turner are intent to emphasise, is not in any serious sense "parasitical" on the formal industrial and commercial sectors of a city's economic life (even if the occasional law or regulation is being severely bent). "Formal enterprises with expensive plant, and high locational and welfare commitments, are often too inflexible to expand easily in an environment characterised by uncertainty and instability. In contrast, informally organised economic enterprises are flexible in their commitments, using social networks and informal exchanges to generate marketing information and inter-firm co-operation and co-ordination. . . . They allow people to become economically active without the need of capital or of technical skills. Small resources are taken from one place and from another and they are combined to form the basis of an enterprise. Another impor-tant aspect of such activities is that they tend to labour intensive-ness; not only do they use labour to substitute for expensive machinery, but they also delegate work and responsibility. The owner of the enterprise expands by taking in co-owners, sharing responsibility for a new piece of plant, truck or contract with several others, who in turn may sub-contract maintenance and other work. These practices impede the rationalisation of an enterprise but they expand the number of people who share the possible profits and risks."

In addition, the existence of these informal business services often contributes quite largely to the efficiency and profitability of their more elaborate and conventional rivals. Cheap marketing, credit and distribution are provided for the big companies' products – and also cheap goods and services for their employees. Measuring the true "productivity" of such contributions is a difficult technical feat, and some economists, obsessed with abstract ideas of optimal efficiency, would argue that they are not productive at all – a line of thought which often makes it very difficult for politicians to see the case for backing them, or at least getting off their backs. But the fact remains, it is precisely this sort of activity – created and extended by people's own initiative – that keeps more than half the population of most Third World cities in remunerative work at all.

In particular, of course, it is responsible for keeping unemployment rates for the illiterate very significantly below those for the classes which can read and write. In Asia, said Buu Hoan at Oxford, "only 1 per cent or 2 per cent of those with no education are without jobs of some kind, with conspicuously lower rates in Taiwan, India, Sri Lanka and Thailand". In his view, and that of many other observers, the plight of the literate is intimately linked with the spread of educational systems that are almost wholly misconceived in relation to what are still predominantly rural societies. Their effect "is more often to alienate the student from his society than to make him a more useful member of it".

According to Paul Bairoch, a prime cause of the high levels of joblessness among the literate urban young is "unquestionably the large flow of migrants, particularly young migrants, into the towns". This generates such pressure that anyone hoping to make use of his newly acquired education finds enormous difficulty in getting a suitable job. In one study of South America, and another more recently, of Africa, as many as 62 per cent of the unemployed between fifteen and nineteen had still to find their first paid post. But this is by no means always due to the recalcitrance of employers. Not only does the teaching available to the children of peasants and small farmers in most countries tend to make them totally unfit for work on the land, but it so raises their expectations and their ideas of status that they are extremely unwilling to seek careers outside the narrow confines of formal business, industry and the bureaucracy. Not only do the syllabuses provide no new ideas or skills for doing agricultural work more effectively, they are more often than not designed as the first part of a logical chain leading right through secondary schools to the universities. Those who drop out along the way – and at the moment barely 1 per cent or 1½ per cent of students in the developing countries achieve a degree – are left with the incompleted torso of an education, fitting them for little but frustration and discontent. It is the worst of all possible worlds, with the rural areas suffering a "brain drain" of vitally needed intelligence, while the cities, with the structural rigidities of the formal economy, can only absorb a small fraction of the inflow. This is one of the most intractable and potentially disruptive of all the problems facing the "cities that arrived too soon", in Barbara Ward's evocative phrase.

Roberts and Turner go so far as to say that, "when city dwellers are left to themselves to make do with what resources they can get, they create a flexible environment that makes for survival, even in the gigantic cities of the under-developed world. Cities of even 20 million people will still work in under-developed countries, provided that their environment is not over-organised."

But today, too often, the educated young have been conditioned to reject the cut and thrust of the unorganised – even if it means years of waiting for an "organised" job to come along. And tomorrow, when the best of them have reached positions of high power and responsibility in the "organised" sector, it is doubtful if they will have much sympathy for or understanding of the virtues of loose structures and the flexible approach. Far more likely, they will join the army of middle-class bureaucratic and academic "experts" that Professor Rios, reflecting on his Brazilian experience, sees everywhere battening happily on the "problems" of urban poverty (and blithely applying to them the "systems" whose main virtue is that they guarantee plenty of expert employment).

In any case, the Roberts-Turner approach does not solve the central problem of urban job-provision – the structural gulf that Bairoch calls, for want of a better word, "over-unemployment". Even apart from the question of under-employment, which permeates large parts of the "informal" economy, there is, in most of the developing world, a gap averaging around 20 per cent between the number of productive city jobs and the people available to fill them. And that gap, though it appears to remain pretty constant in percentage terms, neither shrinking nor noticeably widening, is in absolute numbers growing as fast as the cities themselves.

There are a number of possible solutions – some long-term and gradual in their impact, others of a more immediate-emergency

Already the private car is turning Third World city centres into great traffic jams, even where per capita income is under $200 a year. But in China, personal transport is deliberately restricted to feet and bicycles – and even two wheels are taxed.

Students, Peradeniya University, Sri Lanka; A lucky five per cent can expect to find the jobs they think they've trained for.

nature. Increasing the degree of labour intensity in manufacturing; slowing down, if not actually reversing, the flow of rural-urban drift; and of course moderating the underlying rate of population growth, fall into the first class. Turning the unemployed on to major construction schemes; setting up crash retraining programmes to build up a stock of saleable skills; imposing heavy tariffs to dynamise instant "import substitution" industries; and enforcing through police and military action an effective ban on all in-migration to the cities, have all been put forward, at various times, as examples of the second line of attack. Almost certainly any really successful programme would contain modified elements of all these ideas. And South Korea's extremely aggressive and effective export campaign, which itself has produced some 300,000 jobs – half Seoul's and Pusan's new employment – over the last decade, shows yet another set of possibilities.

Superficially, the huge labour reserves possessed by most developing countries should be their greatest economic asset. But actually finding means to activate these reserve battalions presents great difficulties. As R. A. Berry said, in a 1974 International *Labour Review* article, we now know a great deal about optimising the outputs from capital intensive technologies, but about the efficient use of labour-intensive methods we know almost nothing. All the research effort, both in money and in brain power has gone the other way. Some authorities, like Dr Elizabeth Jelin, of the Buenos Aires Torcuato di Tella Institute, are inclined therefore to dismiss the whole approach. Speaking at Oxford, she said: "The usual solution offered by many of the international agencies is a return to labour-intensive technology. This, I would say, is impossible. The most dynamic centres of production in these countries have got beyond the stage of labour-intensive techniques: cars, colour televisions, nylon fabrics and synthetics cannot be produced with labour-intensive technology. And these have been the dynamic sectors of production, the leaders of growth and industrial development."

Unfortunately this, though largely true as far as it goes, is not very helpful to a developing government. Growth rates alone do not necessarily create jobs, and still less do they always lower unemployment. Non-agricultural openings in eight out of ten African countries studied in the 1960s remained either stagnant

6

or actually shrank, despite the fact that several of them recorded overall economic growth of up to 8 per cent a year. In Berry's somewhat gloomy words: "Rural-urban migration is so elastic that for every good urban job created, more than one person will migrate, and total unemployment in the towns will increase." The pursuit of labour-intensity, therefore, is something that the Third World can hardly avoid. The only real question is whether it can be organised, or must merely be allowed to happen, through the absorptive powers of the "informal" economy.

One very interesting experiment in organisation has been going on for thirteen years in Morocco, under the name Promotion Nationale (PN). So far, its techniques have been applied mainly to the countryside, but there seems no inherent reason why they should not work in the towns and cities to equal effect. Morocco's unemployment figures normally run between 10 per cent and 20 per cent of the country's just under four million active males. Since 1961, the PN scheme has been providing at least some paid and useful work each year for about half the men who would otherwise have been totally without a job. Essentially, the idea is to set up a large number of desirable projects – soil erosion control, flood barriers, village street repair, wells and water-hole boring, the building and planting of fruit-tree terraces, construction of tourist roads, holiday hotels and so forth. These are then each divided into 12-day periods, so as to spread the work as far as possible. Labourers were originally paid about 16p a day in cash, and five kilos of wheat, at about the same value (since 1970 the money has increased and the grain decreased). All the work is intended to be valuable, though obviously some is much more long-term in its effects than others, and the overall profitability to the government has averaged at 14 per cent. Wage costs take up about four-fifths of the investment, and the income-generating effect of the PN programme has been surprisingly high. Morocco is a very poor country, and the pay for working even five two-week periods under the scheme comes out at £40, which is a quarter of the average *per capita* national output. The main difficulties, it appears, have been much more administrative than economic, and even here there is a pay-off, in that PN projects give valuable planning and supervisory experience to Morocco's growing group of young, educated, but often under-utilised officials. H. A. Turner and Dudley Jackson, the two Cambridge economists who have written extensively about the subject, think there would be considerable scope for extending the approach to an urban environment – especially for improving tourist facilities, where there can frequently be very high returns on relatively low-cost projects. They would like to see, too, more combined urban-rural developments, particularly in the essentially labour-intensive area of food processing.

Much more dramatically successful, so far, though, has been the deliberate cultivation of exports, in one or two countries, as a source of large-scale high technology, high-productivity employment. The "city state" examples, like Hong Kong and Singapore, are fairly well known, but widely regarded as inapplicable to the very different circumstances of larger, more open societies. South Korea however has very clearly demonstrated that export promotion can be a very potent tool for job-creation. Between 1963 and 1970, urban unemployment dropped from 8·1 per cent to 4·5 per cent, although the active population grew by a fifth to 9·6 million. Agriculture and mining employed 200,000 less people at the end of the period than they had at the beginning, but manufacturing jobs increased from 631,000 to 1,260,000, with half the extra coming straight from the export industries. Writing in 1973, a Japanese investigator, Susume Watanabe, calculated that for every $1 million of additional foreign orders, 500 jobs were directly created; another 150 sprang up in supporting industries; and another 150 were made available in the consumer goods and services sector. Even this understated the full effect, as it allowed nothing for the longer-term demands generated by this growth in the capital goods and construction areas. Particularly striking and significant, also, was the very large contribution made by industries working mainly with local raw materials, like silk-weaving, chemical fertilisers, cement and tiles.

Following South Korea's example thus holds out considerable promise. But not many countries are yet in a position to rely on systematic export promotion policies as a major contribution to solving their problems. There is considerable evidence that they will make some contribution, if only because potential mass-export industries, like furniture, clothing, footwear, and, in a slightly different sense, tourism, are inherently more labour-intensive than the import-substituting manufactures, like car-assembly, on which so much government care is often lavished.

But the export manufacturing base is mostly too small for its expansion to have a major impact – only in five developing countries, at the moment, including South Korea, Hong Kong and Singapore, does this sector account for even half of all exports.

A much more promising approach for many nations (though it is not one that many have yet actively explored) could well be through the essentially labour-intensive sector of housing and construction. For reasons already discussed, there is little chance that all the 200 million new homes that the Third World's swarming cities look like needing before the end of the century can actually be built, to anything like conventional standards, from the resources available. But that does not mean that a very large number of them will not have to be built anyway, with all their multiplicatory consequences for the suppliers of light, power, chattels, decoration, and a vast array of related services.

Unfortunately, governments and their advisers almost everywhere habitually underestimate the economic importance and potential of the housing sector. As the World Bank says: "There has been a tendency to minimise the contribution of housing to national output and welfare because of its high capital-to-output ratio. Such a simplistic approach, however, may considerably underestimate the importance of housing, partly because both 'capital' and 'output' are ambiguous in this context." In other words, the rent that can be realistically charged, in relation to the total cost of erection, makes a house a pretty unattractive form of investment. But, particularly from the point of view of a developing country, this is a very narrow way of looking at the situation. Building houses and supplying their supporting services require relatively little in the way of expensive capital equipment; most of the input is labour. Much of the work is unskilled, and moderately cheap and simple training schemes are sufficient to supply those skills that are needed. Materials tend to be local in origin, with, again, a highish labour content. Timber often comes most economically from the poorer areas of the countryside, giving the possibility of creating yet more jobs. And the savings required to finance an on-going construction programme are largely generated by the house-building process itself. People save more, all over the world, when they see the possibility of transmuting thrift into bricks and mortar (or even mud and corrugated iron).

Careful fostering of this habit, with an active policy to encourage buoyant housing development, offers many countries their best chance to mobilise both cash and human resources, as Brazil has gone a long way towards demonstrating. Now Colombia too is giving the housing sector a key role in its drive towards 95 per cent employment by 1985. To keep up with population growth, and the low absorptive power of the local farm industry, this will mean creating some five million new jobs – 4·25 million of them in the towns and cities – and the labour-intensive sector, predominantly housing, is scheduled to show just as much productivity growth as the country's more conventionally-dynamic manufacturing firms. There is a monstrous and, some would say, unbridgeable gap to be filled here. But if the task is to be tackled at all, if the Third World's cities are ever to be more than unwanted reservoirs of idle hands, the use of local energies to transmute local materials and local savings for the satisfaction of local demands must play a large and central part. There is little sign yet that the responsible governments, dazzled by modernity and technological brilliance, have seriously grasped the point.

CHAPTER 15

Supporting the Insupportable

> The mobs of great cities add just so much to
> the support of pure government as sores to
> the strength of the human body.
>
> THOMAS JEFFERSON

If urbanisation continues along present lines, we shall all be living in concrete or mud-hut jungles by the year 2031. If the proportion of people living in cities of over 100,000 continues to augment at the 1950–70 rate, the 100 per cent mark will be reached seventy years from now, in 2045. These calculations lead Kingsley Davis, presumably on the notion that the hypothesis must somehow be punctured short of the realms of utter fantasy, to conclude that we may now be witnessing the peak in the process. But when will the growing stop? when Calcutta has reached 50, or 70 million? Or when the whole of industrialised Northern and Western Europe coalesces into some kind of Doxiadian continent-city, or much, much sooner than that? And why will the growing stop – because of plenty in the countryside, the expansion of rural and small-town services and the universalising of the "good life"; or because of total breakdown in the cities?

The earlier images of nightmare and of breakdown in the metropolis conjured up by artists, from H. G. Wells to the great concrete vision of Fritz Lang, have had to do with the tyranny of the machine, with the suction of men into economic flywheels and an automated existence. The modern fear, conditioned by the vast scale of urban unemployment and the evident failure of developing countries' economies to absorb, feed and house their populations, is more closely geared to pestilence and starvation, to chaos, than to mechanised tyranny.

The head of the house of Rothschild, asked why he had refused to insure the *Titanic*, explained: "I thought it was just too big to float." The temptation, as Kingsley Davis comments, is to think the same of the cities – to assume a natural cut-off point. On this reading, "The presence of millions of people in a small area could poison the atmosphere, facilitate infection, induce psychoses, and multiply accidents; these calamities could progressively raise the death rate. Or the crowding of millions together could demoralise the populace and weaken social controls, thus impairing family life, causing people to want fewer children and/or to suffer impaired fecundity, with the result that the birth rate would be reduced. Or again, crowding in huge numbers could increase the costs of production and distribution and the costs of public health, crime control, recreation, and education – with the result that migration to the larger cities would be depressed."

Unfortunately for this argument, as he points out, chances of survival remain substantially greater in the city than in the country in most of the developing world. Death rates in many developing countries (and some developed ones) are consistently lower in big cities than in smaller ones. Fertility differentials between town and country are not great enough to make a significant difference to the cities' growth. And, because cities do not grow by adding more people to the same congested area (world-wide, cities have been growing faster in area than in population, so that their inhabitants have been living in conditions of *declining* density), the theories of behaviour in over-crowded conditions must be set on one side. Davis concludes: "The time when size alone impedes growth, if it ever comes, is still two or three generations away."

With any reduction in birth rates heavily dependent on the kinds of social and economic change which are hampered precisely because the birth rate continues to be high, city growth will be accelerated rather than retarded by rural economic stagnation and the failure of agricultural land to keep up with the extra population. How then are the people of the cities – whose poor now obtain under 1,800 calories a day to the rural poor's more than 2,000 – to stay alive? One agronomist, Walter H. Pawley, in a 1971 paper for *Ceres*, published by the Food and Agricultural Organisation, offered a rosy long-term prognosis. Assuming a population of 36,000 million by 2070, of which around 33,000 million would live in the "low-income countries", he claimed that all could be fed at the standard of the present Western European diet.

The conditions would be the continuous cultivation of soil in tropical countries after the removal of tree cover; the desalination of sea water at costs low enough to use it for irrigation; and cheap, plentiful power to pump it inland and "up to considerable heights". This would enable up to half the world's land surface to be cultivated, in contrast to the present 10 per cent. From this area, Pawley subtracts the 10 million square kilometres needed for cities and roads if 90 per cent of the population is to live in cities at a density of forty persons per hectare. He implies that 10 per cent of the population – about the same number as the present world total – would cultivate the remaining 60 million square kilometres, half of it on a three crops per year basis. With the Amazon, the Sahara and Australia thus under plough, and assuming 4 per cent growth in productivity, food output would increase fifty times. Assuming a global equilibrium between supply and demand, every family would be able to eat their peas with honey in blissful content. And, if synthetic foods were added, "it is futile to try to estimate how many people our globe could feed".

It is a fine polemical counterweight to the prophets of imminent starvation. But it glosses over the need to augment fresh water supplies and the probability that such crop yields would mean "an annual run-off of chemical residues into the lakes and oceans 100 times the present levels". It does not explore the severe and so far unresolved difficulty of preventing soil erosion in tropical zones once the tree cover has been removed. And, while it admits that distribution may present formidable problems, it rather cavalierly assumes away their full extent. If the 55 per cent of the world's population living in South and East Asia is to be fed a hundred years from now, "it is possible to conceive of vast movements of food, running into hundreds of millions of tons, paid for by exports of industrial goods from Asia, on a scale so far unprecedented in the most industrialised and largest powers. It is equally possible to imagine a transfer out of Asia into all parts of the world with a more favourable land-man ratio, on a scale without parallel in human history – nothing less than several hundreds of millions would do."

Retreating a step from the crystal ball, Pawley concedes that timing is crucial – that the population could outrun the cultivable area before the breakthrough to permanent and universal irrigation. But his basic claim is that employment, not food, is the "danger point" in ninety to a hundred countries comprising 70 per cent of the world's population. With 9 per cent annual growth rather than the 6·5 per cent objective of the Second Development Decade, purchasing power could keep ahead of population increase, and agricultural unemployment – which in Latin America he claims amounts to 60 per cent of the un- and under-employment – be absorbed in new growth sectors. With an annual transfer of 20 per cent of the developed countries' incomes, he argues, the road to economic and social betterment (and 90 per cent urbanisation) would be open.

In the year Pawley's article appeared, world harvests produced enough to provide 730 pounds of grain *per capita*. In the crisis year of 1972 which followed, food production was still 20 per cent up on 1966. Throughout the Fifties and Sixties, the developing countries were expanding agricultural output at the same rate as the rich countries. Yet 61 out of 97 developing countries were short of food energy supplies in 1970, and in 1974 400 million were "conservatively" estimated by the World Health Organisation to be suffering from "significant malnutrition". Without taking account of distribution within countries – and the top 10 per cent in India and Brazil consume twice as much as the poorest 20 per cent – *per capita* consumption of grains in the developing countries is just over 400 pounds a year, while the average American absorbs nearly a ton – 150 pounds of it direct, the rest in terms of protein. As A. H. Boerma, Director General of the World Health Organisation, summed up the distribution question, "the 374 million tons of grain used annually for livestock feed" in the rich countries "in 1969–71 is greater than the total human consumption of cereals in China and India together".

The disastrous harvests of 1972 forced a realisation that, Green Revolution notwithstanding, food stocks were frighteningly vulnerable to weather. In 1974, despite a good harvest in the previous year, world grain stocks were down to a month's supply. In the Third World, the WHO reported signs that productivity increases were slowing down, since the "most efficient" farmers had already been mobilised, inflation was eating into the higher prices they had received in the late Sixties, fertilisers were scarce and expensive, and shortage of diesel oil for irrigation pumping

6*

equipment was seriously affecting harvests. But despite the short-term crisis, immensely serious though it was, world-wide food supplies were still expected to balance out with population increases in the 1980s.

"World-wide", however, means everything and nothing, when the gross "cereal gap" of the developing countries will rise by 1985 to three times their gross imports in 1969–72. The cost at 1974 prices has been variously estimated at between $16 billion and $20 billion; either way, well beyond deficit countries' capacities to pay. And Boerma justifiably warns that restriction of consumption "would depress their whole economies". Already in 1974, the increase since 1972 in the food bill for the sixteen countries which account for more than 40 per cent of the developing world's total food consumption was expected to absorb more than 30 per cent of their gross export earnings. That world food supplies would be available at all was dependent on the success of each single year's harvest.

In the decade of the Green Revolution, world supplies had not left the danger point behind. More significant for the continued pattern of flight from the land, the rural poor had become relatively poorer. More than increased harvests had been hoped for from the Green Revolution. As the Soviet agronomist, Georgy Skorov, put it, in theory it "causes a marked rise in agricultural production and makes it possible to satisfy the growing demand of the urban population for food. By raising the income of the upper stratum of the rural population, it enlarges the potential market for consumer goods" and "stimulates the development of services, such as commerce, transport and banking". But, he says, it could equally be described "as the catalyst of further exacerbation of social inequality in the Third World". The Filipino peasants, he recalls, dub the high-yield varieties (HYVs) – which demand an input per hectare of $200 instead of the ordinary $20 – the "Cadillac variety". Boerma agrees that the Green Revolution "has probably tended to widen disparities in agricultural and rural incomes", largely because of the failure of concomitant agricultural policies to integrate the small farmers into the programme and to provide credits.

The costs meantime are still being counted. In the Philippines, chemical fertilisers in some streams have killed the fish and thus removed the farmers' main source of animal protein; world-wide, irrigation is increasing the incidence of the debilitating disease, schistosomiasis. And half of all children in the developing world remain what the WHO calls "malnourished" – meaning that they have less than a minimum 1,900 calories a day to live on. The peasants continue to leave the land, and rapid urbanisation, says Boerma "is not only accentuating the unsatisfactory nutritional status of the population but also modifying the characteristics of this phenomenon, with severe malnutrition appearing at an earlier stage". The urban poor eat least, and of these, children and pregnant women are the most deprived groups.

The overall food shortage of the early Seventies has not obscured the fact that poverty is the root cause of malnutrition, poverty embedded in under- or un-employment. The WHO does not expect increased availability of food to diminish the incidence of "severe protein-energy malnutrition, unless there is a parallel improvement of the environmental conditions, particularly the sanitary conditions, in which children live". In practice, higher incomes in the city offset for the migrant the probability that if unemployed – as around 30 per cent of African city dwellers are – he will have even less to eat. His belief that he will be better off in the city, as Professor William Brass, of the London School of Hygiene and Tropical Medicine, emphasises, is well founded: "Services *are* better, in terms of water supplies and general sanitary conditions, than in the rural areas. The cities may appear more sordid; but they are not necessarily more sordid in ways that militate against health; even in India, even in Calcutta."

The diseases of poverty overwhelmingly affect the children under ten who make up a third of the developing world's population. Half or more of all deaths occur in children under five (as against around 10 per cent in the United States), from malnutrition, diarrhoea and pneumonia (12 per cent of child deaths each), from measles, whooping-cough and malaria (8 per cent). Most of these diseases are not fatal to a well-nourished child. The cost of malnutrition to economic development is impossible to calculate; but one African country rapidly suppressed a recent report by its leading doctors that half its population must, through the prevalence of malnutrition, of bilharzia and cholera, be considered incapable of "normal" economic activity. One British medical expert calculates that nearly all children in low-income families "show retarded growth and development by the time they reach school age" and that adequate diet in school years cannot make up the deficit. John Bryant makes the obvious point in his examination of health policies in poor countries, *Health and the Development World*, that "one of the strongest economic arguments in favour of health programmes is that sick and disabled people do not necessarily die; the cost of poor health to a nation is intellectual and physical disability".

But if the pace of urbanisation puts impossible strains on health services, and slum areas are chalking up an increased incidence of venereal disease, mental illness and other "social illnesses" according to a 1970 article by Oscar Gish in the *Journal of Development Studies*, it is interesting to note that these are diseases principally related in world health statistics to the rich countries. The fact is that health budgets which are hopelessly inadequate, and health systems frequently tailored to the expensive Western model, often imply that adequate health facilities are only available in or near urban areas.

Bryant estimates that perhaps half the world's population receives no medical care at all. Nigeria, allocating 10 per cent of government expenditure to health last decade, had to spread it at a rate of $0·50 *per capita* per annum. Not surprisingly, this budget tended to be concentrated in the cities; in the mid-Sixties, infant mortality was high in Lagos – but perhaps five times higher in rural areas. The national average ratio of doctor to patient in the late Sixties was calculated by Gish at 30,000:1; but when the medical school was started in Zaria to serve the Northern Region in 1967, the population of 30 million was catered for by 120 doctors in government service and 55 in missions – about one to 177,000 patients. In Thailand, in the same period, there were 6,900 patients per doctor in the country as a whole; but the ratio sank to 940:1 in Bangkok, and climbed to around 200,000:1 in the "truly rural areas".

The investment cost of a large teaching hospital in the primate city is likely to exceed the entire annual health budget of a developing country; capital costs per bed might range from $3,000 to $10,000 in a country with a *per capita* income of between $140 and $200. In Zambia, Gish claims that 250 health centres could have been built for the same cost as the Lusaka teaching hospital – enough to reach the entire population and to cover most health needs. He estimates that only one case in a hundred would have to be referred from such health centres to a district hospital, and barely 1 per cent of these to more specialised regional or national hospital care. The theory behind the capital's teaching hospital, he concedes, is that it is the peak of such a referral system. But in practice, 80 per cent to 90 per cent of its patients will come from the capital city region. In addition, almost all hospital-trained doctors will, inevitably, stay in the capital city (or emigrate, as many have done, to richer countries where openings in conventional hospital-based medicine are more widespread). What is urgently needed are systems based on health centres and medical auxiliaries; but these have little political appeal.

The problems of reaching rural areas are generally appreciated. During the wide-ranging tour of health facilities in the Third World on which he based his book, John Bryant and his team found that in Uganda, out-patient attendance "halves for every two miles that people live from a hospital". With clinics each covering a radius of ten miles, perhaps less than a fifth of the people will be reached. As Buu Hoan told the Oxford conference, "A different disease pattern, a different population structure, a scarcity of resources – these are three of the main reasons requiring developing countries to plan for health care in a way radically different from that of the Western world." If three beds per 1,000 people were taken as an acceptable standard, he pointed out, capital expenditure for hospitals alone would range from $9 to $30 in South-East Asia, where most countries spent less than an annual $2 a head on total health care. Health centres might cost about $2·40 a head in capital and recurrent costs per year, would reach most of the population and "might turn out to be one of the most profitable investments public authorities could ever make".

But the problems of effective health care in cities have received less attention, simply because so large a share of the health budget (frequently more than half the total, for a capital city) is devoted to them. Favourable ratios of doctors and nurses to patients do not necessarily mean efficiency. "In the great cities of the world," writes Bryant, "people are without health care when it seems to be available. Forty per cent of the people of Bogotá die without having been seen by a physician, yet there is more than one physician for every thousand people." In Cali, another Colombian city, there were forty graduate nurses to 600 beds in the late Sixties, although 60 per cent of Colombia's nurses worked in its three major cities. Seventeen per cent of Cali's children were not seen during their terminal illness, and a further 19 per cent had no medical attendance in the last forty-eight hours of life.

The missing links within town and country health services are different, just because medical care is available in the city much more readily than in the country. But "curative" medicine which in practice is only a superficial treatment of symptoms; the failure by the people to use the system, often vitiated by the "social distance" between patient and health officer; and the general ignorance about illness which can mean fatal delays in seeking treatment – all result in mortality and morbidity rates in the cities of the poor which are still unacceptably high. Yet the difference in standards of medical care between city and rural area remains so marked as to be absolute.

Ill-fed, ill-housed, suffering from a depressing range of curable but endemic diseases; between a sixth and a third of them un-employed, all struggling to raise families; so the urban poor of the developing world will cluster in cities which in twenty years could cover four or five times their present total area. The city as "suction centre" will continue to operate so long as the pressure on the land continues; new migrants will compete for the diminishing number of available jobs in relation to labour supply. The children for whom the earlier migrants hoped so much will find more difficulty in securing jobs than their parents – and the more difficulty, the greater have been the supposed benefits of education showered on them by the city. Economic growth may be achieved; but the poor will discover that its visible effects are greater in terms of private automobiles, flyovers and freeways than in buses to get to work, or work to get to. "Site and services" schemes will provide some form of order and minimal amenity in some cities; but the £150 million needed for the first stage of the Lagos sewerage system will not necessarily have been forth-coming. In cities of 20 million, more than the total present population of London will have to find roof and keep in the tertiary areas which governments have shown themselves anxious to ignore or eradicate, where they are not destructively pater-nalistic in trying to organise them.

Such a recapping of a few of the problems, however carefully
balanced with reminders that human beings constitute a country's
assets, that progress is being made in almost all the major areas
of city planning, must raise the question: how long will the people
stand it? And, when they decide that they cannot, what form will
their impatience take? The workers in the film, *Metropolis*, when
they revolted, were cunningly incited by the Master's robot to
attack the central generating system. Their action flooded the
whole of the workers' underground city where they and their
own families had their homes. As Rios asked at Oxford, what is
meant by "social justice in urban conditions? Of course I am not
in favour of revolutions because we know they are too costly.
Urban reform means for me giving more bargaining power to
the poor, strengthening their groups and leadership." But what
becomes of leadership among people living at bare subsistence
level? If revolt is self-destructive, what alternatives do we see?
Will the rice riots of Indonesia or Burma remain sporadic and
isolated incidents?

The Roman Empire viewed the victualling of Rome as a
political necessity, overriding all immediate economic considerations. In recalling the policy of "bread and circuses", the assumption that the "urban mob" must be appeased has always carried
with it the rider that the urban poor may be quite as distinctly a
threat as an asset. Yet the remarkable characteristic of the
exploding cities is that it is not their poor inhabitants who
explode. They proliferate, but quietly.

The fear, however, is that without marked amelioration of
urban conditions, this quiescence cannot last. The workers of
Metropolis were armies of the despairing but resigned, who had
found expression only in the dragging footstep of defeat. But
they could be aroused and, despite much evidence to the contrary, it is often argued that the urban poor of the Third World
must one day cease to tolerate the intolerable. The notion that
appalling conditions not only explain but justify the breakdown
of order easily conflates with the conviction that it is bound to
happen. Thus it is not so much concern over bad housing, but
fear of the urban guerrilla that has motivated several governments
to clear urban slums and shanty settlements. But the results are
not always so beneficent. In Detroit, Stephen Aris comments,

it is fear of crime which eats into confidence and paralyses daily life even more than the reality.

As Joan Nelson remarks in her study of poverty's relation to unrest in the developing countries, it is tempting to draw some parallel between the ghetto conditions which allegedly produced the American city riots of the Sixties and the still more squalid conditions of the *favelas* and *pobladores*. If there were indeed a link between deprivation, limited opportunity, politicisation and revolt, then it should certainly lead to mass violence and political instability in cities where the first two are the rule. But the facts have so far failed to bear out this reading. P. K. Sen, retired chief commissioner of police in Calcutta, reported at Oxford that although that city offers all the textbook conditions for a flourishing underworld, "conventional crime has never assumed alarming proportions". Despite the existence of organised and violent crime in some cities of the developing world (linked, in Hong Kong for example, to the South-East Asian drug traffic), this statement could be made of many.

But Sen's point was that Calcutta's problems are not robbery, or assault, or even murder: the significant peril is the breakdown of law and order. A Bombay journalist, Khushwant Singh, voiced at Oxford the widely held view that: "the pattern of crime is different. You walk about Bombay at all times. There are thousands of people on the streets. In the daytime there are thousands of them sleeping on the pavements; so you can't really commit a crime. You can't snatch a handbag in the middle of the day. . . . There are other patterns . . . vagrancy, mendicancy, prostitution, diseased people on the streets fouling the highways and causing enormous dangers to health . . . and the new pattern, pre-eminently, is organised mob violence. In a city like Bombay, day after day massive processions break up cars, burn cars, break up streets and shop window signs."

Leaving aside the question as to whom the "crime" of diseased persons on the streets should be ascribed, the direction of anxiety is clear enough. Sen spoke of "an enormous body of potential trouble-makers", principally found among "a generation of frustrated and cynical youth ready to resort to desperate methods to fulfil their desire for a better life". In politically volatile West Bengal, extremist political parties found it easy to raise support across the social spectrum, he pointed out; and "any popular cause is magnified a thousandfold by the participation, active or passive, of very large numbers of people. Calcutta's dense population and the curiosity of the people are potent factors."

In stressing that the social conditions which, astonishingly, do not seem to father the common criminal, yet have the power to generate mass violence "which cannot be contained" without social and economic reforms, Sen none the less did not confuse the bread march with political protest. Much of the violence for which Calcutta has achieved notoriety has had a strong political emphasis; a great deal of it has been inspired by students and educated youth, and manipulated by politicians. Calcutta's experience would not seem to prove that the urban poor are in full revolt. Lévi-Strauss perhaps overstated the case when he found that in Calcutta, Western concepts of class differences in terms of struggle and tension were irrelevant; "here, the word has no meaning. Nothing is tense, since everything that might have been in a state of tension snapped long ago." He was writing in the mid-Fifties, years marked by frequent agitations by refugees and by students. Yet he perhaps caught the essential point – that, as Joan Nelson puts it, "those at the very lowest levels are preoccupied with survival".

In her study of *Migrants, Urban Poverty and Instability in Developing Nations*, she takes issue with two *idées reçues*: what she calls "the myth of the disruptive migrant"; and the radicalisation of the urban poor. The first theory is based on the notion that the migrant, torn from the social certainties of village life, frustrated in his efforts to exchange the grinding poverty of rural life for anything approaching secure urban employment, will vent his frustration in mob violence. She argues, convincingly, first that the migrant may not have come from the village nest at all; step-migration is still a more common trend, and the typical migrant to the capital city is in all probability a thorough urbanite. Secondly, available evidence does not suggest a strong involvement of migrants either in riots or in extremist political life. Thirdly, conditions which appal the bourgeois sociologist, represent for the migrant in almost every city an improvement on his former way of life. To a generally low level of political consciousness, a high degree of adaptability to urban existence, and a sense of personal progress, most migrants add a determination to "get on". Far from being "the core of local despair and disaffection", as Barbara Ward saw them, they are determined to extract from the city the services, and the opportunities for their children, which brought them there in the first place.

But, as Joan Nelson points out, there is a real danger that the urban poor, completely urbanised and generally born in the city but not assimilated into its economic social structure, may revolt against the failure of the city to satisfy the aspirations it has heightened. She quotes the sociologist Daniel Goldrich's warning that the children of the self-help home-builders of Santiago or Lima, if these communities are not integrated into society as a whole, could force the nation to count the cost by venting their frustrations in political opposition or across-the-board delinquency. Given the extent of un- or under-employment likely to continue in most of the exploding cities, the implications of such *anomie* would be extremely serious. But it is harder than one might expect to demonstrate that radicalism is a function of economic marginality.

The major Calcutta riots were predominantly middle class; the experience of most politicians is that greater, rather than lesser efforts have to be made to arouse the low-income groups; improvements in living conditions which look marginal to the outsider may have immense importance to the person who benefits. If the many earnest surveys in this area are to be believed, the poor are normally disinclined to assume the revolutionary and violent stances anticipated by the sociologist Samuel Huntington when "the children of the city demand the rewards of the city". There is a gap between the aspirations that might logically be aroused by the visible affluence of a few city dwellers and the actual expectations against which most people are likely to measure their achievement. It is not evident that urban dwellers tend to get less satisfied the longer they have been in the city.

And finally there is the factor of innate optimism, reinforced by a degree of upward social mobility from one generation to another. Findings in several Latin American cities and in India are quoted by Joan Nelson. Asked whether their economic situation had improved over the previous five years, between a third and two-thirds reported actual deterioration; yet asked about their prospects for the future, the degree of hope was astonishing. Whereas 74 per cent of the respondents in a Caracas *rancho* felt things had stayed the same or got worse in the previous five years,

69 per cent believed in a rosier future, and only 7 per cent thought it would get worse still.

Belief in the openness of society, where one's child might become a small shop-keeper or even, in certain countries, a government minister, is fairly widespread. Such thoughts, however illusory, diminish the tendency to translate personal disappointment into political activism or violent despair. But disaffection, if conditions actually deteriorate in the cities of the poor, can probably only be postponed. The revolt of the young Janatha Vimukthi Peramuna in Sri Lanka in 1971 was dubbed "Guevarist". It could more accurately have been ascribed to frustration and boredom – and as such gave a warning of the outlets which better educated, unemployed urban youth may seek.

Violence and organised crime are "natural" safety valves for unemployment and the continued precariousness of life. Evidence that the urban poor, rather than the new middle classes, are prone, yet, to disruption and political extremism is rare. But, as Mr Sen emphasised, they could be mobilised. And Harold Dunkerley, at Oxford, put the challenge to governments:

> There is for institutions a natural speed of evolution, a rather sluggish speed of evolution. But the big cities are changing in their social structures, in their economic structure, in *mores*, in their size and land area, in every respect; and with such rapidity that institutions are with great difficulty adapting to the challenge – sometimes not adapting, sometimes collapsing.

The threat of mass violence may be hard to document or quantify; there are other outlets for frustration than the political. But the proponents of the "time-bomb" theory emphasise the urgency of integrating the poor into the development process, if the "urban cancer" is to be turned into a benign multiplying of cells.

SECTION IV

Communes and Communism

China is to my knowledge the first country to have conceived *industrialisation without urbanisation*. . . . In the USSR, on the other hand, the policy has always been *urbanisation on the cheap*.

PETER WILES,
The Political Economy of Communism

CHAPTER 16

The Two Shanghais

If you are dealing with a time bomb – and I think we all agree that there is an element of this in the urban crisis – you solve the problem by defusing it, by stopping the mechanism working. Now that has been achieved in China.

NEVILLE MAXWELL

Workers in urban state enterprises are paid several tens of yuan or several hundreds . . . We peasants are paid only ten, twenty or thirty yuan a year. Many workers in towns live in blocks of flats . . . we are exposed to wind and rain. Just what attitude do the dogs of officials responsible in the towns have towards the peasants?

Red Guard poster, Shanghai, January 14, 1967

The month of March 1949 was set aside for the People's Liberation Army to learn the secrets of city administration. For four years, Mao Tse-tung had been calling on the Communist Party to "shift the centre of gravity" of the revolution to the cities. Now, on the eve of the Liberation, he called on the army to become a school as part of an emergency campaign to prepare a core of urban leadership. The revolution, he emphasised to the overwhelmingly rustic cadres – the men who were to assume responsibility, as the word implies, for China's development – could not limit itself to benefiting the peasants.

The energy with which this change of emphasis was promoted illustrates the difficulty of separating discussion of the city in modern China from Mao's overall development strategy. The question is further complicated by the dissensions within the leadership over the role of the city, by the fundamentally city-centred convulsions of the Cultural Revolution and subsequent fluctuations in policy, and by the often awkward conjunction of vigorous urbanisation and calls to "support the countryside". Mao, while he recognised that the cities must afford the initial impetus for development, was openly apprehensive of the power of the "sugar-coated bullets" of urban living to puncture the Party's revolutionary zeal. His goal was to create a new urban model which would realise, as the distinguished student of the Communist Party leadership, Professor John Wilson Lewis, puts it, "in hundreds of cities at different stages of industrialisation an ideal of local self-reliance and rural-urban co-operation". It is by this criterion that China's urban strategies and successes should be judged.

To many scholars and visitors to China, that new urban model has come to exist. There are three widely held views about the Chinese city. The first is that the Chinese have achieved industrialisation without urbanisation. A planner who toured parts of China in 1972 reported that "the Chinese have very self-consciously avoided the pattern which has characterised industrial development in the West: the pattern of industrial and urban concentration; the growth of mega-cities with their attendant problems; and the pattern of regional imbalance in economic growth".

The second is that the Chinese have succeeded, where everybody else has failed, in stemming urban drift. The cities' growth has been frozen, runs this argument, by efficient measures to limit migration, by birth control and, above all, by creating conditions of prosperity in the countryside. Neville Maxwell told the Oxford conference that behind these policies to stabilise city growth was a strong anti-urban bias: "They don't like the city. The cities that they are left with are the bequest of the period of imperial investment, the domination of coastal China. They have to live with them; but as far as they are concerned there will be no – or very few – new ones." Estimates by the Population Division of the United Nations Department of Economic and Social Affairs put the number of million-cities in China at thirty-four, as against eight in 1950. Yet the assumption of an anti-urban current in Chinese planning is encouraged by the Chinese themselves. (Local officials were assuring visitors in 1973 that the population of Sian was being frozen at 1·3 million, when United Nations calculations had estimated it at 2·1 million by 1970.)

Along with assertions of Chinese antipathy to the city, there are paeons of praise for their order and cleanliness – the third, and visually convincing, argument for the success of China's urban policies. Maxwell drew thumbnail sketches of "two Shanghais": the pre-revolutionary city where, "in addition to the familiar evils of slums and overcrowding, of mass unemployment, of filth, disorder and mendicancy, there was also a particular shamelessness of vice and crime and exploitation"; and today's Shanghai, "still greatly overcrowded, but not intolerably so, . . . a city of cleanliness, order and co-operation . . . a working city again, not an out-of-control agglomeration of mankind, but an ordered community". To have effected this transformation, it is argued, the Chinese must have devised entirely new and fruitful ways of running the cities they have.

To what extent do the Chinese have the answers which elude the rest of the world, and how far would any claims to success be predicated on either coercion, or on a revolution of "hearts and minds" so great that the young become pioneers, the workers dedicated to production, the society honest and its leaders clear-headed enough to find their way round the urban dilemma? Has Mao Tse-tung written, on his "poor and blank" country, the blueprint whose secrets planners across the globe should be trying to decipher? And what, if these observers are correct, could the Red Guards conceivably have had to complain about?

The plight of the cities in 1949 was dramatic enough to make reconstruction and the restoration of order urgent priorities. A century of turmoil had resulted in an almost complete breakdown of services; sufferings under the Japanese occupation had been accentuated by famine and economic disruption. The ravages of war aside, amenities were traditionally minimal. From the southern walled city of Peking, today's officials tell visitors, 600,000 "official" rubbish dumps, many in use since the Ming dynasty, had to be cleared; Sian had no urban water system; in Shanghai, fire-lanes had to be cut through the hovels before any rehabilitation could begin. Organised crime flourished in conditions of widespread starvation, unemployment and overcrowding.

Sian's transport system boasted seventeen buses, of which six were operative, and Shanghai's and Peking's were little better equipped to serve their larger populations. (Transport remains the Chinese town planners' most marked failure: Shanghai today has only 1·45 times the number of buses and trams that it had in 1949, while the number of routes has been trebled and their length increased ten times. Frustrated commuters are deterred from purchasing bicycles because their cost is deliberately kept artificially high, but one in every five or six urban residents still finds the means to possess one.) Other services, where they existed, were similarly overstretched.

The worst housing was replaced either by selective demolition or by redevelopment of complete districts. In Shanghai, two million people had been rehoused by 1972 and the equivalent of the entire 1949 housing stock rehabilitated. Although little attention was paid to aesthetic standards or to integrated environmental development, basic services had been assured throughout many Chinese cities by the Seventies. In new housing, each unit generally was provided with a lavatory; families often shared kitchens, and bathrooms remain the exception. Slums were supplied with pure water, from neighbourhood-serving stand-pipes. The cities are still crowded enough to prompt comment by a British architect that "the stress areas of British cities appear idyllic by comparison"; but the improvement was steady and rapid.

Emergency reconstruction moved ahead more rapidly than formal city planning. Not until 1955 was a comprehensive scheme of urban development drawn up, and the generality of its provisions perhaps reflected the strong differences between Chinese planners, on everything from the regulation of trade to the planning role itself. In the following years, the concentration on development of heavy industry entailed the expansion of both coastal and inland communities, the creation of new towns and upgrading of western provincial cities. During the First Five-Year Plan (1953–57) it was also possible to tackle urban living conditions in detail. There was intensive discussion of amenities and services, pollution control and health, crime and education in the national press. The urban proletariat was given the favoured status in terms of welfare and education that it was to maintain in relation to the countryside, and which was to have important consequences.

China had already entered on a process of rapid urbanisation from an overwhelmingly rural base. Franz Schurmann, in *Ideology and Organisation in Communist China*, estimates that when the Communists took over in 1949 there were only five million-cities in China. The entire urban population was 57·65 million. Only five years later, the *People's Daily* revised the figure to 92 million, and the official People's Handbook estimated that two-thirds of the cities' growth was due to rural-urban migration. Particularly in the north and north-west, intensive urbanisation continued up to the Great Leap Forward. The United Nations' estimate that by 1960, 122·3 million were living in urban areas, may even be conservative, since the official plans formulated in 1962 after the failure of the Great Leap involved cutting back the urban population from 130 million to 110 million. Strenuous measures to limit urban growth through the Sixties did not, according to the United Nations' most up-to-date calculations, prevent the cities' populations nearly doubling between 1960 and 1975, bringing urban population up to 246·5 million.

None of this accords perfectly with the notion of a leadership united in distaste for urbanisation. In the northern industrial areas, and in the new inland development centres, Mao encouraged urban growth to match industrial expansion. The old centres continued to flourish: the eight million-cities existing in 1950 housed 17 million; by 1975 they accommodated 41·4 million. But the leadership's efforts to diversify large-scale urban development bore dramatic fruit. Seven of today's million-cities started with less than a quarter of a million in 1950; Tsupo, a city of 1·2 million, which is expected to double by 1985, did not then exist. Although all figures, Chinese or otherwise, on the country's population and its distribution need to be viewed with caution – Chou En-lai openly admitted the shortcomings of China's head-counting machinery to Edgar Snow, and in 1974 an urgent campaign to improve statistical expertise was launched – the trend is unmistakable. And over a third of this urban population lives, for all the emphasis on decentralisation, in million-cities.

The pressures that this growth placed on urban planning and existing resources during the Fifties were exacerbated by troubles with the urban bureaucracy. At the outset, this machinery was almost totally out of order. Over two million officials fled the cities in 1949, and the Communist Party could mobilise only

750,000 people even remotely qualified to replace them. Few of these were from urban backgrounds. The shortage directly threatened the twin policies of stabilising the cities and mobilising the urban populace behind the revolution. Mao was forced to authorise "a coalition of classes", with guarantees to those administrators trained under the previous régime who were prepared to co-operate. In Shanghai, the government appealed to "politically pure" Nationalist officials to stay on the job; over 70 per cent complied, and in 1952 70 per cent of the city's major administrative posts were still occupied by non-party cadres, despite 1951's "three-anti" campaign against corruption, waste and bureaucratism, and its successor, the "five-anti" campaign against urban businessmen and their bureaucratic supporters.

Peking and Shanghai were placed directly under the State Council; other cities came formally under the provincial administrations. The municipal administration covered the entire urban area, and its City Construction Bureau was responsible for town planning. Beneath it would be the district administration, responsible typically for a quarter to half a million people; reporting to it was the street office with a bailiwick of 50–100,000. All three levels had informal ties of co-operation with areas largely independent of their jurisdiction, such as industry. But the roots of city organisation were the residents' committees and the residential small groups. In essence, writes Ezra Vogel, Professor of Social Relations at Harvard, "what the Communists have done is to expand downwards the municipal police organisation and to give it more authority in supervising informal associations". The interaction of police and these informal groupings was the key to the orderliness that so often strikes the foreign observer.

Each family was represented in the residents' small groups, whose leaders commonly were members of the residents' committees. In this way, the neighbourhood was to be firmly linked with the public security apparatus. The police station was the dominant institution at precinct level, responsible not to the municipal government, but to the district public security bureau, which equalled in size the whole of the rest of the district government apparatus, and operated entirely independently. All members of each household had to register at the police station, and absences or arrivals had to be reported there. The full-time director of the residents' committee worked under the supervision of the policeman assigned to the same area.

The committees mediated in disputes, organised rationing, and undertook various community health and welfare functions. The first were formed in Tientsin and Shanghai in 1952, but it was more than two years before they were established in other cities. The reason was their unpopularity, resulting from their close links with the public security apparatus. The committees were never a formal part of the city government, and were designed as a channel for the propagation of government policies, and also for residents' grievances. They existed in the twilight world between informal and formal government, a vital element of the campaign to spread control downwards through the residential areas and to organise those not controlled at a place of work. Under the eye of the "Uncle Policeman", social control was enforced. It was a system that placed its main emphasis on controlling deviance through "maintenance of the class line" and deterring future disorder. The method involved short but intensive campaigns, followed by relaxation. The citizen, unable to predict the timing of campaigns, uncertain of his rights, and knowing that actions permitted today could be "crimes" tomorrow, trod carefully.

But if citizens were inhibited by unpredictable changes in the rules by which the urban game was played, these also largely paralysed official initiative. Between rounds of mobilisation and slogan-wielding, urban cadres left people much alone, retreating into a safe, comfortable and increasingly overcrowded bureaucratic world. A "revolution of hearts and minds" implied more than the mere maintenance of order; but the risks of falling foul of a new line through over-energetic action were unacceptable. When Mao called on the people in the Cultural Revolution to "dare to rebel" and criticised cadres for slavish obedience to the Party machine, he was specifically attempting to tackle the superficiality that had so far characterised the revolution in the cities.

Shortage of administrators had turned to a glut by 1954, when the State Council complained that cadre recruitment had far outstripped the expansion of state functions and economic growth. Energetic drives by the Communist Party resulted in the expansion of Canton's municipal government cadres by 84·4 per cent a year between 1949 and 1957. Ten years after Liberation, at least 5 per cent of all urban dwellers were cadres and China, whose entire history makes it the perfect candidate for allegiance to Parkinson's Law, was again afflicted with a self-procreating bureaucratic machine. The State Statistical Bureau complained in the mid-Fifties that a third of all administrative employees were "non-productive"; the maintenance of state cadres alone cost 9·6 per cent of the national budget; and the bureaucracy had developed a "heavy head with light feet". The cadres headed for the cities and rapid promotion, while the shortage of grass-roots cadres in the countryside was inhibiting the progress of collectivisation.

In the later Fifties, massive campaigns to "streamline" the bureaucracy by permanent transfer to industrial complexes and to the countryside, and by temporary rustication and down-grading, resulted in the re-locating of over three million cadres. But as the *People's Daily* reported, "those who were assigned to organise co-operatives and to work with the masses thought they were doomed"; recruitment regularly followed these periodic drives and cadres crept back into the city bureaucratic apparatus. One of the most violently emphatic slogans of the Cultural Revolution was "thoroughly smash all bureaucratic structures". The leadership had discovered that lesser measures were soon circumvented.

The city-based bureaucracy sabotaged one of Mao's prime tenets for urbanisation: that city and rural hinterland should be closely linked. In practice, the countryside was neglected. In the mid-Fifties, an industrial worker in urban areas earned three to five times the wage of an average peasant. Campaigns to "support the countryside" masked the steady exploitation of rural re-resources. There was more communication between cities than between city and rural area, and officials tacitly assumed a break between the two worlds, with rural collectivisation and city organisation operating as exclusive systems.

The peasants voted with their feet, in what by 1957 was de-scribed by the Central Committee as a "blind emigration of peasants from the rural areas". They came, overwhelmingly, in response to hardship; and they brought their families. A govern-ment survey of fifteen cities for 1953–56 reported that the "basic" (i.e. employed in the formal sector) population had risen by 28 per cent. The dependent population had however increased by 70 per cent, and now constituted 60 per cent of the urban populations – and nearly half these additions came from rural areas. A succession of social, political and economic crises in the countryside, together with the disparity in living standards and resistance to collectivisation, resulted in a formidable implosion. In 1958, at the outset of the Great Leap Forward, 10 million swarmed to the cities. Government directives repeatedly urged measures to curb immigration but, as Professor Lewis comments, "travel permits, area-specific ration cards, the 'sending down' of cadres, enforced population registration – nothing stemmed the tide".

Urban economic growth could not keep pace. During the First Five-Year Plan, about a million persons annually were added to the urban working-age population from natural increase alone – and to this were added an annual 800,000 working-age people from the countryside. Statistics on additions to the number of jobs suggest an annual shortfall of around 300,000. "Contract labour" exacerbated the situation: urban enterprises recruited labour from the co-operatives at rates well under the wages paid to city workers. It was a system which came under peculiarly bitter attack during the Cultural Revolution. But it received official blessing because these workers, at least, were not permanent migrants.

Many did not register. Chinese cities offered underground jobs, and family networks remained stronger than the vigilance of the public security apparatus. The influx put impossible demands not only on urban services but on urban organisation. The problem was no longer simply one of order, but of how to mobilise this vast population for economic development. The leadership borrowed from the countryside to find a new form of organisation. The most radical experiment in China's urban policy began in the summer of 1958. It was the urban commune.

Units of production had been specifically excluded from the control of the residents' committees. The urban commune, by contrast, was to integrate industry, commerce, cultural and law-and-order functions, household activities and agriculture. In cities where many workers still lived miles from their factories, and where, under the pressures of population increase, housing projects were not going forward fast enough to link the scatter of industrial and residential enclaves, the urban commune was to bring about the "unity of living and working" by integrating production, administration and family life.

The inherent difficulties were immediately obvious; communes were set up round central cores of already existing organisation – factories, schools or offices. Yet the most urgent need for the system was in primarily residential areas. Again, conflicts rapidly arose because production units did not necessarily coincide with administrative boundaries. In the model Chengchow commune, for example, the nucleus textile factory was state-owned, but the commune as a whole was not. Satellite factories, commune-supporting agricultural brigades and production materials now came under state ownership, administered by the Honan provincial government. But stores, banks, post offices and other supporting parts of the infrastructure, although transferred to commune control, were still units of city government. Elements of collective ownership further complicated the picture.

The system was to work from the bottom up and to offer a new kind of urban living. Schurmann describes its impact: "The ordinary citizen found himself in the grip of a new way of life. Private life was decried as old-fashioned, women were mobilised for labour and collective life supplanted home life. The street, not the home, became the central focus. . ." But the experiment was over almost before it had begun. By December 1958, the Tientsin Party Committee was admitting that conditions in the cities were "different" from those in the countryside. The Sixth Plenum, lamenting the prevalence of "bourgeois thought" in the cities, abruptly announced in the same month, that with the exception of a few model cases, urban communisation was to be halted.

The urban commune failed because it was economically too small, in terms of the complex interrelations of city structures. By fragmenting the modern sector of the economy along residential lines in the name of local self-reliance, it not only failed to make the best use of available labour but sharpened the divisions between city and rural hinterland which it was Mao's aim to eradicate. As a bid to change the nature of the cities, it exposed the lack of genuinely city-based policies in the Chinese leadership. Although in name some survived – Sian boasts that its organisation is commune-based, and the theoretical journal *Red Flag*

Bangkok's floating market: Much-maligned, the bazaar economy still offers the best hope of a job for most city workers.

Unplanned city: the teeming Tondo slum of central Manila, where birth control is still left to nature, or Vatican roulette.

claimed in July 1960 that 1,064 such communes were in existence
– they were much larger, and had become a medium simply for
the promotion of street industries. This organisation of the tertiary sector, and of the urban unemployed, in backyard production created out of "waste materials, idle hands and organisation"
related more to the obsessions of the Great Leap Forward than
to any urban ideal. In the general shortage of raw materials after
the Great Leap foundered, many withered and others quietly
reverted to private ownership. Paradoxically, the most enduring
legacy of the urban commune was to be the reintroduction to
China's cities of small-scale Chinese enterprise of the kind
familiar in Hong Kong or Singapore. It brought new liveliness
and flexibility to the cities – as the accidental by-product of a bid
to achieve greater regimentation. The urban commune did not
radically change the nature of city living; and it was to be China's
unique experiment with revolutionary urban models.

The most pervasive weapon in China's armoury against the
rural-urban influx was neither the urban commune, nor the
subsequent Maoist experiments with the "economic region", but
the more universally applied system of "planned re-location".
A mixture of returning migrants to the home village and sending
city dwellers "down to the countryside", it has been canvassed
as a major feature of national planning to urbanise the countryside. It was also an emergency measure, a policy of last resort.

During the Fifties, when the influx was at its greatest, the policy
was largely confined to the "non-productive" urban population –
young workers whom the labour market could not accommodate,
offenders shipped out for "labour reform", and surplus cadres.
Occasionally more drastic measures were taken: the year after the
huge migration of peasants fleeing to the cities from rural hard-
ships in 1954, 700,000 involuntarily returned to their villages from
Shanghai and Tientsin alone. And in 1962, thousands of small
urban factories were forcibly closed and urban workers, employed since 1958, when 21 million non-agricultural jobs had
been created, were abruptly dismissed under the "return to the
home village" emergency measures. From then until the Cultural
Revolution in 1956, an estimated 40 million were sent to the
countryside.

Their welcome was far from assured. The peasants regarded
the returnees as people who had failed to make good, and urban

newcomers – often correctly – as downright "bad elements". All were extra mouths to feed. When in the Cultural Revolution millions of young people took advantage of relaxed travel restrictions to return to the cities, wall posters were covered with vehement complaints of their treatment in the countryside – and complaints, too, against neighbourhood cadres' deceptions and false promises to get them to "volunteer". In Shanghai, "Revolutionary Parents of Shanghai Aid Sinkiang Youth Revolutionary Rebel Headquarters" groups were formed in each district to mobilise parents, who were to persuade their children to return. But angry parents, protesting at rural conditions, challenged cadres to practise what they preached by volunteering themselves or sending their own children. Although between 1966 and 1973 an estimated 20 to 25 million were sent either temporarily or permanently to the countryside, social persuasion was an even less cogent factor than before. The young were widely alienated. Many graduates, reported a 1973 article in the *Far Eastern Economic Review*, "simply refuse to leave the cities. Jobless, they become 'social parasites', a term which the government uses to disgrace hostile graduates. Roaming in the cities, the troops of 'parasites' enlarge over the years and finally become unmanageable, threatening the welfare of the society." To resolve problems generated by the increased necessity for forcible "planned relocation", the government reportedly has had to cut some communes' compulsory grain delivery quotas in return for accepting urban "mouths".

China's achievement in the decentralisation of industry and the diversification of the rural economy has been considerable, and has to some extent taken the pressures off its cities. But if the "down to the countryside movement" is, as Neville Maxwell found, "an on-going and effective phenomenon" which "works to narrow the gap between city and country", development remains markedly uneven – and the pivot of China's industrial revolution is basically urban. The vaunted primacy of agriculture is directly related to the cash-flow which agricultural output makes available for industrial development, and official policy towards rural industry has been highly variable. The Chairman's aim of balanced rural-urban development has been chiefly impaired by the slow progress in improving agricultural output. For all the impressive performance in achieving self-sufficiency

in grain production, for example, 1972 showed how far this could
be set back by severe weather conditions. China was not in fact
much nearer the goal of adequate safety margins than it had been
in the late Fifties. Recent cutbacks in the promotion of rural
industry have been related to the urgent need to concentrate on
food production and on flood control. In 1974, senior officials
in Canton, capital of the agriculturally prosperous Kwangtung
Province, acknowledged that "the biggest problem China now
faces is food; any major drought would still be extremely
serious". Despite notable successes, reafforestation and irrigation
schemes in the arid central provinces have a long way to go. So
far, the countryside has markedly failed to parallel the urban
industrial take-off.

So long as the sharp disparity between rural and urban living
standards remains, Maxwell and other observers may be over-
optimistic when they contend that the problems of the "exploding
city" have been faced and solved in China. The Chinese for many
years now have been adjured to "learn from Taching", Taching
being the best-known example of the "system of widely separated
townships . . . each agriculturally self-supporting . . . each self-
sufficient in services" which Maxwell argues is the leadership's
preferred recipe for industrialisation without urbanisation. But
the lesson, in many cases, has been less than enthusiastically
received. The cities continue to exercise their pull.

The Cultural Revolution was centred on the city with good
reason, for it is in the city that the Chinese revolution has most
markedly failed to remould society. For all the achievement in
physical terms, in welfare and in education, Schurmann is
probably right to say that "the Chinese have yet to create
effective economic institutions to resolve the dilemma of population, and effective social institutions to resolve the dilemma of
community". Mao Tse-tung's recognition of the importance of
the cities as revolutionary catalysts was re-emphasised after the
Cultural Revolution in his insistence that Party organisation
"should be composed of the advanced element of the proletariat".
But the cities continued to function on a system of inter-group
bargaining which had little to do with the new urban model of
the theorists.

After the experiment with the urban communes, the Chinese
made no further radical moves to remake the cities. Whether

under the pre-Cultural Revolution system of organisation, or under the Revolutionary Committees, the emphasis remained order – and avoidance of crisis. When the turmoil of the Cultural Revolution had subsided, in 1968, Hankow Radio betrayed the failure of its central aim in lamenting, "the iron broom of revolution has not yet reached the towns". The basic problems of political transformation were not solved: the cities remained residential areas for a vast labour force, rather than integrated communities spearheading a countrywide revolution.

The competing claims of ideology and the *ad hoc*, which have mixed slogan-laden campaigns with pragmatic response to a variety of economic and social problems, have produced in China's cities a paralysis of the will in the medium-level leadership. Caught between rhetoric and mundane urgencies, the cadre is aware that today's declared policy may conflict with tomorrow's new "revolutionary line" – that Chairman Mao's famous utterance about the dangers of "lifting up a stone to drop it on one's own foot" may all too readily fit his case.

This ambiguity, which is the direct effect of the leadership's refusal to establish well-defined, consistent norms for administrative action, is deliberate. It serves, even, certain purposes in controlling a society so poised between the traditional and the modern. But it leads to confusion in officialdom, and in the Chinese case deprives cadres of the confidence to innovate – the confidence essential to social revolution. What one political analyst of the Chinese scene has called the "fudge-factor" has not prevented Chinese cities from operating efficiently; but it has spelt death to Mao's dream of eliminating the "three great differentials – between brain and hand, worker and peasant, city and countryside". In the quicksands of institutionalised unpredictability, the bureaucracy continues to seek refuge in immobility.

The Chinese can point to considerable achievements in the government of their rapidly growing urban environments. In terms of containing that growth, they have done no worse than any swiftly urbanising country. But they are not about to patent the model society.

CHAPTER 17

Smog over Magnitogorsk

Soviet urbanisation, in tempo and scale, is
without parallel in history.

ISAAC DEUTSCHER,
The Unfinished Revolution

The more rapidly capital accumulates in an
industrial or commercial town, the more
rapidly flows the stream of exploitable human
material and the more miserable are the
improvised dwellings of the labourers.

KARL MARX, *Capital*

Soviet planners, in the first, heady days of Marxist-Leninist self-
assurance, distinguished sharply between two basic varieties of
city-dweller – the "city formers", who were essentially the
directly productive labour-force, and the "city servers", who
merely facilitated urban existence for their more important
neighbours in the factory or the regional-government complex. As
the Soviet state owns all the land, capital and resources, city
development could from then on be regarded as a fairly straight-
forward process. First the desired output of manufactured goods
or administrative services that the city was expected to provide
was laid down by the State Economic Planning Commission
(GOSPLAN). This in turn gave the required number of workers,
who would make up the "city-forming" base. Once that was
established, the appropriate complement of "city-servers" was
derived from a simple mathematical formula – usually in the
proportion of three or four to one, "according to the concrete
conditions". Then, with the total population known, the settlement's physical layout, housing density, street pattern, utility
network and so forth could be read off from whatever was the

current book of standards, normally known as "Regulations and Norms for the Planning and Construction of Cities".

That was the theory. It rarely worked quite so neatly in practice. Soviet cities exist, in the overwhelming majority of cases, to meet the needs of Soviet industry; and industry, driven forward by the lash of Stalinism in the Thirties and by the imperatives of "catching up with America" since the war, could not often wait for the niceties of the planning text-book. But planned or random, one thing is incontrovertible – since the Revolution, the USSR has achieved a quite staggering population switch, from peasant countryside to industrial townscape. In fifty years, the number of Russian cities with over 100,000 people has risen from 31 to 221. Many of these have grown from nothing at all in that time: they are included among the 1,464 "new towns" which did not exist before 1917; some are even among the 600 or so which have sprung up in the last fifteen years. From a land of infinite rural horizons, the Soviet Union is now almost as urban as the United States, with well over half its 242 million inhabitants established, at the latest, 1970, census, amid the smog and tension of Commuter-grad.

The Russian authorities, in principle, dislike large cities. Almost the only reference to urbanisation in the 1848 Communist Manifesto comes when Marx and Engels advocate "the gradual abolition of the distinction between town and country, by a more equitable distribution of population over the countryside". That is still, in some sense, official policy. But for the moment draconian powers, elegant formulae, internal passports and ubiquitous central-planning are still, it seems, insufficient to halt, or even significantly moderate, the now often unwanted cityward surge. Nor are they always able to achieve tolerable conditions for those already in residence. Many people, including Americans, have observed that Moscow is not only Russia's largest, but also, on the whole, most successful city, while New York, for all its dominance, is among America's most deplorable. But at least it is possible to escape from New York to the suburbs, which contain some of the most attractive attributes of American existence. The outskirts of Soviet cities, Moscow not excepted, often have difficulty even acquiring adequate water and sewage facilities.

Despite this, though, the inward flow continues. In the first great period of Soviet urbanisation, between 1926 and 1939, Stalin's brutal drive to collectivise the farms and develop heavy manufacturing forced more than 18 million peasants to the work-benches and one-room apartments (for the lucky) in the teeming new coal, steel and chemical settlements, on the Don, and the Volga, and beyond the Urals. Since 1945, although the element of compulsion has virtually disappeared, the flood of rural–urban immigrants has merely broadened and deepened. More than 40 million people have made the move – as many as left Europe for America and the British dominions in the whole of the nineteenth and twentieth centuries. Inevitably, many of these fetch up at the boundaries of already-overstrained administrative areas, and even the resources of a fully-planned society are hard put to it to cope.

Much of the problem stems from the fact that Stalin's Russia, where many of today's officials and planners, after all, received their training, always tried to get its urbanisation on the cheap. The supreme praesidium, then as now, strongly supported the formation of new towns, and trumpeted the achievement that they represented. But behind the shiny steel works or the capital-intensive oil refinery, which in most cases was the *raison d'être* for these towns, living space, services and even the most modest amenities were held to a rock-bottom minimum. Such one-industry settlements – like Gus-khrystal-nyy, east of Moscow, where 73·4 per cent of the active population is engaged in glass-making – were a characteristic product of Russia's ferocious economic drive, and despite numerous ambitious but ultimately rather half-hearted efforts at reform, their inner contradictions continue to scar the everyday lives of all Soviet citizens.

Such contradictions are not noticeably diminishing. As recently as 1969, one of *Pravda*'s correspondents, discussing the development of the new Siberian oil towns, described the two main schools of Soviet thought:

"The first says: begin by creating normal housing conditions for the workers; provide necessary consumers' services; build roads and electric transmission lines; lay water mains, etc. Then start regular oil production.

"The second school says: The main thing is production. Every-thing else is subsidiary. Normal living conditions can be created while oil is being drilled. In time, the contrast between production and the quality of life will be eliminated and everything will be put right."

He was writing about Gornopravdinsk, established in 1964, by a geologist planner who insisted on following the first route; arguing effectively that in Siberia, where conditions were so tough that even clay had to be transported by air, it was more than ever essential to be "concerned about housing and services". But the point of the passage was to emphasise the uniqueness of Gornopravdinsk, where a tiny population, only 2,000 people, made experiment possible. "The proponents of harmful, one-sided development have taken no heed of its example," reported *Pravda*. "They still sing the same old tune."

That tune has been heard most loudly, perhaps, in Magnito-gorsk, the most famous of the Soviet Union's economic-miracle cities. Founded in 1932, round a huddle of tents, ramshackle barracks, and a brand-new blast furnace, in the Second World War it produced steel for half Russia's tanks and shells, and is now a sizeable community of 364,000 people. Yet it remains a classic example of the "company town" – that concept, now so widely and justifiably discredited in the West, which has taken deep and often pernicious root in the USSR. When industry is virtually the only excuse for a town or city's existence, its managers are frequently made responsible also for providing the employees' living needs – housing, shops, electricity, water, sewerage, roads, public transport. But its main task remains production, and these social services, being essentially "unpro-ductive" (at least in the Marxian calculus, as interpreted in Moscow) always tend to be starved of funds.

Thus, in 1960, the huge Magnitogorsk Metallurgical Combine owned 52 per cent of all the city's state housing and ran most municipal services, including the mass transit system; the Magnitogorsk Construction Trust and a calibrated-gauge factory another 32 per cent of the houses; and the remaining 16 per cent of "bits and pieces" was shared among seventy other organisa-tions, of which the city soviet, representing the Soviet equivalent of local government, controlled rather under 2 per cent. As William Taubman says, in his recent book *Governing Soviet Cities*: "The large industrial enterprises not only planned for insufficient services, but had not fulfilled their plans." The city's heating, water, and sewage systems were painfully inadequate.

While large factories provided themselves with poor services, small plants could not afford any: their tiny housing projects – one or two apartment houses each – often lacked heat, water and electricity. And the combine cut off electricity to homes whenever production required extra power – which prompted little girls skipping rope on street corners to sum up the politics of urban development in the following verse: "*Na ulitse Lugovoi sveta ne emeetsia; Predsedate!' gorsoveta na lunu nadeetsia.*" Which means: "On Lugovaia Street the lights are out; the mayor has to rely on the moon." Water, pumped from dangerously near a local ore-enrichment plant, was frequently cut off without notice, even at the height of summer. Tram repairs were so slow that two-thirds of the fleet was often off the road, while managers endlessly procrastinated over building a new depot, or re-routeing to pass the city's painfully acquired new schools and hospitals. They refused to transfer jobs like garbage collection or snow clearing to the soviet, but then claimed they could not afford to buy the equipment themselves. And to reinforce the mess, the Ministry of Municipal Services found that its regulations forbade it to allocate the necessary trucks or snow-ploughs to the combine – they could only go to a soviet which was running its own services.

The overall result was described by Vladimir Chivilikhin, writing in the *Literaturnaia Gazeta* of 9 August 1967. "I remember one spring. Black streams flowed down black slopes, while the hard-working city suffocated in an agglomeration of fumes. The commendable, prizewinning, etcetera, etcetera, Magnitogorsk Metallurgical Combine throws off a monstrous quantity of sulphur dioxide in these fumes. If this quantity were calculated in terms of sulphuric acid, it might constitute a considerable percentage of the country's total sulphuric acid production! Animals, plants and the soil suffer; buildings deteriorate before their time; clothing is ruined; and even metal does not last as long as it should. Flowing into the rivers with the rain and spring floodwaters, the sulphur compounds contaminate the fish and diminish the already diminishing number of sources of drinking water. Who has taken all this into account? And most important, what is the monetary cost of the actual losses arising from people's lower working capacity?"

The fact that such questions can be, and are, frequently raised

7*

in the Soviet press (*Izvestia*, in particular, often throws in whole teams of reporters to probe the more flagrant outbreaks of citizen discontent) at least shows some sort of awareness that there is a deep-seated malaise. But progress, at all levels, remains desperately slow, as puny and in many cases almost resourceless local soviets carry on the twin battle with enterprises who will neither transfer power nor divert materials, and with superior bodies in the regional, national and ministerial hierarchy, who are usually playing an elaborate and impenetrable chess game of their own.

Back in 1960, three years after the first serious effort at postwar reform, V. Kucherenko, the chairman of GOSSTROI, the Soviet State Construction Committee, which is the highest body directly concerned with urban affairs, summed up the main shortcomings of the system as it then operated. Regional planning, he said, with its careful co-ordination of industry and urban growth, should be one of Russia's greatest strengths, but in fact was a prime weakness. Not enough people were practising such planning, and those who did were frequently ignored. GOSPLAN essentially confined itself to industry-by-industry planning and had lost contact with the localities. Urban plans, which were theoretically mandatory for every city, often did not exist. At that time, out of 1,700 substantial Soviet cities, half had no plan at all – including Kiev, Sverdlovak, Novosibirsk, Gorkiy, Kharkov and Odessa, all of which are now near or above the one-million population mark. Other plans were more or less useless – inaccurate, insensitive to local conditions, or out of date. Architects were in perpetually short supply. Only two institutes specialised in the training of town planners and only forty students had graduated in the previous year. And the party line, that 50,000 to 200,000 was the optimum size for a city, while over 500,000 was highly undesirable, had been wholly ignored. Not a single part of the supposed control mechanism was not being breached on the largest possible scale.

Most of his concern here is still highly relevant today. The 1957 reforms were supposed to take sizeable chunks of power and responsibility away from the vast industrial enterprises, and put them into the hands of the local city soviets. But this was one of those changes that, like desegregation in the United States, was allowed to proceed "at all deliberate speed", which in many cases turned out to be barely perceptible. Moscow and Leningrad certainly acquired control of their own housing and many services, but it remains difficult to identify any other major successes, behind the vague but unspecific official assurances that they exist. Indeed, much tentative advance went into reverse in 1965, with the renewed call for increased industrial output – one result of which was to shut down a lot of the small plants which had been successfully turning out low-technology goods, like building supplies, for local consumption, and forcing the already-impoverished soviets to buy much more expensively from "efficient" factories far away. Money remains a constant bone of contention. City authorities, in most cases, get some income from the supply of local services, and this they can apply at will. But even in the largest and best run settlements, such "independent" funds have shrunk as a proportion of total spending over the years – even Moscow is said to get only 10 per cent of its needs this way. The rest – cash, advice, consents, materials, manpower – all supposedly comes from higher entities in the great Soviet bureaucratic jigsaw. But the downward trickle is often so slow that the soviets find it necessary to cut corners, if they are going to keep their charges from seizing up. That is where the deals are done with the local industrial giants, whose "incentive funds", built up by over-fulfilling their production targets, are usually the most effective source of alternative finance. And the form of these deals – roubles in exchange for soft-pedalling on anti-pollution protest, or a less-demanding line on the deficiencies of enterprise-provided services – constitutes one of the most effective brakes on municipal improvement.

The latest batch of reform proposals came out in March 1971. The basic indictment remained much the same. The city soviets, it was said, were "still not making full use of their rights and possibilities to improve services to the population". There had been a failure to provide "integrated urban development" by "co-ordinating the work of enterprises and organisations of different departmental subordination". And while "the constant numerical growth of urban population makes ever higher demands on housing and municipal services . . . in many cities the soviets have no direct relationship with the maintenance, repair and improvement of public housing, almost two-thirds of which belongs to non-soviet enterprises, institutions and organisations".

The upshot was a series of proclamations and enactments urging the city soviets to step up their efforts, to co-ordinate and implement upgrading programmes for housing and services; to take over non-soviet activities and acquire control of everything that "primarily" concerns the city's population, rather than the workers at a particular plant. A "right" was also established for soviets to share in the various profits and funds earmarked by enterprises for city-development purposes. There was much talk of deadlines and new supervisory bodies to get all this moving, but the general impression of foreign observers is that there is still plenty of room for compromise, delay and foot-dragging on both sides (after all, not all soviets are keen to take responsibility for, say, a collapsing tram-service, when they know that without the most generous provision of investment money, all they can expect is to shoulder the blame for its final breakdown).

Soviet cities form a hierarchy of discontent. The smallest, including most of the thousand or more founded since the Revolution, envy the provincial centres, with their greater autonomy and their easier access to the support and concern of the higher political authorities. But these too have their troubles – notably their almost universal inability to stave off additional industrial expansion, however unwanted and irresponsible. And they, in turn, jealously covet the supposed wealth and independence enjoyed by the city fathers of Moscow and Leningrad.

However, excessive growth remains a constant concern all the way-up the pyramid. War was first declared on the unchecked sprawl of major cities by the Central Committee of the Communist Party in 1931, and since then it has never let up. But it has not noticeably achieved very much either – the best that can be said of the USSR's counter-growth strategies is that the results might have been even worse. For instance, much of the potential expansion of Moscow, Leningrad, Kharkov, Kiev, Tashkent, Baku and Gorkiy has been deliberately channelled into an often dense ring of satellite towns and subsidiary settlements. But they are all now in the million-plus class – five times the supposed optimum – and many of their satellites are also well past the danger level. Certainly the "big seven" share of Russia's city population has dropped significantly, from the 60 per cent of 1926 to today's mere 23·4 per cent. But this merely means that, since December 1969, it has been necessary to impose an absolute ban (which in its turn is being almost universally ignored) on all industrial construction, new or additional, in thirty-four cities of European Russia.

Moscow itself, despite its dominant status close to the heart of the party power machine, is by no means immune from the general woes of the Soviet municipality. In some ways it is rather a paradox among cities. Although its population is now just over 7 million, it is, in fact, rather small for the capital of one of the world's largest and most populous countries. Applying the Zipf analysis to the hierarchy of lesser Soviet centres, it should be roughly twice its present size, paralleling the 16 million of metropolitan New York. Certainly it accommodates a far smaller proportion (2·9 per cent) of the USSR's total census roll than, say, Greater London, where 22·5 per cent of all Britons are crowded, or Paris, with 16·8 per cent of all Frenchmen. But from its own planners' point of view, Moscow is very much the city that got away.

It was in 1935 that the limitation of its growth was erected into a central planning objective, under the General Plan of Reconstruction for the City of Moscow. Already, three years earlier, severe restrictions had been placed on industrial expansion, and now, with its population standing at 3·66 million, it was laid down that the ultimate, impassable target, to be reached by natural increase alone, must be fixed at 5 million. Immediate preparations, largely through the close supervision of work permits, were made to cut net immigration back to zero.

In the event, this has never looked even remotely realistic. Even by 1939 the limit was drawing uncomfortably close and, although the war's ravages slowed things down a bit, the 5 million barrier had already been well and truly crossed by the census of 1959. Then, in 1960, the whole notion was tacitly abandoned when a stroke of someone's pen brought the whole of the inner suburban ring, with its million extra people, within the boundaries of Moscow proper. By 1985, the United Nations predicts, Moscow, like Jakarta, will be nudging the 8 million mark.

One almost uniquely intractable problem that Moscow now faces is the area over which this central-city population is now spread. Since the 1960 decision virtually doubled the physical extent of the place, Muscovites rattle about in an urban space which is fully three times as big as that of only slightly more heavily populated London, and nine times that of the city of Paris. This, as Soviet commentators bitterly observe, ought to mean the enjoyment of much greenery and fresh air. What it actually means, however, is a quite inordinate time spent getting to and from work or any kind of social activity. Detailed comparisons have been made between Stockholm and cities in the USSR, which have the same number of people (750,000) but are physically four times the size. These show that where the Swedish citizen spends 76 hours a year on his average 322 trips by municipal transport, his Soviet opposite number needs 796 trips and 365 hours – a difference of 35 working *days* a year, spent hanging on tram straps, squashed into overcrowded vehicles, or desperately keeping a toe-hold on the running-board.

Moscow, where the distances are much greater, demands a far greater travel toll – so much so that, as one critical researcher said, "few workers have the energy to enjoy the greenery and the fresh air even when they get home to them".

Moscow, in comparison with all other Soviet cities, has very great powers to control its own destiny. It owns the bulk of the houses, it builds the roads and the schools, and from time to time its spokesmen boast "in general, the enterprises do not make trouble for us". It confiscates land when planned development is too slow; it warns, and in extreme cases fines polluters; it holds factory officials personally responsible for their errors and omissions. But still it grows. All its careful land-allotment procedures and its overseeing of project planning, even when national ministries are involved, cannot disguise the fact that when it comes to the point, Moscow cannot, in the words of its own Executive "influence the planning of non-soviet capital investments, or evaluate the expediency of this construction". On a famous occasion, in 1967, the Mayor of Moscow, V. F. Promyslov, asked "Do we really need seven higher institutions studying the seas and oceans? Wouldn't it be better to move some of them closer to the seashore?" But up to now he has been no more successful in discouraging the great mass of Russia's scientific and educational institutions from establishing themselves in Moscow, than in re-routing the government departments, and the water-, fuel- and electricity-hungry industries that "contribute to the backwardness of several branches of the city economy". In theory Moscow's growth pattern is fully set out in the document, prepared in the 1960s, under the title "Technical-Economic Bases (TEB) for the Development of Moscow until 1980". But it took almost five years for this to accumulate the full necessary range of state and ministry approvals, and even then the representatives of industry remained ominously silent, and the committee men of the great professional and educational institutions openly hostile. It is clear that, even in Moscow, the prerogatives of the "company town" will not be given up without a very long struggle.

In Russia, as to some extent also in such thrusting new city-dominated economies as South Korea, Japan or Singapore – or indeed, Britain in the early nineteenth century – productive investment has been consciously and deliberately allowed to outrun the provision of social overhead capital. To see such a policy as benign means believing that, in the fullness of time, those who suffer from the system will assemble sufficient power and voice to amend it. It certainly worked that way, to some extent, within the relatively loose and free-enterprise-dominated societies of Britain and the United States. But in the case of Russia, and similar centrally organised societies, it is very possible to share Taubman's concern that, within the intricate and intensely competitive mechanism of the Soviet bureaucracy, people find: "that old evils have a powerful inertia, that institutional arrangements devised to implement one set of priorities resist efforts to set new goals, that bureaucratic interests that gain from an old order fight to perpetuate their position, that even a powerful central leadership may find it difficult to overcome these obstacles, especially when the leaders themselves cannot bring themselves to break fully with the assumptions of an earlier era, of which they themselves are a product." Until that inertia is broken, the Soviet cities will offer few models, and even fewer solutions, to the rest of the world.

The Intolerability of Topsy

by Barbara Ward

Where you find both good and evil,
there you find a city.

Hindu proverb

I should like to explore in this final chapter the ways in which the context of city development has changed over the past hundred years. What we confront now is an acceleration on the one hand of the process of urbanisation, but on the other an almost complete break with the patterns which have characterised it to date. It is this discontinuity which I think accounts for some of the greatest problems with which we have to cope.

There are two commonly held assumptions which we should first examine. The first, clearly, is the persistent belief that the unfolding of the technological order is a single continuous process. First the Atlantic world goes through it, followed by Russia and Japan, and now that everyone is being drawn into this upward movement science and investment will solve all the problems. Thus the world's trend towards urbanism and the "exploding city" is both cumulative and irreversible.

The second assumption is that the city as it has been shaped in the technologically advanced societies represents "the urban norm". Its typical form is the metropolitan area – the urban region with centre-city and vast penumbra of semi-urban and suburban fringes in a continuous system. Up to a point the figures bear this out. Yet I would like to suggest that both major assumptions have to be re-examined. In the late twentieth century, something quite different is happening. And many of us are beginning to have some questions about the ultimate model, in other words about the Metropolitan Region: is it inevitable, is it workable, is it compatible with the kind of energy constraints, the kind of food constraints which, with the first cold chill of possible limits on resources, we begin to sense? Since the city on the whole is a very involuntary thing – like Topsy, it "just growed" – have we inadvertently grown ourselves into something that does not necessarily work? If this is the case, the course of wisdom for those who have to build, in the next twenty-five to thirty years, the equivalent of all the building that exists in the world at present, is surely to take a long cold look at this model and ask themselves whether other patterns would not be more desirable and, if so, whether it is possible to work them out.

One reason why we assume that urbanism is a continuous process is that, for all its horrors – and, God knows, the horrors were acute – early industrial urbanism produced a system that more or less worked. But, leaving aside such "unworkabilities" as wars and slumps, the assumption omits the degree to which particular, not always repeatable conditions determined the nineteenth century's urban growth. First of all, the technological revolution came at about the same time to the urban industrial and to the agricultural sectors, so that as the movement which concentrated people in the towns and the factory system went ahead, a very large increase of productivity in agriculture made it possible for workers to be released while food supplies grew. There was a kind of orderly moving belt from agriculture to the city.

Then, within the city, early forms of industrialisation were labour-intensive. Manchester was not calling for trained artisans but for "hands" – hands for the looms, hands for the mills. Thus not only were the numbers roughly in balance. So were the needed skills.

The movement was further eased by 40 million migrants going from Europe to new lands overseas. It was also helped – tragically – by the fact that the death rate in the cities remained high. There was cholera in London up to the 1860s and by the time the sanitary revolution began – incidentally, a most extraordinary feat of engineering – urban populations were beginning to stabilise (in part because having ten children in a tenement is not very comfortable). The farm worker's desire for the larger family had begun to diminish and female emancipation had at least started, with women beginning to work outside the home. All these changes were reducing family size before any real improvement in health, infant mortality and life expectation.

By historical chance, in developed lands industrialisation, the beginning of urban culture, the beginning of workers' education, the beginning of settled urban industrial life came *before* the expansion of health services and sanitation, before any population "explosion" could take place. These coincidences gave us a trouble-free or a relatively trouble-free transfer from traditional to industrial society. The enormous obstructions inhibiting this process have faded from our memories. The fact that urban culture became the dominant culture is the thing we remember. Dickensian novels fade. The "Year of Revolutions", 1848, slips away. We think of the transfer from pre-industrial to industrial on to post-industrial society as orderly and reasonably successful. We take it for granted that no special efforts by public or private agencies were needed to guide or cushion the process. Certainly, population policies hardly seemed necessary when demographers were predicting the disappearance of Britain and Sweden by 1980 – or was it 1984?

So much for our first assumption – that urbanisation is a continuous and self-repeating process. Now let us take a look at the second assumption – of the "Urban Region" as the norm. From the beginnings of the industrial order, not everyone has been convinced. Manchester, the "fabulous city" of early Victorian society, was the place where Engels found the evidence of deepening class division upon which Marxist theory was later built. The split which goes back to the early nineteenth century was symbolised in a physical split of rich from poor by residential space. It began about 1820 with the first suburbs – St Cloud, Clapham, Brooklyn. The more affluent, escaping from the dirt and noise and toil of the inner city, began to spread it thin all round the outer circumference. Spread, sprawl, conurbations – out they went to meet each other, reducing the sense of multi-class, multi-cultured, functioning communities and cutting off more and more people – rich and poor – from the choices and variety the "urbane" society had seemed to offer. And wherever this split was reinforced by racial segregation, deeper unease and increasing pressure grew up in the cities. During and after the Second World War this was reinforced in the United States by a massive move to the North from the South and, more recently, by the sudden increase in "guest workers" in the cities of Europe.

We should not exaggerate. In the long boom of the last twenty-five years, the city dwellers in advanced technological societies have seen the visible class differences of style and language greatly reduced. Perhaps three-quarters of society could now be called middle class. Suburbs are more mixed. Middle-income people are moving back to the inner city. But where the districts of poverty remain, they are more ugly and intolerable because of surrounding affluence. Moreover, the "spread city", created by people escaping from poorer industrial quarters, has developed other evils which also lessen its claim to be a genuinely workable urban model.

Let me pick out two. In market economies, a private land market in urban areas has spun the suburbs out by the attraction of land sales on the fringes and complicated the life of the centre cities by vast increases in the cost of land. The increment of wealth thus created has not been sufficiently available for the community whose growth was its cause. Henry George is as relevant and as neglected as he was half a century ago. In these conditions, between high cost work places and distant dormitories, it is difficult for recognisable communities to keep old roots or develop new ones. Urban "villages" like Chelsea or Trastevere are evidence of what a genuine social entity can be like. But they are easily swamped by careless expansion or equally careless "renewal".

A second evil also springs from the desire of many citizens to escape the city. It has made the escape first apparently more successful and then, paradoxically, more obstructed. We cannot go into all the shortcomings of the private automobile operating in the urban region. Let us simply say that it is the enemy of community by condemning too many people to lengthy, lonely commuting, by requiring road systems which tear towns apart and eat up the land, by its deaths and pollutions and, increasingly, by its excessively wasteful use of the world's valuable and shrinking stock of petroleum. Of all the symbols of waste, there is little to beat the single commuter in a station wagon (which uses only 25 per cent of its energy) sitting in a queue along with a million others in city streets where the horse went faster.

Over the last five years, the efficiency of the metropolitan area has begun to be questioned more and more sharply. Can the degree of social division be tolerable in the long run? Are there ways in which the community can be re-created on a multi-class basis? Are there ways in which, by the designing of communities, we could end the enormous wastage of energy in movement and mobility? These doubts go to the very heart of the question: is this a good model? Is the "inadvertent city" with which developed societies are burdened, a wise or possible precedent for those whose major building programmes lie ahead?

What in the urban experience of the developed world is relevant to developing countries? The road to urban society was a particular historical road with unique conditions and events which may not be repeatable. And along the road, an urban pattern developed which is so far from satisfying a number of man's basic needs that fundamental reforms are increasingly called for.

I believe the first point to be made in looking at the developing world is to understand that the transfer process to the city is simply not occurring in a tolerable way in the late twentieth century. We are looking at a "system" that is not adding up to a workable strategy. It is this relatively blocked system we must tackle if we are to do anything about our explosive cities.

The first "block" is the fact that, owing to colonial and imperial control in developing lands, big cities existed well in advance of any industrial development. In Europe, by the eighteenth century, the capital city usually had the beginnings of commercial and money markets. But very few of the other settlements numbered much more than 5,000. In fact, when America was settled, apart from 30,000 people in New York and 50,000 in Boston and Philadelphia, no other settlement had more than 2,500 inhabitants. In fact, there were only about 5 million people in the whole vast continent, when there were already 100 million people in India.

The sudden expansion of city after city – Pittsburgh, Manchester, Dusseldorf, Milan – reflected the concentration of power and people in new *industrial* centres. But look at the developing continents; their vast cities – many of them already far beyond the million mark – are nearly all ports. This is the key. They grew up in the late eighteenth and nineteenth centuries to serve the commercial and imperial interests of Europe. They were the transmission belts for mines and plantations in a small modernised sector, transferring out the raw materials and bringing in Western manufactures for a small urban élite. Père Lebret, the

great Dominican economist, called countries in which these great
ports – Bombay, Lagos, Rio de Janeiro – grew up, the "milch-cow
economies". The cities drained but did not serve the local community. They did not stimulate local industrialisation. They
grew as appendages first of the European, and later of the
American, world trading system. At the beginning of this century,
Latin America was more urbanised than Europe, yet not even
5 per cent of its people were employed in industry.

Besides, the colonial system only changed that part of agriculture that produced materials for export. Subsistence food production continued to be organised on feudal or tribal lines with
little or no surplus for the market. There was thus no large increase in productivity available to cushion the transfer of workers
to a growing industrial system. The great cities could be said to
be plugged into a foreign circuit and to bypass most of the
potential growth in the local economy. When independence began
to loosen the old ties, they became magnets for migration – but
lacked the economic dynamism to sustain it.

This new feature of urbanisation – the big city existing *before*
the transformation of the economy – is reinforced by another
contradiction, the profound disproportion between the factors
of production. No longer do unsophisticated machines need
"hands". One hundred and fifty years of technological development have left far behind the labour-intensive industries, like
textiles, which characterised Meiji Japan or early Manchester.
The new investment patterns in industry call for sophisticated
machines and capital-intensive methods. Similarly the "Green
Revolution", hailed as the great breakthrough in agricultural
productivity, is orientated to capital and machines, not to
maximising labour use. The result has been a transfer out of the
country into the cities of an explosive kind, in which rising
unemployment burdens both communities. This reinforces the
results of the sanitation and health measures first introduced by
colonialism and extended during the Second World War. The
ending of the colonial regimes coincided not with high death
rates but the beginnings of the "population explosion". Also, it
should be added, nearly all migrations were now *internal* because
there was no longer open land overseas to which migrants could
go.

Putting all these factors together – cities before industry, populations exploding, capital-intensive technologies in labour-rich societies without any outlets for migration – we can see the degree of blockage in the system. Critical links, which operated in the nineteenth century, are missing. The process is not creating out of pre-existing agricultural society the beginnings of an effective urban technological order. Instead we have massive pressures of people moving into relatively unprepared cities. There is no final mystery about our exploding cities. What we are seeing is a particular set of historical circumstances working themselves out, in a transfer of population which bears little relationship to what went before. We are increasingly forced to recognise just how unsatisfactory a basis this provides for the cities of the future.

Nor are the pressures connected solely with the obstructed transfer from rural to urban society. In addition to the unemployment, the illiteracy, the lack of opportunity created by over-migration, developing cities are showing signs of adopting some of the more unhealthy aspects of the fully modernised metropolis.

The strategies which, in still-constrained societies, imply a lavish use of energy – cars and highways before 5 per cent of the people have cars; high-rise buildings and air conditioning before the poor even have piped water – all these energy-wasting tactics are questionable even in the richest societies, and are certainly unsustainable in the poor.

If we want an all-embracing symbol, we might take the shanty town, springing up throughout the developing world and growing at twice and three times the speed of any other form of settlement. Here all the problems come to a physical and visible head. On our present figures, the shanty town is going to grow by 8 per cent a year for the next thirty years. It is fairly unworkable now. How much more so when it is doubled? How impossible if we add to its troubles the near-certainty of rising future constraints on such basic means of life as energy and food?

This is a formidable set of crises to face. But Cassandras must recognise that a foreboding sense of multiple disaster is not the best basis for constructive action. Already the feeling that nothing can be done is becoming a dangerously prevalent excuse for doing nothing. Inertia, nourished by lack of hope, then turns into a certain cynicism which dismisses even those policies that have proved effective on the grounds that they are not relevant, or not normative, or not possible to repeat.

However, all is not wholly dark. Whether the issue is the un-satisfactory nature of the urban model or the "obstructed system" underlying the developing world's urban migrations, there is far more awareness of the problems and dangers than was the case even five years ago. And the new processes of recognition can be mutually reinforcing. If developed societies start changing their models and the developing world starts mastering the transfer of populations, the urbanism of the next thirty years could be in-comparably more creative and humane than the inadvertent city building of the past. And there are signs that the sorting out of models and systems has at least begun.

Let us look first at the developed society and the "unintended city". There is a certain weakening in the traditional notion that the whole of a nation's urban pattern can develop as the by-product of other decisions – on industrial location, on transport, on trade routes. Above all, there is growing scepticism about allowing urban patterns to go wherever land speculation may lead. In 1974 there was a land use planning bill before the US Congress. It would have been inconceivable even ten years earlier to have said in America: "Listen, you simply have to have some control, not simply over patches of land for zoning, but over the whole strategy of how your land is to be used." In Britain, there is a continuing study of development strategies for land in cities and beyond. I would suspect that the idea of allowing an un-controlled land market to be the final determinant in the pattern of settlements is something we shall see fade in the next ten to twenty years. Certainly, if socialist societies produce satisfactory results, market planners may begin to beat a path to their door.

This concept of control over land use is linked with another change. Over the last four or five years a growing interest has developed in the idea of re-creating multi-class, multi-cultural communities within the urban spread. Is it necessary to endure mega-regions which are so separate, so spread, so thin in the suburbs, so neglected in the centres, so overloaded in their office districts, so given over to all the strains of mass commuting that they become the focus of rejection, *anomie* – and even violence? The idea of decentralised communities, within a region deter-mined by patterns of mass transit, looks much more interesting than it did only five years ago. Actually the two concepts of creative land use and of the planned urban region come together in mutual reinforcement. In France, it is central government policy to divert further economic growth from Paris and to drag it out to "poles of growth" in other parts of France. Britain has its regional policy. Holland has brought all its land use under a central Planning Act, and the national grouping of its major centres of population in a planned decentralised Randstadt shows what might be done in the most densely populated of developed societies. Some socialist countries are devising challenging models planning the distribution of centres so that explosive urban growth can be contained. Rumania is one of the examples. There, the capital city is no bigger now than at the end of the war, despite a 14 per cent annual rate of industrial increase. Growth has been spread all over an "urban grid" worked out in relationship to topography, climate, resources and transport patterns. China's decentralisation, whether or not it is yet working, is specifically designed to keep the giants – Shanghai, Canton – from further growth.

In other words, the concept of the derivative city has to some extent given way to the idea of the city which is planned and thought of as actually being a habitation for human beings. Instead of being the place where the "hands" are put in order to supply industry, it becomes a place where employment is developed to support the community. And this incipient reversal of ends and means is likely to be reinforced by the energy crisis.

One consequence of the shock of nearly rationing and fully trebling the price of energy has been, at least temporarily, to give us a sense of our own wastefulness. There is an undercurrent of questioning whether we can go on with our spendthrift economy and still endure for another thirty years. The question is not fully articulated yet. It is "a morning's war" between light and dark, between obscurity and conviction in men's minds. Yet the sense of the need for conservation, the sense that we are intolerably prodigal is beginning to edge into the centre of public discourse. People are a little less pleased with the extravagances; a little more inclined to raise their eyebrows at buildings which must be air-conditioned and heated at the same time because nothing can be turned off; a little less happy about 100-storey offices with continuous elevators which serve perhaps 20,000 users and, like the Trade Towers in New York, use up the energy equivalent of a city of 200,000. These questions about the proper use of energy have a direct bearing on new thinking about urban models. The idea of decentralised communities within a wider "urban region" acquires an added validity when scarcity of energy may compel us to think of more journeys on foot or bicycle, and less commuting in that single station wagon.

I do not pretend that any of these new concepts – land use planning, decentralised development, energy conservation, the workable and walkable community – yet add up to a total programme for the new urbanism. But I do believe they represent a very sharp break from the accepted wisdom of the last fifty years which has given us the "unintended city" and with it something that does not by any means fit all the human intentions we bring to our urbane ideals.

And perhaps this questioning of our basic assumptions is one of the most helpful aspects of the modern urban scene from the standpoint of developing countries. It can help to break down two widespread and dangerous notions. The first is the developed city as model. The second is that urbanisation is a force to be allowed to follow its own course. If there are no workable models, leaders and planners can feel much freer to invent new ones.

For if we look at the chain, something can be done about each link. First of all, the overwhelming primacy of the inherited big city can be countered if land speculation is checked and land use planning is systematically developed. Many developing societies now look far more carefully at the siting and distribution of population. Land use plans, land use maps, the idea of the nation's endorsement as a whole as the basis for planning appears to me at least to have started to emerge in the development picture in the last decade. This change can have a direct effect on another link in the fatal chain – the lack of sufficient agricultural employment and productivity to balance migration to the cities. In earlier planning, agriculture, too, was often left out of the central focus of planning. As Robert McNamara pointed out at Nairobi in 1973, the intermediate services needed to make the small farmers productive have been largely overlooked. They and their families make up 40 per cent of the world's peoples and it is on their small farms – five hectares and less – that productivity is low enough to make a tripling and quadrupling of world food supplies possible, provided the inputs can be increased. This is where credit, fertiliser, tubewells, co-operatives, extension services, banks, storage, health and veterinary services and more advanced education are critical elements in raising the sights of the small farmer. All these, clearly, demand a *spatial* distribution of small and intermediate urban areas where it is economic to provide the proper range of modern services. At this point, land use planning and decentralised urban growth can underpin rising agricultural productivity and a better life on the land.

This, in turn, could stem the Gadarene rush to the big cities. It could do this in two ways – through slowing down migration by creating more employment on the farms and more work in intermediate centres, and by increasing the demand for consumer goods of an unsophisticated kind which can be produced by labour-intensive workshops and small factories in the cities. The building of intermediate centres could also increase the scope of unskilled work in construction away from the big cities. These are not utopian exercises. Taiwan has proceeded along these lines. So, in part, have South Korea and Yugoslavia. The prime model of local self-sufficiency is probably China. These are examples. They can spread.

All these policies together can begin to have some impact on the rate of population growth, since one rule at least does seem to prevail among all the uncertainties about the Malthusian dilemma – that population begins to stabilise as hope and opportunity increase. Any policy that neglects the interests of the 40 per cent of the world's population who live on the frontiers of destitution is certain to have no answer whatever to the problem of explosive growth.

If some of the intolerable pressures of continuous deluges of migrants can be taken off the big cities, there, too, policies are available to lessen the tragedy of unemployment and the loss of hope. It is a labour-intensive and income-generating task to accelerate the rehabilitation of many of the shanty towns, along the lines of providing them with elementary sanitation and water services and then encouraging, by security of tenure and the right kind of loan associations, the people's capacity to build for themselves. We already know from a number of settlements how much this approach can achieve. Notice, too, that in the shanty towns, as in the developed world, it is the group co-operating, working together, sharing a common social experience that begins to create the sense of a genuine community. If these lively centres of self-help were then incorporated, by mass transit, by better distribution of industry, commerce and services, as decentralised units in the wider urban region, the developing world could conceivably come up with something worth teaching the already-settled societies. Then the sterile one-way flow of unworkable strategies from rich to poor might give way to a much more lively exchange.

None of this work is possible without control over land use, without an end to urban speculation, without the highest possible priority for the citizen's work and shelter. In societies in which there is no commitment whatever to social justice, no such controls are possible. It would be fatuous to suppose that those societies which still operate on the principle that rapacity can be encouraged and then controlled, will be given time for this particular philosophy of development to bear fruit. It might have been possible in the nineteenth century when the pressures were so much less. In the twentieth century, governments which have no commitment to any form of agrarian change, to any kind of land reform, to any emphasis upon the prime needs of citizens, will not carry out these programmes. And I doubt whether they are going to survive. Governments with such a commitment – whether they are Tanzania or Cuba or China or Peru – have a possibility of breaking what I call the "blocked system" and beginning to create urban centres where better incomes, greater opportunity and hence responsibility and family choice become socially conceivable. Without these changes, I do not think there will be any move towards a lower rate of population growth; therefore the built-in crisis will simply continue.

Nor is it simply a question of social justice within the developing societies. The issue is also posed at the planetary level. The difficulty in taking the optimistic view is that the whole development process, with greater decentralisation and with its stronger emphasis both on agricultural productivity and on efforts to build up the whole range of smaller industry needed for the rehabilitation of urban areas, is extremely expensive. Energy now costs three and four times as much as it did before – adding US$1,000 million a year to India's current deficit for example.

The forty poorest countries in the world – including the whole Indian subcontinent – are also crippled by the tripling of grain and fertiliser prices which added £5,000 million to their balance of payments shortfall between 1973 and 1974. They can, less than ever, afford the whole investment package. But the developed world can. It still has 80 per cent of the world's resources for 20 per cent of its people. The ratio of rich to poor has been slightly enlarged to include oil producers, but generally speaking the distribution of resources of the planet is not very much changed. The combined national incomes of the Organisation of Petroleum Exporting Countries is about $2,000,000 million. But for developed societies it is nearer $3,000,000,000 million. There is still a margin. Indeed, the United States earned $2,000 million from the poor in 1973 by selling them high cost grain.

There is a wry story going around that at one of the recent meetings of OPEC, one of the representatives of the developed oil-consuming countries actually said to the oil sheiks: "You know, oil is so important to the entire life of the planetary community, we think it should come under international control." To which the oil sheik replied: "What an admirable idea. We'll put the northern plains of America and Canada under international management because food is also very important to international society." Between our food concentrations and our energy concentrations, there are problems of planetary management which we have to confront in quite new ways. And we must do so in the context of a new era of doubt and anxiety. It becomes clearer that the stock of basic materials is dwindling, as it must in a finite planet. We have to reassert our faith in the transfer of resources and creative development and investment, just at a time when the richer countries are going to be less willing because it may mean some sacrifice for them.

I do not know any way round this dilemma. But let us first take the argument from history. Suppose we had said at any time in the late nineteenth century: "No, we are not going any further with our transfers of wealth and sanitation and education. Forget the whole welfare budget. Forget the idea of creative income tax. Justice is out. We are not going ahead." I do not believe our society would have survived in any form at all. If we now say that there are to be no more transfers at the planetary level, that for example, United States Congressional action in rejecting the International Development Authority's replenishment fund is to be the norm for the future, again social violence and collapse lie ahead.

Nowhere in history have societies run up against the scale of social disintegration that is threatening us in the world's cities and come through simply on drift, without a single creative policy. On the contrary, the record is of the collapse of cities and disintegration of social systems. Our crisis happens to be on a planetary scale, but I do not think history has been in any way rescinded because of this. Therefore I would say that the first thing we have to link with any discussion of the whole population-related pressure of the next twenty years on food, on energy, on our cities, is the simple proposition: do we share? Is justice relevant – or are we so tied up in our national preoccupations that we feel no obligation to the city of Man?

Secondly, there is the question of the availability of resources. I will not put much stress on aid as such – although I do not share the popular rejection of its efficiency. I simply admit that at the moment, inflation and shortage are weighing on us so heavily that we forget how much more heavily they weigh on the poor. So, for the time being, I will mention but not press such policies as the International Development Authority's low interest loans, support for raw materials prices, or the proposal that the Special Drawing Rights of the International Monetary Fund might be allocated to the poorest 40 per cent of the planet's peoples to give them a permanent surplus for which the other wealthier countries could compete.

There is, however, one particular possibility which is also instantly relevant to our problems of inflation. Surely our bankers, our financial advisers should be reminding us that US$215,000 million to $230,000 million spent each year on arms and arms sales is the most inflationary possible use of resources. During the war we fully understood the principle that if you create something which cannot be purchased, for instance, tanks and bombers, at the end you are creating purchasing power which slops about in the economy, pushing up prices, if it is not mopped up. If $230,000 million is slopping around now, and only a tenth or a twentieth of this sum could, by international agreement, be transferred to the exploding cities, what a very different prospect the world would take on. Is it so inconceivable to insert into the SALT talks or into the conversations between Washington and Moscow the possibility that the world needs more bread, more homes, more restored cities and rather fewer multiple re-entry vehicles? We should think not of the acceptable instruments of death, but the absolutely essential instruments of life. It is a big switch, but are we not in fact aware that this is the biggest decision of all? We are not going to get through the next twenty-five years on the basis of the systems, the policies, the interests – and the disloyalties – that have brought us where we are now. If they were enough, there would be no crises. If the cities were already working, then we would not have to change. But the policies that we need now are policies to confront crisis: and they include justice, sharing, all the things which in our domestic society just contrive to contain our drives and our dreams. But they are absent at the planetary level and therefore we are getting a largely unworkable planet.

We are not going to drift into solution. We are not going to slide through a series of adjustments and just come out happily on the other side. We have to have policies, we have to have justice and we have to have a vision. It may be difficult to say it because it has to be said again and again and again – and there is nothing more tedious to people than thinking they have heard it all before. Yet from the beginning of time they have heard this "still, small voice" of obligation and brotherhood. When they have listened, society has worked. When they have refused to listen, society has broken up. Whatever our conscience may say, the voice of realism is going to accept the fact that by the year 2000 there will be 3,000 million more people here whatever we do. Either they are going to make this into a planet of hellish confrontation, of total disruption and technological disaster, or we are going to feel our way towards a society in which people can be neighbours and friends. It is as simple as that. The people are going to be there, the changes are going to come; cities are exploding, resources are under constraint. Either we have policy and generosity or we have disaster. The voices of reason, of realism and of conscience all urge us to choose that generosity shall prevail.

Bibliography

This book evolved, as stated in the Preface, out of an international conference on the world's cities, organised by the United Nations Fund for Population Activities and The *Sunday Times*. From among forty-three speakers, and several additional hours of open discussion between delegates, more ideas, and a greater variety of opinions, emerged than we have been able to reflect in this book. All who spoke, whether directly quoted or not, contributed importantly to the shaping of this summary of a multi-faceted subject.

To offer a comprehensive bibliography of even the major works on world-wide urbanisation and its attendant problems would have required a companion volume. What follows is a short-list of books and articles which have particularly assisted us in writing this book – some of them, again, directly quoted, others essential background material. It will be apparent that in some sections – that on the cities of the West, for instance – we have kept more closely to the papers presented at the conference than in others; the suggestions for further reading have been correspondingly shortened. We have divided our references under general subject headings, rather than under sections, since cross-reference has inevitably been a characteristic of the book's organisation.

General Demography

The most remarkable and scholarly statistical analysis of urban population is unfortunately not widely obtainable. It is Kingsley Davis's *World Urbanisation, 1950–1970* (two volumes, Institute of International Studies, University of California, Population Monograph Series Nos 4 and 9, 1969, 1972). Also basic are the United Nations Demographic Yearbooks, especially those for 1971 and 1972; *The World's Million-Cities, 1950–1985* (United Nations Population Division Working Paper ESA/P/WP. 45, 1972); *The Determinants and Consequences of Population Trends* (UN, 1973), and Sidney Goldstein: *An Overview of World Urbanisation, 1950–2000* (Liège, International Union for the Scientific Study of Population, 1973). Useful but less up-to-date analysis is contained in *Growth of the World's Urban and Rural Population, 1920–2000* (UN, Department of Economic and Social Affairs, Population Studies No. 44, 1969), and in *Urban and Rural*

Population: Individual Countries 1950–1985 and Regions and Major Areas 1950–2000 (UN Population Division Working Paper ESA/P/WP 33/Rev. 1, 1970).

On the city at large, Max Weber's *The City* (New York, The Free Press of Glencoe, 1958) and Peter Hall's *The World Cities* (London, Weidenfeld and Nicolson, 1968) make excellent introductions. The collection of essays from *Ekistics*, edited by G. Bell and J. Tyrwhitt, *Human Identity and Urban Environment* (London, Penguin, 1972), covers subjects from the question of supplying megalopolis with water to strictly theoretical aspects of city-design for the future. For solid information on the actual workings of cities, a classic work is William A. Robson and D. E. Regan (eds.): *Great Cities of the World: Their Governments, Politics and Planning* (London, Allen and Unwin, revised 1972 edition).

The Size, Distribution and Organisation of Cities

The seminal work in this area was probably Feliz Auerbach's *Das Gesetz der Bevolkerungskonzentration*, and the modern mathematical and statistical arguments have been developed by many people, notably G. K. Zipf in his *Human Behaviour and the Principle of Least Effort* (Cambridge, Mass., 1949) and by J. Aitchison and J. A. C. Brown in *The Lognormal Distribution* (Cambridge University Press, 1957). The best all-round discussion of this and many other aspects of city scholarship is Harry W. Richardson's excellent *Economics of Urban Size* (Saxon House, London, 1973). There are also a number of very interesting monographs bearing on various particular questions. These include M. Jefferson's essay *The Law of the Primate City* (*Geographical Review*, 29, 1939); C. L. Leven's *Determinants of the Size and Spatial Form of Urban Areas* (Papers and Proceedings of the Regional Science Association, 22, 1969); and two papers which first appeared in Chicago University's outstandingly valuable periodical, "Economic Development and Social Change" – Koichi Mera's *On the Urban Agglomeration and Economic Efficiency* (21, 1973); and N. V. Sovani's *The Analysis of "Over-Urbanisation"* (12, 1964). For city models, we have also leaned substantially on Jay Forrester's *Urban Dynamics* (Massachusetts Institute of Technology, 1969).

The Cities of the West

Classic works are Lewis Mumford's *The Urban Prospect* (London, Secker and Warburg, 1968) and Jane Jacobs's *The Death and Life of Great American Cities* (New York, Random House, 1961); together they illustrate the variety of approaches to big-city development. We also drew on Jane Jacobs's *The Economy of Cities* (London, Jonathan Cape, 1970) and, more specifically, on Robert Kolodny's research paper on *Self-Help in the Inner City* (United Neighbourhood Houses of New York, 1973). An interesting conservative analysis of the problems of America's cities is Edward C. Banfield's *The Unheavenly City* (New York, Little, Brown, 1970). We are grateful to Ui Jun for making available the extensive paper entitled *Environmental Pollution Control and Public Opinion*, which he presented with two collaborators to the 1st International Symposium for Environmental Disruption, held in Tokyo in March 1970. Among many works dealing with the question of governmental responsiveness, and the matching of planning to individual needs, a useful current contribution is Michael Young (ed.): *Poverty Report, 1974* (London, Temple Smith, 1974). Daniel Bell's *The Coming of Post-Industrial Society* (New York, Basic Books, 1973) provided many helpful insights, as did Sir Karl Popper's *The Open Society and Its Enemies* (vol. 1, London, Routledge and Kegan Paul, 1972. 4th Edition, revised).

Cities in the Developing World

Particularly valuable general works are D. J. Dwyer (ed.): *The City as a Centre of Change in Asia* (Hong Kong University Press, 1972); T. G. McGee: *The Southeast Asian City* (London, Bell, 1967) and the admirably unbureaucratic World Bank Sector Working Paper on Urbanisation, published in 1972. Less well organised, but full of interesting material, are Gerald Breese (ed.): *The City in Newly Developing Countries* (New York, Prentice Hall, 1969) and D. J. Dwyer (ed.): *The City in the Third World* (London, Macmillan, 1974). A helpful study of a rapidly-urbanising continent is W. D. Harris: *The Growth of Latin American Cities* (Ohio University Press, 1971); and N. V. Sovani, in *Urbanisation and Urban India* (London, Asia Publishing House, 1966), sensitively outlines the future prospects for that country's hungry cities.

On housing, aside from the contribution by John F. C. Turner and Bryan Roberts, we have drawn on a number of sources covering particular geographical areas: among the most important, both in detail and originality of general conception, were the seminars published by *The Monthly Symposium* (New Delhi, 1973) on mass housing, Calcutta and mass transit (Nos. 162, 163 and 171). Charles Correa's papers on cheap housing and on mass transit were particularly distinguished. Morris Juppenlatz, the Australian social economist, is the author of *Urban Squatter Resettlement, Sipang Palay* (United Nations, New

York, 1965), and also provided us with documentation on the BNH housing development schemes in Brazil. Shankland Cox Partnership gave us their two reports on low-cost and site and services housing in Jamaica, prepared in 1970 and 1973. Professor Buu Hoan's paper on the South-East Asian city, presented at the Oxford conference, supplemented his article, published by *Kajian Ekonomi Malaysia*, on "The National Housing Problem and International Development Assistance". Aprodicio Laquian, both in his book *Slums are for People* (Manila, 1968) and as Director of the International Development Research Centre, which published *Town Drift: Social and Policy Implications of Rural-Urban Migration in Eight Developing Countries* (Istanbul, 1973), has provided some of the most cogent analyses of the social and economic implications of the rural-urban migration and squatter settlements. A good detailed study is by Barrington Kaye: *Upper Nanking Street, Singapore* (University of Malaya Press, 1964). The quotation showing Claude Lévi-Strauss's reaction to Calcutta was taken from the excellent new translation of his *Tristes Tropiques* by John and Doreen Weightman (London, Cape, 1973).

The chapter on urban employment drew extensively on Paul Bairoch's distinguished study, *Urban Unemployment in Developing Countries* (Geneva, International Labour Office, 1973), and on the latest ILO statistics. Clifford Geertz is the author of *Peddlers and Princes: Social Change and Economic Modernisation in Two Indonesian Towns* (University of Chicago Press, 1963), a sensitive portrayal of the virtues of the bazaar economy. On transport, a particularly useful study was produced by Wilfred Owen of the Brookings Institution: "Automobiles and Cities: Strategies for Developing Countries" (OECD Environment Directorate, Working Paper No. 5, August 1973. U/CKO/72.900). The most important source for the outline of the food position was the United Nations *Preliminary Assessment of the World Food Situation*, published in May 1974 as a forerunner to the World Food Conference. Others were the address to the Washington Institute of Foreign Affairs in October 1972 by A. H. Boerma, Director of the FAO, Georgy Skorov's critical article on "The Green Revolution and Social Progress" in *World Development*, vol. I, no. 11, 1973, and Walter H. Pawley's futuristic "In the Year 2070", published in *Ceres*, vol. IV, no. 4, 1971. In more general terms, William Alonso's article on "Urban and Regional Imbalances in Economic Development", in *Economic Development and Cultural Change*, vol. XVII, no. 1, 1968, challenges some accepted pieties.

Published material for the general reader on the health situation, aside from WHO Technical Reports, tends to be highly technical and over-specific. Useful material is contained, however, in John Bryant:

Health and the Development World (Cornell University Press, 1969), in articles by Oscar Gish, including "Health Planning in Developing Countries" (*Journal of Development Studies*, vol. VI, no. 4, 1970), and in a recent essay by Ole David Koht Norbye, "Health and Demography" in *World Development*, vol. II, no. 2, 1974.

Any assessment of the potential for civil disorder and mass violence in the developing world's cities must be tentative. But Joan M. Nelson has written a sceptical and detailed essay on the evidence which backs commonly-held assumptions of imminent chaos, which shows how little this corresponds with empirical findings, and puts the whole subject in cool perspective. (*Migrants, Urban Poverty and Instability in Developing Nations*, Harvard University Center for International Affairs; Occasional Papers, no. 22, 1969.) Also of interest is Samuel P. Huntington's *Political Order in Changing Societies* (Yale University Press, 1968).

Soviet Union

Two very valuable and complementary books have come out fairly recently, which help greatly in tackling this rather forbidding area. Chauncy D. Harris's *Cities in the Soviet Union: Studies in their Function, Size, Density and Growth* (Chicago, 1970) distils a staggering amount of factual, statistical and descriptive material into manageable form, while William Taubman's admirable and sympathetic study, *Governing Soviet Cities* (Praeger, New York, 1973), disentangles and analyses an almost equally massive amount of material on planning, investment, organisational reform, city finance and similar topics, as they have evolved in post-revolutionary Russia. More general insights are to be found in Isaac Deutscher's *The Unfinished Revolution: Russia 1917–1967* (Oxford University Press 1967) and in P. J. Wiles's earlier *Political Economy of Communism* (Blackwell, Oxford, 1962).

China

The most up-to-date survey of China's cities after 1949 is the collection of papers edited by John Wilson Lewis: *The City in Communist China* (Stanford University Press, 1971). Another brilliant and detailed recent work is the revised, 1968 edition of Franz Schurmann's *Ideology and Organisation in Communist China* (University of California Press). Other useful sources were Ezra F. Vogel: *Canton under Communism: Programs and Politics in a Provincial Capital, 1949–68* (Harvard University Press, 1969), A. Doak Barnett: *Cadres, Bureaucracy and*

Political Power in Communist China (Columbia University Press, 1967) and A. Doak Barnett (ed.): *Chinese Communist Politics in Action* (University of Washington Press, 1969). In attempting to give some statistical picture of the growth of China's cities, H. Yuan Tien's *China's Population Struggle* (Ohio State University Press, 1973) is helpful, although disappointingly it deals, despite the publication date, principally with the Fifties. The demographic studies by the UN and by Kingsley Davis were invaluable in this connection. Much of the material on post-Cultural Revolution China is found in periodicals such as the *China Quarterly* (which in particular published an interesting analysis by Audrey Donnithorne on "China's Cellular Economy" since the Cultural Revolution in its Oct/Dec issue, 1972). Also useful were the essay by John Wilson Lewis, "Political Aspects of Mobility in China's Urban Development", published in the *American Political Science Review*, LX, 4 (December 1966), and articles in *The Far Eastern Economic Review*'s China Focus, October 1973. Enthusiastic accounts of China's city planning appeared in articles by a British visitor to China, Graham Towers, in the *Architects' Journal* (December 1973) and the *Journal of the Royal Town Planning Institute* (March 1973). Extremely valuable advice was given by Chinese friends who are frequent visitors to the People's Republic.

Index